THE FORTUNATE ISLANDS

THE STORY OF THE ISLES OF SCILLY

by

R. L. Bowley

BOWLEY PUBLICATIONS LTD
P.O. Box 1, St Mary's, Isles of Scilly, TR21 0PR

THE FORTUNATE ISLANDS

First edition by E. L. Bowley	1945
2nd edition	1947
3rd edition	1949
4th edition	1957
5th edition, revised by R. L. Bowley	1964
6th edition	1968
7th edition	1980
8th edition, revised and enlarged	1990
reprint (with amendments)	1996
9th edition, revised	2004

ISBN 0 900184 40 X

CONTENTS

FIRST THOUGHTS

Awakening on a bright summer morning on holiday in the Scillies, one's first thoughts are not of the day's work ahead or commuting to it, or of cleaning the house or shopping, or even of a good read; there are, of course, still decisions to be made, such as which island shall we visit today and where shall we eat – but they are of quite a different and pleasanter sort from the more pressing and exacting ones of everyday mainland existence. Of course, there are a few who think mainly of the bare necessities of life, like Winnie-the-Pooh when asked by Piglet what were his first thoughts when he woke in the morning:

"What's for breakfast?" said Pooh. "What do *you* say, Piglet?"
"I say, I wonder what's going to happen exciting *to-day?*"
said Piglet.
Pooh nodded thoughtfully.
"It's the same thing," he said.'

Winnie-the-Pooh, Chapter 10 – A.A. Milne

ILLUSTRATIONS

PREFACE TO THE SEVENTH EDITION (1980)

The first edition of *The Fortunate Islands* was written by my father Ernest Lyon Bowley at Star Castle in 1945, and subsequently he produced three more editions of the book, which became the standard work on the Isles of Scilly. Since his death in 1959, there have been three further editions, in each of which I have carried out some revision to keep the text up to date. I am most grateful to Mr John G. Pickwell for the help he has given me in this task, and for making very many useful suggestions and comments which have much improved the book.

PREFACE TO THE EIGHTH EDITION (1990)

In this edition the opportunity has been taken to enlarge, revise and rewrite much of the book; even so, it scarcely does justice to the immensity of the subject matter, but selects those aspects of Scilly's story likely to be of most interest to people who visit the islands.

Except in the introduction, little reference is made to Scilly today, and for this the reader is recommended to consult the latest edition of the *Isles of Scilly Standard Guidebook*.

Thanks are due in great measure once again to John Pickwell for his helpful criticism and for his painstaking checking of the bibliography. I am also grateful to Frank Gibson for allowing me to use some of his superb collection of photographs.

PREFACE TO THE NINTH EDITION (2004)

In this edition much revision of detail has taken place and an attempt made to present a less partisan view of the past, particularly concerning the 17th century. Thanks are due to Glenda Pattenden who has helped with the production, and to Frank Gibson and his family for the continued use of some of their collection of excellent and unique photographs of Scilly.

Companion with this volume is the *Isles of Scilly Standard Guidebook*, an 84 page, pocket-size handbook, designed to be of interest and helpful to holidaymakers. It has extensive maps, colour photographs, with travel and accommodation details, and includes relevant information on walks, cafes, pubs, beaches, boats and so forth, with some advertisements.

The other book which readers may care to consider is *Scilly at War*, the first part of which tells the story of Robert Blake and his conquest of Scilly in 1651, illustrated by some contemporary letters and first-hand accounts. The second part deals with the First World War, and includes the part played by seaplanes at their base on Tresco in helping to counter the U-boat menace. The third part is concerned mainly with the Second World War and its effects on Scilly, and with travel developments to Scilly.

Rex Bowley,
Penzance, 2004

THE ISLES OF SCILLY in 2004

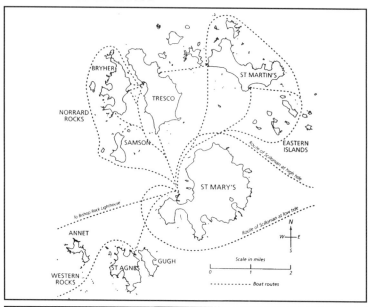

- BRYHER
- TRESCO
- NORRARD ROCKS
- ST MARTIN'S
- SAMSON
- EASTERN ISLANDS
- ANNET
- ST MARY'S
- Route of Scillonian at high tide
- To Bishop Rock Lighthouse
- Route of Scillonian at low tide
- ST AGNES
- GUGH
- WESTERN ROCKS

Scale in miles

0   1   2

------- Boat routes

N
W — E
S

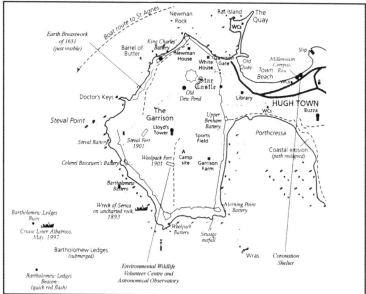

- Boat route to St Agnes
- Newman Rock
- Rat Island
- The Quay
- WCs
- Earth Breastwork of 1651 (just visible)
- King Charles' Battery
- Barrel of Butter
- Newman House
- Garrison Gate
- White House
- Old Quay
- Slip
- Millennium Compass Row
- Town Beach
- WCs
- Star Castle
- Old Dew Pond
- Library
- HUGH TOWN
- Doctor's Keys
- The Garrison
- Upper Benham Battery
- WCs
- Buzza
- Steval Point
- Lloyd's Tower
- Sports Field
- Porthcressa
- Steval Battery
- Steval Fort 1901
- Woolpack Fort 1901
- Camp site
- Garrison Farm
- Coastal erosion (path realigned)
- Colonel Boscawen's Battery
- Bartholomew Battery
- Wreck of Serica on uncharted rock, 1893
- Morning Point Battery
- Bartholomew Ledges Buoy
- Cruise Liner Albatross, May 1997
- Woolpack Battery
- Sewage outfall
- Wras
- Coronation Shelter
- Bartholomew Ledges (submerged)
- Environmental Wildlife Volunteer Centre and Astronomical Observatory
- Bartholomew Ledges Beacon (quick red flash)

THE GARRISON ON ST MARY'S in 2004

INTRODUCTION

The Isles of Scilly are a group of islands and rocks situated about 28 miles west-south-west of Land's End, and therefore a mile or two further from the mainland than Calais is from Dover. In archaeological terms the present islands, which spread over an area of sea roughly eleven by five miles, are the surviving hill-tops of a much larger land area which over a considerable period was reduced by inundations of a rising sea. The extent of this land we can surmise from the fact that, at a sea depth of fifteen metres, most of the present islands form part of one large one, which would include the Seven Stones, and which some may call Lyonnesse.

It is not known when the present islands became separated, but field walls of former farms can still be detected on the beaches running out to sea, particularly on Samson (inhabited until 1855) and on Par Beach, St Martin's. This suggests that some of the inundations occurred in comparatively recent historical times – and the sea is still rising. In 1989, sixty-eight ancient monuments on Scilly were scheduled as such – so giving their preservation specific legal protection – and eleven of these are managed by English Heritage. These sixty-eight are less than half the ancient remains in Scilly so far identified, and more probably exist, particularly in the shallow waters around the islands. Some national designations have been made in recent years to help protect the environment: in 1974 Scilly's coastline was declared a Heritage Coast; in 1975 the islands as a whole were made a Conservation Area, giving the Council more power to control the demolition as well as erection of buildings; between 1971 and 1976, 23 sites of Special Scientific Interest were established covering over half of Scilly's land area, and in 1976 Scilly was designated an Area of Outstanding Natural Beauty.

Only six of the present fifty-six islands in Scilly are inhabited, and all are small – the largest, St Mary's, being less than three miles across at its widest point and only ten miles around its coastline. In winter, Scilly offers visitors the sight and scent of early flowers, and a mild climate which makes their early growth possible; in summer there is sea, sun, sand and relative solitude to be enjoyed.

1

Small islands have an advantage for summer holidaymakers in that they possess relatively more coastline than mainland seaside resorts, and so seem less crowded; in Scilly, visitors can usually find an unfrequented beach even in high summer, for there are so many from which to choose. The small size of the islands also enables shelter to be found nearby on a leeward shore when a stiff breeze is blowing – the direction of the wind being easily determined by a glance at anchored boats, whose prows tend to turn into wind. There is also much open land available for walking in Scilly, which, as Alfred Wainwright says of fell walking in the Lake District, "should be done slowly; beauty is too rare to be hurried past".

The islands are part of the possessions of the Duchy of Cornwall which maintains a land steward on the islands, and an office at Hugh House, St Mary's. In 1949 sitting tenants were given the right to buy the freehold of their properties in Hugh Town, but much property elsewhere on St Mary's and all property on the off-islands is held on lease. Dorrien Smith has the lease of Tresco, while the uninhabited islands and untenanted lands are, since 1985, managed by the Isles of Scilly Wildlife Trust, which has sixteen trustees all residing in Scilly.

Today the islands are administered by a council composed of 21 councillors (who sit without party labels), thirteen of whom are elected from St Mary's and two each from the off-islands of Tresco, St Martin's, Bryher and St Agnes. It has been said that the council has the powers of a county council with the size of a parish council. There are two doctors, a dentist, district nurses and a small, well-equipped hospital on St Mary's. There is also a water ambulance, one of the first of its type anywhere. A veterinary surgeon resides on St Mary's and there are seven justices of the peace. However, St Mary's has no road traffic lights, beacon crossings or speed limits (other than the statutory 60 mph.), but car parks and yellow lines testify to modern traffic pressures as elsewhere.

Among the people in Scilly there are distinctions. A 'tripper' is one who comes for a day visit; a 'visitor' is one who usually stays a week or more and before he leaves has entered into the spirit of the place – and sometimes learnt to side in its politics; a 'resident' is a mainlander who has come to live in Scilly usually to work or retire; and a 'local' is one who has lived in Scilly a long time. But not all locals are 'Scillonians'. This last description is reserved for those forty or so families who have lived in Scilly several generations, to which are often added nowadays all those who were born and brought up in Scilly. This forms a sort of hierarchy which newcomers sometimes detect, though less so than formerly. For some years now the Council of the Isles of Scilly has consisted of more former mainlanders than Scillonians.

One of the difficulties which the Council of the Isles of Scilly faces is in the provision of housing; not only do they find difficulty in finding sites for building, but the high costs of construction in Scilly have made it difficult to fix rents on an economic basis and provide housing for a skilled work force. There are, typically, about 100 names on the Council's housing waiting list and, by 2004, about a quarter of all housing was used for holiday letting. Moreover, the cost of living in Scilly is high, and much has to be imported from the mainland including meat, vegetables, fruit, and (perhaps surprisingly) fish. Prices tend to be higher than on the mainland partly owing to freight charges, but the islands have been helped by EEC grants. The islanders suffered two economic setbacks in recent years, when they were assessed for the first time in 1954 for income tax, and for motor taxation in 1971. They escaped income tax for so long because the Council of the Isles of Scilly is not really a county council nor a borough council; indeed, it is the only one of its kind – an all-purpose authority.

Today the inhabitants of the Isles of Scilly form a relatively prosperous community of around two thousand persons. They have come a long way since the time in the early part of the nineteenth century when their inhabitants petitioned the public through the columns of *The Times* to relieve their 'extreme distress'. Then they were anything but the 'fortunate islands' they can claim to be now. There are problems today – transport costs, housing development, etc. – but the long-term economic future in Scilly looks promising, for the islands have so many natural advantages for the tourist trade – unspoilt beauty, clean air (its purity evidenced by the richness of lichen flora on rocks in Scilly), wonderful beaches and sea, favourable climate, interesting fauna and flora, a small, friendly population, etc. – that they seem hardly able to fail. Moreover, forecasts that the flower industry would not survive have proved exaggerated, and flower growing still provides the inhabitants with a winter livelihood to supplement that from summer visitors. As an indication of the continuing development of the flower-growing industry, a fast-cooling facility owned by fourteen growers was

3

opened in 1989 close to the airport. It is in a shed capable of storing about seven thousand boxes of flowers at low temperatures so that they are sent away from Scilly in perfect condition. However, flower-growing – as with potatoes, another crop from Scilly – does have one handicap; it does not benefit from price support under the European Community Agricultural Policy, and is therefore vulnerable to competition. Scilly also has a somewhat longer holiday season than on the mainland – from March, when visitors may come to see the flowers, through to the end of October, when they come to see the migrant birds. In high summer most accommodation in Scilly is full, and those who love Scilly are conscious that development to provide modern amenities, even for the current over 100,000 visitors a year, might be at the expense of some of the unspoilt beauty and unique atmosphere in the islands, which is what attracts many of those visitors and helps make Scilly different from mainland resorts. At present the twenty-eight miles of sea separating Scilly from Land's End serves as a moat defending the naturalness of the islands from caravans and too many cars and campers, and the Council of the Isles of Scilly, the Duchy of Cornwall and the Isles of Scilly Wildlife Trust all try to take a long-term view of what is best for Scilly. But the task is not easy, for there are many conflicting interests and views, and what seems desirable development to some can appear as ill-judged spoliation to others. Yet, the islands cannot stand still; the skill will be in welcoming the new at the same time as preserving the best of the old; and whatever changes do come in Scilly, the particular qualities of self-reliance, intelligence, industry and foresight, which are most marked in Scillonians, should serve them well in the future in these fortunate islands.

CHAPTER I – HISTORY OR LEGEND?

When the history of Scilly is so rich in incident and so interesting in story-line, it is sad that some of it continues to contain invasive speculation, based on little or no evidence, but which is often expressed as if it were the relaying of proven facts. An example is the story about the Viking sea-raider and King of Norway, Olaf Tryggvesson, who also ruled what is now Denmark, Iceland and much of Sweden. After Olaf had undertaken a four-year-long plundering voyage around the coasts of Britain – something which is easy to accept as later we hear of other raids (almost an economic necessity for many Northmen) including that of Svein Asleifsson, King of Orkney and Caithness, who raided Scilly in AD 1155 and 'took immense plunder' – Olaf is said to have dallied some time in the Islands and been converted to Christianity by one of the holy men of Scilly during his stay, subsequently carrying his new religion back to his people in Norway at the point of his sword. As Longfellow later put it:

> King Olaf from the doorway spoke:
> 'Choose ye between two things my folk
> To be baptised or given up to slaughter!'

Olaf was the subject of many such fanciful stories, this one apparently originating in the *Heimskringla* (meaning Round World), a saga written by the Icelander Snorri Sturlason in 1222, and therefore over two centuries after the event. It is hard to prove a negative, but there are no reliable sources for the story and, fine though it is, there is too little evidence to accept it as history.

One especial local difficulty about writing about Scilly – and indeed about all Cornwall – is that many readers will have come to believe reports that the county is different, a mysterious even mystic land, when actually it is surprisingly unpeculiar, and its people refreshingly practical and pleasant in every way. There may still be pixies on the shop-shelf for sale, but the shop-assistant is invariably welcoming, smiling, and willing to pass the time of day – although, admittedly, the absence of the impersonalising effects of large cities in the county today may partly account for this.

However, to attempt to write about any part of Britain in the Dark Ages before the Norman Conquest is difficult because proven facts are few – as are written sources – and much necessary detail is either missing or unreliable – a real challenge to sort history from legend.

Incontestable evidence for Arthur and his Round Table, Alfred burning the cakes or Canute defying the waves is unavailable, the stories being enduring speculations rather than certain history. We like to think of them as verbal history passed down through the generations, something to cling on to in the want of hard evidence or convincing written testimony. But one has only to be reminded of the old Music Hall joke of the First World War about the message that was passed by word of mouth from soldier to soldier from the front line back down the trenches, which began as 'Send reinforcements, we are going to advance' and ended up in the rear at headquarters as 'Send three and four pence, we are going to a dance' to be reminded how subject to distortion verbal communication can be.

In this connection, a salutary lesson for a schoolteacher is to read aloud an Aesop fable two or three times to a class of the age range 8 to 18 or beyond – for convenience, three examples have been included in this book's appendix – and then to require the class to write the story down by themselves individually without further aid or discussion. The result will often be almost as many different versions as there are members of the class, with some even missing or misunderstanding the essential points of the story, and this even when difficult-to-spell words, such as 'Aesop' or 'moral' are written on the blackboard for the younger ones – an action which has the incidental benefit of helping with recall for those of the class who claim to be 'stuck'. The point being made is that, although written history is often inaccurate, verbal history tends to be infinitely more so.

A much earlier story than those of Arthur, Alfred, Canute or Olaf, concerns Joseph of Arimathea, who is believed to have come to Britain to buy tin. In some versions he visited Cornwall and was accompanied by his young nephew, Jesus of Nazareth, with even a suggestion that they could both have come to Scilly. There is no historical evidence for any of this, and even the identification of

Scilly with the Cassiterides is now discounted, for there are no signs of past extensive tin-mining in Scilly, at least not on land now above sea-level. Most of the tin of Roman times probably came from the Iberian Peninsula rather than Cornwall, so the story that Julius Caesar's invasion army of Britain in 55 BC came 'with shields and breast-plates made of metal from Cornwall' is most unlikely. Even the widespread belief that St Michael's Mount was Ictis is unlikely speculation; the Mount has been the called 'the high, grey rock in the wood', which seems accurate, as it may not have been an island until the 11th century, when the sea is believed to have flooded much of Mounts Bay, possibly at the same time as the valley between Tresco and St Mary's was also flooded. As evidence of the woodland, forest tree trunks sometimes appear in Mounts Bay today above the sand at low spring tides.

* * * * *

Another difficulty – and this applies to writing almost anything about the past – is that history is not as static as some people like to believe, but is largely formed from what has been written down and accepted about the past at the time it was written. But then times change, and views of the past become subject to amendment according to the new standpoint from which the past events are observed, and it is particularly noticeable that, in a conflict situation, the accepted version of events has, more often than not, been that of the eventual victor.

Much that has been accepted as true of the past often rests on flimsy evidence, but even a proven fact can sometimes give rise to misleading interpretations – one well-known example of this being the bald claim that the *Titanic* – the liner which sank in the Atlantic far to the west of Scilly after hitting an iceberg on her maiden voyage in 1912 – was such a great disaster in terms of the numbers of lives lost because she had an insufficient number of lifeboats – the actual number on the *Titanic* being 16 plus 4 collapsables. One can almost sense the reader's anger at the revelation of this fact, and blame being prepared to be heaped somewhere, perhaps upon the White Star Line, the owners responsible for what seems to be a culpable omission. To modify this criticism requires the reception of a host of other information – such as that compliance with Board of Trade regulations in this matter was complete; that many of the lifeboats rowed off from the *Titanic* with passenger spaces in them unfilled; that the number of lifejackets and lifebuoys on *Titanic* was considered by all authorities before the disaster as more than adequate; that the number of lifeboats, although inadequate to hold everyone, was relatively high relative to passenger numbers, as *Titanic* was only two thirds full on her maiden voyage; and that, although quite aware himself, Captain Smith failed to inform the passengers or most of the crew that *Titanic* was sinking, an omission leading to confusion, although intended to allay panic, some passengers therefore remaining on *Titanic* by choice rather than – as they saw it – needlessly embarking on a small open boat on that cold night; 2nd officer Lightfoller later testified he could only persuade 24 passengers and 2 crew to enter his 65-seat lifeboat. Indeed, criticism of the *Titanic* for carrying too few lifeboats must also imply censure of all other liners of that time for doing the same thing, which is a little like in 1912, after there had been a number of road accidents involving casualties, criticising car manufacturers of that time for not fitting seat belts or air bags or head restraints.

To dwell upon this criticism – which was undeniably one factor in so many people drowning – is to overlook other possible contributory areas of censure, such as the mislaying of the binoculars in the Crows-Nest, whose use could have provided more time for the bridge to alter course – or the action by Murdoch, the officer on the bridge, who tried to alter course, but the bulkheads of *Titanic* might have survived had he not done so.

Few blame Robert Hichens of Newlyn, the helmsman (and first cousin of Joseph Reseigh, famed captain of the 1st *Scillonian*, 1931-53), who steered the *Titanic* into the iceberg, for he 'was only obeying orders' and steered other liners safely in his subsequent career. He was in charge of a *Titanic* lifeboat (No. 6) which had over 50 empty seats, and he could have picked up strugglers in the water, but failed to do so because he said he feared his boat would have been overturned in the press of desperate people. But the popular Captain Smith, who was warned and aware of the ice-flows, yet failed to reduce speed, seems an eminently blameworthy candidate. After all, *Titanic* took hours to sink, yet he did little, not even to warn people of the danger they were in. To allege, however, that he took risks for reasons of personal glory – proceeding at full speed in order to make a record Atlantic crossing – or in deference to his Company's Managing Director who was on board, is speculation and not evidential history, even if it may be true.

Another problem with history is that – as Hitler is once said to have remarked – if something is repeated often enough, people will come to believe it. Indeed, that alleged remark of Hitler's may itself be an example of this. More famous is Marie Antoinette's reply on hearing of the hunger for bread of the people of eighteenth century Paris; she is alleged to have said 'Well, let them eat cake' – thus apparently revealing that she had no idea of the abject poverty in which most of her subjects lived. The memory of the remark survived partly because it was useful to the political opponents of royal despotism and of unegalitarian societies. However, if uttered at all, it was more probably from Louis XIV's wife rather than Louis XVI's and, in any case, the remark loses its point somewhat when it is pointed out that 'cake' at that time in France – and properly translated – is likely to have meant a different form of bread rather than luxury food.

Marie Antoinette was the victim of many such calumnies, even being censured for grieving too long when her 11-month-old daughter Sophie died. Her reply to this was to say 'She might have grown up to be a friend', a response which has a sad authenticity likely to win hearts. As for her husband, Louis XVI, he was even criticised for writing 'Rien' in his diary on the day the Bastille fell, July 14, 1789, although nobody at the time seems to have realised that the entry was only in his hunting-diary, and that no hunt was held that day.

In Scilly's history there are many stories and legends which possess little evidential support, yet gain credence because their repetition continues. Among these are King Athelstan's supposed visit to conquer Scilly in the 10th century (he is also often said to have founded the priory on Tresco), the story of a Scillonian called Nance, who, in 1651, is said, deliberately and for political reasons, to have piloted troops in boats to Northwethel instead of to Tresco, when in fact his accusers were trying to shift blame on to him for their own inept bungling (see *Scilly at War* p. 41), the repetition of the name of the Dutch Admiral Tromp as 'Van Tromp' when he never had 'Van' in his name, and the oft-repeated allegation that Tromp 'declared war on Scilly'. He did bring a fleet to Scilly seeking recompense for Dutch ships against whom piracies had been committed – not by Scillonians but by rebel occupying forces in the Islands – but he never fired a shot. He was under orders at the time not to do anything which might offend the government in London. Mention could also be made of one island in the Scillies which has an undeserved reputation; this is Hangman's Island whose name derives from the Middle Cornish *An Main* (meaning 'The Rock') and is not associated with capital punishment (see Padel's, *Cornish Place – Name Elements*). In English, sloppily pronounced, the Cornish sounds vaguely like 'hangman' – and that name for the island has stuck, occasioning unjustified speculation about executions. The 'an' in Cornish names is much more common than is 'the' in English names.

There has also been a story that in 1707 there was a Scillonian sailor serving on Rear Admiral Shovell's flagship *Association*, who warned the Admiral that his fleet was heading into danger onto the rocks of Scilly, but was ignored. The story is unlikely to be true and impossible to confirm. There was also at one time a belief that Shovell managed to come ashore at Porth Hellick, exhausted but still alive, and was then murdered by an Island woman who stole a ring from his finger. The evidence for this colourful story is slight, and, although Shovell may have succeeded in leaving his stricken flagship in his barge (it is said together with some relatives, his valuables and pet greyhound), it is more likely that he drowned on the Western Rocks with the rest of his crew because of the heavy sea running, and at the time the *Association* foundered. The number who lost their lives that night in all the ships is more likely to have totalled nearly 1,500 rather than the 2,000 originally estimated.

The most important long-term historical consequence of the 1707 disaster was that the Government was persuaded to offer a reward to someone who could invent a clock which would keep reliable time on a swaying ship at sea. This prize was eventually won by Harrison, an innovative watchmaker, and, as a result, ships' captains from that time onwards have been able to calculate longitude accurately – one of the greatest advances in navigation. Ironically, it was Shovell's error in calculating latitude – more than longitude – which seems to have been responsible for what happened to his fleet in 1707, for his navigators believed the English Channel was clear before them. This error may have been partly due to a failure to allow for the effect of Rennel's Current, which would have placed the fleet to the north of its charted position.

Another confusion is over the use of the term 'wreckers' or 'shipwreckers'. This is meant today to describe people who have salvaged goods from distressed or abandoned ships, some of the goods declared, others perhaps not. It is not meant to describe persons who have deliberately lured vessels to destruction on the rocks, so that they can loot the valuables aboard. It is not that such a horrific practice may never have occurred in Scilly in the past, but that examples of it, by their nature, were hard to prove, and the possible few such nefarious acts have been so much outweighed by the many hundreds of humane rescue services – both of human lives and of goods, and sometimes undertaken in circumstances of great danger to the rescuers – all of which have been well documented and attested throughout the years in Scilly.

Another example of a words problem is the ponderous description of the Islands by some visitors as the 'Isles of Scilly'; that is certainly their correct postal address but, in normal everyday parlance, people talk of 'Scilly' or the 'Scillies' or even of the 'Scilly Isles' without giving offence. Another difficulty lies in answering the question of how many islands there are in Scilly; it seems a bit absurd to include every bare rock, so, if one agrees that some variety of vegetation must grow permanently on an island for it to be counted as an island, then the answer is 56, of which five are inhabited. Another error – although grazing the edge of pedantry to label it as such – is the assertion that Scilly is in the Gulf Stream. Strictly speaking, the Gulf Stream does not come within a thousand miles of Britain's shores, because, far out in the Atlantic and heading north-eastwards, its warmer waters mingle with the cooler Labrador Current heading southwards from off the coast of Greenland, and it is this mixture, known as the North Atlantic Drift, which reaches Britain. But it is still accurate to claim that the Gulf Stream has a beneficial effect on Scilly's climate, as its waters do form a constituent of this North Atlantic Drift. Another error is the belief that Germany did not attack Scilly in the Second World War because of gratitude for the sterling work done by Scillonians when the German liner *Schiller* was wrecked on the Western Rocks in 1875; in fact, early in the war, German aircraft bombed Scilly several times and two Scillonian civilians were killed. It was only after a flight of six Hurricanes were based on the aerodrome on St Mary's from 1941 that German aircraft were deterred from encroaching on Scillonian airspace.

Other examples of Scilly's myths and misunderstandings can be found, but those above have been mentioned partly because an

11

apology may be called for where previous editions of this work and others have – regretfully – strayed into an easy acceptance of some of them. But study is nothing if it does not expose the limitations of one's knowledge, and lead to some attempt being made to put matters right; and Scilly is too wonderful and special a place to continue unnecessarily to suffer from correctable erroneous beliefs ascribed to its past.

CHAPTER II –
ANTIQUITY, ATLANTIS and LYONNESSE

In Greek and Latin mythology, frequent mention is made of islands situated beyond the Pillars of Hercules (now called the Straits of Gibraltar) and referred to variously as the Isles of the Blest, the Hesperides, the Elysian Fields, or Atlantis. None of these can satisfactorily be identified with Scilly, even though at that time Scilly would most likely have been one large island, with a few smaller, outlying ones, rather than the larger number of much smaller islands which exist today. The current belief seems to be that Atlantis was of a large size and, if it existed at all as a fabulously rich land, was situated in mid-Atlantic and was destroyed by undersea volcanoes, leaving today only the Azores and the Canary Islands to mark its former presence. An alternative calamity theory postulates volcanic eruptions at Santorini, 70 miles north of Crete in the Mediterranean, but Plato was sure its location was in the Atlantic.

Speculation about Atlantis intrigued adventurers such as Christopher Columbus, one of whose aims on his first voyage westwards in 1492 was to discover Atlantis – he even altered course twice to be more likely to encounter what remained of the land he believed was rich with gold; but today only a chain of islands, called the Antilles, preserves the name – if not the position – of the fabled land, for Columbus was looking primarily for India, which he imagined he had found when he made a landfall in the West Indies.

The American historian Samuel Eliot Morrison wrote in *The Oxford History of the New World* 'History is very chancy. America was discovered accidentally by a great seaman who was looking for somewhere else; when discovered it was not wanted; and most of the exploration for the next fifty years was done in the hope of getting through or round it – and America was named after a man who discovered no part of the New World'. Morrison describes Columbus as a great seaman; but as a navigator – using the word in the sense of knowing where you are on the globe – he could hardly have been more wrong, for he believed until he died that he had reached Asia, and, ever since, his error has been perpetuated by naming as Indians the original inhabitants of most of North America.

* * * * *

One reason why Scilly was at one time thought to be identified with the Hesperides or Islands of the Blest was because Celtic legends referred to a land of the dead called Avalon or Glasinnus, with old manuscripts locating this vaguely to the south-west of Britain. Some support for this view seemed to come from the large number of chambered barrows of the megalithic period that have been found on Scilly – many more than in the whole of Cornwall. These barrows or ancient burial mounds are out of proportion to the number and style of persons who, according to the archaeological evidence, are likely to have been living in the islands. Hence grew the belief that the graves were erected for princes (and possibly their families) of greater renown than could ever have lived and ruled locally. It used to be argued that the relative inaccessibility of the islands would have made them a safe depository for sentimental and material treasures, and a suitable place for the remains of a departed chief to rest undisturbed and in peace. Moreover, since it was believed that the spirit of the departed could not cross water, a dead chief left on Scilly would be unable to return to his native land to embarrass his successor.

All this, however, was speculation and is now discounted, the large number of ancient burial grounds in Scilly being explained by the practice of inhumation persisting longer in Scilly than on the mainland, and by the fact that the valleys, where many people lived, have been covered now by the sea, whereas the hilltops, where burials were common, still survive. Moreover, mainland farmers are likely to have cleared more ancient grave sites for agriculture than occurred in Scilly, where the high ground is exceptionally stony and difficult to work.

The stone tombs in Scilly are generally of two main kinds; the chambered entrance graves of massive granite slabs were for communal or family burials, and the smaller cists, kistvaens or stone-boxes were for single burials. Many have been destroyed or despoiled, including three on Round Island when the lighthouse was built, and it was not until 1901 that George Bonsor carried out the first systematic excavation of Scilly's tombs. He started with one on

14

Obadiah's Barrow on Gugh

photo K Dibley

Gugh, named after Obadiah Hicks, the St Agnes man who found it; inside was an urn (now in the museum on St Mary's) containing cremated remains, and a bronze awl, one of the first bronze objects found in a preserved chamber in Britain.

Below the cremated remains of Middle Bronze Age people, human bones from an earlier period were often found. This is because the practice of burying the body in a sitting posture, and later in a lying position, lasted until about 1700 BC when it was superseded by that of cremating the body first and then placing the ashes in urns, often in existing barrows. There are also several monoliths or standing stones in Scilly, the most impressive of which, *The Old Man of Gugh*, stands in a solitary spot on the downs on that island. Their original purpose can only be surmised as being connected with religious ceremonies. There are about 14 ley lines emanating from this stone, which has led to further conjecture. On the other hand, such stones could have been territorial markers at some time in the past.

From pieces of pottery, funeral urns, stone mace-heads, flint instruments, holed stones, saddle querns, and stone mortars which have been found in Scilly, it is clear that the islands were inhabited as far back as 4,000 years ago. The remains of a few huts dating from the Bronze Age have also been discovered, and one on English

15

Passage Grave at Porth Hellick

Porth Hellick Down Burial Chamber is one of a group of eight tombs near together, this one being the only one in the group maintained by English Heritage and perhaps the best preserved in Scilly. A passage three feet wide leads to the chamber which has four large cap-stones. Only a few potsherds dating from the late Bronze Age were found in the tomb, so the original contents have long since been stolen or removed. The tomb was probably used many times both for burial and later as a repository for cremation remains during the Bronze Age. It is the largest in a cemetery for a family or tribe living in Scilly between two and four thousand years ago, and probably unused since then; yet a holidaymaker, entering the dark tomb in 1989 to change the film in his camera, picked up what turned out to be a 5th century copper-coin.

Island Carn, St Martin's, has an impressive midden or refuse dump alongside, indicating the diet of the early inhabitants from the great quantity of limpet shells it contains. But these relatively insignificant huts built for the living contrast strikingly with the massive masonry of the tombs built to house the dead. At Bants Carn near Telegraph is what is now thought to have been an ancestral shrine, built about 2000 BC or a little later.

The barrows and other monuments were constructed between two and four thousand years ago, and built with the use of primitive

16

instruments; their construction may in some ways have resembled that which we now believe was employed in the building of Stonehenge, namely by using log rollers, levers, and considerable manpower for haulage. Splitting of the granite stones may have been accomplished by inserting dry wooden wedges into crevices in the sides, and then soaking them with water till the expansion of the wood split the whole stone. Many boulders on the islands show indentations which seem to have been made for wedges in this way.

Unfortunately, quite apart from the destructive effects of weather, many of the barrows have been despoiled, as on the mainland, by farmers looking for shaped stone for hedging and walling, and by plunderers who, particularly in the 18th and 19th centuries, opened many of the barrows seeking the jewellery and valuables which it became believed they contained. These had sometimes been buried with the dead for their use in the next world, by people who believed in the immortality of the body as well as of the spirit. Archaeologists have been fortunate in that the plunderers missed so much, for, besides valuables and jewellery, tools, weapons, and even foods were buried. A visit to the museum in Church Street, St Mary's, is one of the best ways to become acquainted with some of these finds.

One object from the Bronze Age was discovered casually by a holidaymaker on a beach on St Martin's in March, 1989. This was a small, horseshoe-shaped, gold bracelet which was lying in the sand. At first he just slipped it into his pocket as something unusual, and the first mainland museum he took it to declared it to be of no importance and of little value; but, when he had it examined at the British Museum, they declared it to be of gold, and 2,000 to 3,000 years old and likely to have been worn at that date by someone of rank and importance. Another important find was Britain's earliest-known statue; it had been lost, but was rediscovered on St Martins in 1989. It is a roughly-carved stone idol over 3,000 years old, now about two feet high and re-erected on Chapel Down, although originally it must have been on a plinth and much higher. The top consists of a human face – nose, mouth, eyes and neck all faintly discernible in the right light.

Important discoveries of human activity long ago are not infrequent in Scilly. In 1999 a farmer's tractor wheel fell into an unsuspected burial cist on Bryher, in which was a two thousand years old sword, still in its scabbard – and an oval bronze mirror of

Standing Stone on Gugh, ancient ritual site or territorial marker?

photo K Dibley

Kistvaen on Samson: opened by Augustus Smith in 1863 it contained the ashes of human remains

photo Gibson, Scilly

18

similar age – both now on view in St Mary's Museum in Church Street. In 2003, a Bronze Age village of five houses, perhaps over 3,000 years old, was uncovered by contractors creating a new cricket ground at Old Grimsby, but had to be covered by earth again to await future full excavation by archaeologists.

* * * * *

The legend of the lost land of Lyonnesse has persisted for centuries and inspired poets and writers to produce fanciful tales, which help to keep the legend alive. The claim that human settlements once existed to the east of Scilly is believable as there is relatively shallow sea here (mostly not over a hundred metres deep) and some of Scilly's land hereabouts has definitely been engulfed by the rising sea – although an alternative site for Lyonnesse is claimed at Leonois off Brittany. What is claimed with greater certainty is that Scilly has not been joined to Land's End in historical times, not indeed since the last ice age, some ten thousand years ago. This was when the English Channel was also dry land and the River Thames a tributary of the River Rhine, which emptied into the sea to the north of what is now called the North Sea. Formations of flint and chalk today at Land's End have been found similar to those on Castle Down, Tresco, and green sand chert on St Martin's matches Eocene river gravels in Devon – all of which indicates that, before the last ice age, Scilly was part of a table-land over which rivers flowed from Dartmoor into the sea at the edge of the Continental Shelf, some 200 miles west of Scilly. There is no record of a sudden calamity in Scilly in historical times, but plenty of evidence, if not recordings, of progressive minor encroachments of the sea. But elsewhere around British coasts, such happenings have certainly been recorded: in 830 AD, a thousand persons are said to have been drowned on islands near Cork in Ireland, and in the Anglo-Saxon Chronicle it is recorded that on the 11th November, 1014, 'the sea-tide ran up so very high and did so much harm as no one remembered that it ever before did'. In Edward I's reign (1272-1307) there is known to have occurred an inundation at Old Winchelsea near Rye, and in the Welsh Triads there is a story of a great inundation about AD 500 which destroyed nineteen fortified towns in Wales. These incidents may well have been part of widespread disturbances which included Scilly, and floodings have more than once been recorded as having taken place

19

in Mounts Bay. Moreover, doubtful identifications of islands in Scilly mentioned in some medieval documents, could be accounted for if they were victims of subsidence, and the stone hedges and foundations of buildings such as those on Par Beach, St Martin's, and on Nornour below the high tide line, are evidence that the sea has encroached within historical times; moreover, it is traditional belief of Cornishmen that a tract of land called Lyonnesse (or in Cornish, Lethowsow) once existed within historical times, on which was a town called the City of Lions at the Seven Stones (where the lightship is now stationed), the site of which was spoken of as 'The Town'. It is also claimed that ruined parts of houses have been observed under the sea at the Seven Stones. Heath writes that 'at Sennen Church-Town, near the extremity of Cornwall, there is the base of an old stone-column, belonging to a building, which was taken up by some fishermen, at the place of the Seven Stones, about 18 inches height and three feet diameter at the circular base. Besides which, other pieces of building, and glass windows, have been taken up at different times in the same place, with diverse kinds of utensils ...'. Such recordings need not be disbelieved if they are inventories of salvage from habitations which once existed in the drowned valleys within and around the present islands of Scilly. But there is no record of floods in the annals of Tavistock Abbey (founded AD 961), and all the religious foundations in Scilly were certainly attached to Tavistock Abbey by AD 1114. The legend of Lyonnesse was possibly the exaggerated collective folk memory of a succession of comparatively minor floodings taking place over a considerable period, which may have seemed to those who suffered from them and to their descendants, evidence of much greater and more widespread disasters. The story later gained some credence partly from Malory's romantic story of King Arthur and the Knights of the and Round Table, later also used by Tennyson who visited Scilly for a few days on his 'Arthurian journey', and has inspired many poets and writers, in Brittany as well as Britain, including Milton, Spenser, Dryden, Scott, Swinburne, and William Morris. In the course of time fact and fiction have become easily confused and difficult to disentangle.

CHAPTER III – TIN, ROMANS,
KING ARTHUR and INUNDATIONS

For many centuries attempts have been made to settle the question of whether Scilly may be identified with the Cassiterides, the secret islands where the Phoenicians were believed to obtain their tin. Pliny wrote that 'opposite to Celtiberia are a number of islands, by the Greeks called Cassiterides, in consequence of their abounding in tin'. However, there is no evidence of much mining in Scilly, only a few shallow scrapings such as can be found in the northern parts of Tresco, which are most likely 17th century tinner's pits. Certainly a deduction can be made from the fact that the range of granite runs from Devon to Scilly, and that tin is most plentiful on the extreme tip of Cornwall nearest to the islands. Archaeological evidence suggests that the Land's End peninsula was the most densely populated part of Cornwall from the Stone Age till late in the Bronze Age – the tin veins may have been nearer to the surface in that area than elsewhere on the mainland, and probably more exposed still in Scilly. In time Scilly's surface tin could have become exhausted, but by then Scilly might have become a safe place to store mainland tin prior to export, although this is only speculation. Stand today on the coast above the village of Sennen, and, as the tide falls, a reef appears, breaking the sea surface and suggesting that when the sea level was lower, Sennen possessed a harbour, protected from rough water by this natural breakwater. Then, imagine the sea level lower still, when the reef may have been an island with growth on it and was never covered by high tides – it may even have had some of the qualities ascribed to Ictis. Scilly might then conceivably have become a depot from which the tin was shipped elsewhere – the discovery of jewellery from Roman times on Nornour, artefacts which seem unlikely to have been made in Scilly – also suggests that Scilly may have been a depot at some period. But all this is speculation and not history, for the whole story is lost in the mists of antiquity, and Scilly's claim to identification with the Cassiterides is now regarded as most unlikely.

Geoffrey Grigson wrote a most readable book about Scilly in 1948 entitled *The Scilly Isles*. But in his other book entitled *West Country*, part of the 'About Britain' series published by Collins, but sponsored by the Brewers' Society as their contribution to the Festival of Britain in 1951, he wrote: 'Do not believe stories about Cornwall and Phoenicians. They are an invention of the Elizabethan antiquary William Camden, which are not easily killed. Nothing has ever been discovered to connect the Phoenicians with the Cornish tin trade...'. Actually, one of their coins, a Numidian coin of the 2nd century BC, when Numidia was a Carthaginian dependancy, was found on Carn Brea. However, Grigson did recognise that 'the exploitation of Cornish tin seams ... must have begun under the influence of traders or prospectors from Brittany, North-west Spain and Ireland between 2000 and 1000 BC' – far earlier than Phoenician seafaring – and then mentions the 1st century Greek historian Diodorus, who wrote that merchants bought tin at the Island of Ictus, sending the ore across France to the Mediterranean, Grigson concluding – apparently for want of a more likely candidate – that Ictus was probably St Michael's Mount.

* * * * *

The Roman invasion of Britain in AD 43 began under the corpulent Emperor Claudius, and for the next 400 years most of the southern part of Britain was occupied by the Romans. Unlike some previous invaders, however, the Romans did not come to exterminate the inhabitants or to enslave them or to drive them out, but to subdue and rule over them, and acquire for the Roman Empire yet another province. In this way they were successful to a large extent south of the Fosse Way. North of this line was a military zone in which the 'pax Romana' did not always reign and, even after the building of the massive demarcation line known as Hadrian's Wall, the Pictish barbarians to the north and Anglo-Saxon pirates around the coast necessitated constant defensive military activity.

The area of Roman civilian settlement did not extend as far west as Cornwall, so few traces of Roman times survive; but it is possible that a military or penal establishment was kept in Scilly since there are records of islands named Sylina Insula being used as a place of banishment. The Emperor Maximus, is thought to have transported Bishops Tiberianus and Instantius to Scilly for heresy about AD 380,

Round House on Halangy Down

A village of round houses dating from about the 2nd century on Halangy Down, St Mary's. In the photograph one of the round houses can be seen and the cooking hearth and a drainage channel may just be discerned on the left. The hut was probably roofed with a conical covering of reeds or heather thatch. The monument is carefully preserved by English Heritage, and can be reached either by following the coastal path from Porthmellon or by taking the lane almost opposite Telegraph Tower.

and the Emperor Marcus banished a false prophet during the time of the rebellion of Cassius for 'pretending to prophesy, and foretelling of things to come, as if he was inspired', and sent him to 'Silia Insula', which has been claimed as Scilly.

In 1949 excavation on Par Beach, St Martin's, just above the high tide line, revealed the foundations of two clearly defined round houses a few feet below the sand, together with pottery of Roman influence and two fragments of Samian ware. Tradition maintains that a Roman causeway existed joining St Martin's to St Mary's along the top of Crow Bar. This 'road' is more likely to have been a stone hedge around the fields that undoubtedly surrounded the houses on Par Beach. At low tide, a careful look at the rocks on Par Beach stretching seawards, often in remarkably straight lines, certainly confirms the impression of stone hedges.

Porthcressa c1904

photo Gibson, Scilly

Porthcressa 1989

These two photographs taken about eighty years apart (c1909 and 1989) show almost the same view of Hugh Town from Buzza Hill, but in their differences reveal much of the intervening history of the town. The increase in the number of buildings is obvious, and the rising level of the sea can be surmised from the need for sea defences to Porthcressa Bank erected in 1962 and visible in the later photograph.

Close observers can also make out the windmill which used to stand on the site of the modern police station (which before the Second World War was at Hamewith) and was used to help pump water to the Garrison.

In the older photograph four children are paddling, and three of them watch the photographer – it was an unusual sight then to see someone taking photos and worth watching as much because of the paraphernalia involved in setting up a plate camera; in the later photo a few holidaymakers sport themselves on the beach, and some of them are paddling – all unchanged pleasure.

In the foreground of the modern photo is the ancient barrow on Buzza Hill, able to be reached by visitors now that English Heritage has cleared some of the gorse, bracken and brambles.

With the exception of a Roman bronze brooch found on Old Man, a Roman alter found on St Mary's, and a few Roman coins found on Samson, little is known of Scilly during the Roman occupation of Britain AD 43 to AD 410. However, there is a village of eleven huts near Telegraph dating from about 200 BC called Halangy Village and in use in Roman times, but nothing specifically Roman has been discovered there. Then, in 1962, just above the high tide mark on the small uninhabited island of Nornour in the Eastern Islands, was discovered a collection of Roman items, exposed as a result of the storms of that year. Over three hundred pieces of jewellery mainly from the 1st to 3rd century AD were unearthed, but no coins later than the 4th century were among them, probably indicating that habitation (or at least the industry there) terminated then. There were also Roman brooches, pieces of pottery, fragments of a stone statue, and part of the stone wall of a house together with a stone fire-place. Such contact as the inhabitants of Scilly may have had with the Romans during the period of their occupation was at any rate ended in the 5th century AD, when the Roman military forces withdrew to defend the heart of the Empire from invading barbarians from Eastern Europe. The Britons, who had become unwarlike in outlook, enjoying the benefits of Roman law and Roman military protection, now lay defenceless; and Britain presented a rich and tempting prize for pirates. Even before the

The area inside the broken line represents a speculative map of the Isles of Scilly as they might have been in about the time of King Arthur – one large island with a few small outlying islands and rocks. This map suggests that more of Scilly has drowned in historical times than has remained dry land. The higher ground which survived the inundations of the sea are the islands of today, shown marked with their separate names.

The Drowning of the Valleys in Scilly

Romans withdrew there had been plundering raids on the east and south coasts of Britain, and in the next four hundred years we know little of the Isles of Scilly except that they formed at times a base for marauders.

The West Saxon invasion of Cornwall (West Wales) began in 814, but it is not known when they reached Scilly. In 927 King Athelstan is supposed to have embarked with his fleet at Whitsand near Plymouth and to have subdued Scilly, but this story is now regarded as doubtful, for probably Scilly was confused with somewhere else. Later, as a result of the arrival of the monks, the islands adopted Christianity, and a priory to St Nicholas was founded on Tresco. St Nicholas, as the patron saint, was an appropriate choice since he was said to have been able to preserve vessels from the perils of the sea, if his aid was invoked fervently enough. St Nicholas was Archbishop of Myra, a city of Lycia in Lesser Asia, where he died in AD 324. His relics (now in Bari in Italy) were said to perform miraculous cures, particularly with infants.

* * * * *

King Arthur had no chronicler, for few except priests were literate in the sixth century. No contemporary manuscript has come down to us to record his saga, nor even ballad or verse. According to one account he was made King of Britain when he was fifteen and was 'well beloved among all men'. His story belongs to the days when Britain belonged to the Britons – before the English (Angles, Saxons, Jutes) invaded – and his life seems partly to have become a crusade of a Christian leader fighting against the pagan Anglo-Saxon invaders. In history we hear of a British prince of the name of Arthur engaged in what is presented as a noble but losing fight to stem the westward movement of the English. At Mount Badon (in about AD 500) he fought a great battle and is said to have slowed the English advance for a generation. But Arthur seems to have been active in many parts of Britain, which may well indicate a composite figure built up from folk tales of the exploits of many such valiant local defenders. J.C. Walters has written that 'Arthur's graves are so many that it would be easy to reduce the whole thing to an absurdity by saying that, if there were a doubt that King Arthur ever lived, his numerous "graves" conclusively prove that he died many times, despite the tradition, too, that he did not die at all!' With so many

Giant's Castle – the earliest man-made fort in Scilly

claims, there is no means of knowing where he was buried; Cornish legend has Arthur killed fighting at the Battle of Camlann and his body being subsequently taken for burial on the Isle of Avalon (which could be Scilly by an imaginative stretch). This is certainly not history, but there is so little of that in the 6th century, that a fanciful story like this gets credence far beyond what the evidence for it should permit. If Avalon is Scilly, then burial on the western slopes of the island which bears Arthur's name would seem as likely a spot as any. In Arthur's time, early in the sixth century, despite some rise in sea levels, Scilly was still mainly the one large island of Ennor, with St Agnes joined with Annet as a second smaller one. The relative shallowness of the sea separating the islands was demonstrated by John Pickwell of St Mary's when, in September, 1970, at a very low spring tide, he walked from White Island to St Martin's, and on to Tresco; then, on the next tide, accompanied by the very tall Chaplain of the Isles, Bill Rowett, and a local policeman, he walked the most difficult crossing from Tresco to Bar Point, St Mary's, accompanied by a following punt in case rescue was required. This feat would be more difficult to repeat today because the sea level has risen slightly since and continues to rise, although seas which used to sweep across from Porthcressa to the Pool (most devastatingly perhaps on the afternoon of 26th September, 1744) are now rare owing to the raising of the high sand barrier at Porthcressa early last century. But, on 7th March, 1962, a south-easterly hurricane, which caused considerable damage to the sea-wall at Old Town and swept away part of the sandbank on Par Beach, St Martin's, built up the spring tide to such a height that sea broke through the bank at Porthcressa and floated boats down Hugh Street before pouring into the Pool. The sea defences at Porthcressa have been strengthened and a new sea-wall was constructed at Old Town in 1965 which has prevented any repetition, although a storm in December, 1989, severely tested these defences. New walls built since at Porthcressa have much improved safety – for the time being.

An inundation of a different kind, not caused by gales, occurred in 1755 when the great earthquake at Lisbon produced a tidal wave in Scilly so that low water became, for a few moments, high tide. Boats formerly lying inert on dry sand were lifted bodily on the crest of the waves, straining at the limits of their anchor chains. Fortunately, the sea was calm and at low water, so little damage resulted and the sea quickly subsided.

CHAPTER IV – THE MONKS
and THE MIDDLE AGES

Though there is mention in early records of cells and chapels bearing various names on some parts of Scilly, and of holy men who lived in them, the earliest one of which good evidence survives was on St Helen's, known as St Elidius, but, of course, not necessarily an island during much of it's time as an oratory. It consisted of a round building and three rectangular huts, with St Elidius as its solitary tenant in the tenth century. The site was excavated 1956-58, and today an annual pilgrimage is made there each summer.

The cell of priory of St Nicholas on Tresco consisted of monks but it is not clear how far the house had a distinct corporate character. As early as the reign of Edward the Confessor (1042-1066), the Abbey of Tavistock held possessions in Scilly, and it was these which Henry I (1100-1135) confirmed to the Abbey of Tavistock in 1114 and to Turoldus, one of the monks in Scilly. He granted his special protection for them to retain all churches and all land they already held. Little is known of the priory before this charter confirmation, except that it had existed from a much earlier date. One memorial stone, which probably marked a grave of the priory now lies broken and flat and serving as paving immediately under the smaller archway of the priory ruins. What is left of the inscription reads: 'THI FILI...COGVI', which means something like 'the grave of the son of ...' (rest missing). It is the oldest writing in Scilly.

When Henry I made his grant to Tavistock Abbey, he included Elidius's (St Helen's), St Sampson (Samson), St Theona (Teän), Renteman (presumably Tresco), and Nurcho, Nutho or Nullo (unidentified), together with all wrecks except whole ships. (In these grants gold, whale, scarlet cloth and fir or masts were always reserved for the King). In another grant all the tithes of Scilly were confirmed to the monks by Richard de Wich 'for his soul and the souls of his parents, and of Reginald, Earl of Cornwall, his Lord'. Reginald de Dunstanville, a natural son of Henry I, was created Earl of Cornwall in 1140 and confirmed the original grant to Tavistock

Abbey, from which it appears that the islands were then held as part of the Earldom.

From its establishment to the dissolution of the monasteries in 1539, the monastic community of Tresco was controlled at different times by thirty-eight abbots, but little is known of their affairs in Scilly. The traces of the priory which are still in existence on Tresco indicate that it was of some considerable size, and the record of its final destruction is missing, but, from the evidence of charred timber, it was probably destroyed by fire in the Civil War or after. Today, the major relic is a pair of fine archways standing among the ruins.

In a Return of Edward I's Commissioners of 1275 for the Hundred of Penwith (which included Scilly), it is stated: 'They [the jury] say that John de Allet and the Prior of St Nicholas [Tresco], Lords of Scilly, take wreck of the sea in those Islands, but they know not by what warrant, the ancestors of the aforesaid John and the Prior having done so from the time whereof memory is not.' And later in Edward I's reign we find the Abbot of Tavistock claiming 'the ship-wrecks happening in all the Islands' (i.e. the monks' islands), which he and his predecessors had 'enjoyed without interruption from time immemorial'.

The monks must have been sorely harassed by marauders from the sea since the civil authority would not (or more probably could not) give the islands adequate protection. We find the monks complaining of the rigours of their existence on the islands and petitioning to be redrafted to the parent abbey at Tavistock. Possibly a tour of duty in Scilly was regarded as a disciplinary measure or penance. In the reign of Edward III (1327-1377) only two monks appear to have been resident at Tresco; and in the wars against France only secular priests were resident in Scilly.

In the Register of Bishop Grandison, of the 21st September, 1351 mention is made of the impoverishment occasioned to the Abbey of Tavistock from the enormous devastation committed by pirates in the Isles of Scilly – 'ex qua non modica pars subsidii Monasterii de Tavistock provenire consuerit.'

The following document, translated from the Norman-French, gives an interesting side-light on Scilly, as a resort and refuge of fugitive serfs in the time of Edward III. 'Edward the [Black] Prince, etc., to Walter Hull, Constable of the Castle and Keeper of the Isles of Scilly: At the suggestion of our well-beloved Ralph Vyvyan, one of

31

our tenants in Cornwall, we command you that whereas Robert Martyn, Roger Tregarn, Robert Carngonel, and others his born serfs have run away out of his seignory in Cornwall as far as the said Isles, and now remain there. We command that if it be so, you permit that he take them again, and cause them to return to his seignory as Law and Right require, and do not make any disturbance or maintenance by them against him in this matter to his disinheritance. Done under our Privy Seal at London, the 4th February, 27 Edward III.'

This document may well be evidence of the effects of the Black Death, which produced such a shortage of labourers that many of them fled from their village serfdom and took paid employment elsewhere as free men. Before the Black Death serfs were bound to the soil and could not leave their villages without their lord's permission; if they attempted to do so, they would be sent back because it was in all landlord's interests to support this lawful practice. But after the Black Death, labour was in short supply as up to a quarter of the population of England is estimated to have died from the plague in the year 1348-9. Therefore, it became no longer in the landlord's interests to reject such labour and thus, in a sense, the Black Death was a significant factor in the decline of the feudal society and the rise, over time, of a rural wage economy. It is a little remarkable that the three serfs mentioned in the document travelled out of mainland Cornwall as far as the Isles of Scilly, because even journeying to the next village was somewhat rare in the Middle Ages; and the three all seemed to have surnames, which was not widespread before the 16th century.

Secular authority in the islands was vested in the Earls of Cornwall by the time of Henry I, but it is not always easy to draw a distinction between ecclesiastic and secular affairs. One of the earliest known records is that of Pope Celestine III in 1193 confirming to the Abbey of Tavistock its privileges and properties, and amongst them, within the Isles of Scilly, the islands of St Nicholas (Tresco), St Sampson, St Elidius, St Theona the Virgin, and an island called Nutho, with their belongings, and all churches and oratories in all the isles, with tithes and offerings, besides two bits of cultivated land in Aganas (Hagness, now St Agnes) and three in Ennor (now St Mary's).

The rest of Scilly was a Feudal Lordship appurtenant owing allegiance to the Castle of Launceston, and the Tenant owed suit and paid yearly a rent called 'waiternfee' (or 'watching fee') at Michaelmas at the gate of the castle.

The date of the building of Ennor Castle is uncertain, but it probably commenced in the time of Henry III (1216-1272) although possibly even earlier; it is mentioned specifically in a document dated 1244. This castle, of which little remains, has been identified as Old Town Castle and was situated in a commanding position close to what was then the main town. Its name, Ennor or Ynnor, was the secular name for St Mary's.

In AD 1248, Drew de Barrentine was sent to Scilly by Henry III to act as Governor and to administer justice. He received lands to the value of £10 in payment. The noble Norman Barrentines were a maritime family who kept to the sea coast as long as they could, and already held the Channel Islands under the Crown. Their garrison at Ennor Castle would appear to have consisted of armed men supplied by tenants as a condition of holding land.

The next king (Edward I, 1272-1307) granted the Castle of Ennor in Scilly in 1306 to Ranulph Blancminster in return for finding twelve armed men, keeping the peace at all times, and paying at Michaelmas three-hundred puffins, or six shillings and eight pence. This rent seems to have been paid yearly up to the reign of Edward VI (1547), but always in the form of money.

In the reign of Edward II (1307-1327) Ranulph Blancminster was given licence to crenellate the castle. The Caption of Seizin, preserved in the Duchy Office, records that, when the Black Prince took possession of his Duchy (in 1337), the Lord of the 'Manor of Scilly' was Ranulph Blancminster who died in the summer of 1348, leaving, as his heir, grandson Gandewen, a minor of about nine years of age. The Duchy held the Manor during the minority, and after an interval the Black Prince granted its custody and the wardship of the heir to William Morier or Morrers.

In the Minister's accounts for the year 1348-49, the collection of rents by the Duchy is recorded. The rents collected were from bond and free tenants, perquisites of court, heriots, and dues from ships calling at the islands, and a note is appended that the collection was 'no more, because the great part of the Fishermen have died this year by the Pestilence' – a reference to the Black Death of that year.

A further account of the same Roll states: 'The Yearly Rent of l00s, for the Wine Tavern [Taberna vini, possibly a wine booth or custom house] and of 40s. for the Windmill are not forthcoming because both tenements have been destroyed by the Foreigners'.

In 1342, six-hundred Welshmen were sent to Brittany on the King's Service, and probably fought later at the Battle of Crécy, 1346. We learn about them from a petition of the Lord of the Isles of Scilly (Patent Rolls) setting forth that 'whereas these Welshmen were drawn by the sea on to that Island staying there for 20 days and carrying away £500 worth of crops, the Tenants are not able to till their lands and pay their dues'. Whilst becalmed they had apparently plundered Scilly.

From the Inquisition Post Mortem of the 22nd year of Edward III, it appears that 'Ranulf de Blancminster held in his demesne as of fee of the Lord Edward, Prince of Wales, Duke of Cornwall and Earl of Chester as of the Honour of His Castle of Launceston, the Castle of Scilly with the Islands belonging to the said Castle by Knight Service at a yearly rent of 300 puffins or half a mark. The which Castle with the islands aforesaid are worth yearly in all issues according to the true value £18 19s 4½d.'

In the Calendar of Inquisitions Vol III Edward I Cornwall Inq. 30 November 29, Edward I, p. 458, there is the following entry: 'Fee farms pertaining to the gate of the castle of Launceston, to be received by the hands of divers tenants. viz – Sully – 6s 8d from 300 puffons sent.'

This date is 30 November 1300, rather earlier than previously thought, and it suggests that puffins were paid as rent for Scilly in the 13th century – possibly from the time Edward I came to the throne in 1272.

Puffins could he eaten in Lent having been classed as fish to enable their consumption to be lawful because there was some doubt about the puffins' origin. Kenneth Sisam has written that puffins were usually salted, but, 'in New Zealand, seabirds, of kinds that are brought to maximum fatness and then deserted by their parents, were dragged out of their holes, plucked, cooked and preserved in their own fat: these "mutton birds" were reckoned a great delicacy.' Puffins were also valued for their feathers as well as for the edible qualities. Their value seemed to vary over time, for, instead of 6s 8d or 300 puffins, by 1440 the rent of Scilly was 6s 8d or 50 puffins.

Blancminster seems to have been a high-handed individual who, according to William le Poer, Coroner on St Mary's, instead of keeping the peace 'received felons, thieves, outlaws and men guilty of manslaughter', and committed many abuses. For this complaint

Edward I appointed a commission, but nothing came of it, and William le Poer was thrown into prison by Blancminster at Le Val (Holy Vale) and made to pay one hundred marks. Justice could certainly be rough in those days, for instance: 'When anyone is attainted of any felony, he ought to be taken to a certain rock in the sea, with two barley loaves and one pitcher of water upon the same rock, they leave the same felon until by the flowing of the sea he is swallowed up.'

We have another reference to the administration of the Blancminsters, in this case probably that of Ranulph's son and successor, John de Albo Monasterio, Knight, and MP for the County of Cornwall, in the reign of Edward III. During his time, the priory of St Nicholas, having complained that 'for want of proper protection' it was 'wasted and impoverished by the frequent arrival of the seaships of all nations', King Edward III, 'holding it in great esteem as a royal foundation', commanded all dukes, earls, admirals, soldiers, masters of ships, and mariners, and especially the constable of his castle in the isle of Ennor, to extend to the prior, monks, and chaplains and their servants, all possible protection, so that they might be able to bear their proper burdens and offer prayers and devotions continuously for the King, his progenitors, and his heirs, as they had been wont to do'.

The Blancminsters were succeeded by the Coleshills, and St Agnes was held in the Hamley family for a considerable length of time, apparently as inferior grantees. On 25th March, 1351, Ralph Hamley granted to his brother, Laurence, the 'Island of Agnes in Scilly, with the rents and services of the same, consisting of dried fish and wrecks of the said Island, paying yearly for seven years to come one grain of wheat and after that time one hundred shillings Sterling'.

William of Worcester in his *Itineraries* of 1478-80 mentions Scilly, and Richard III ordered an inquisition of them to be taken in 1484, when it appears that they were worth, in time of peace, forty shillings, but in time of war – nothing! This latter value was recognition of the difficulty and danger of holding Scilly in time of war, and of the expense which it entailed.

The next record is taken from the notes of John Leland, the antiquarian, who claimed to have visited Scilly in about 1540, but who was prevented, owing to loss of his reason, from arranging the notes. Some are of interest:

'St. Mary Isle is a five miles or more in cumpace, in it is a poor town, and a meately strong pile (Ennor Castle); but the roves of the buildings in it be sore defacid and worne.

Iniscaw longid to Tavestoke, and ther was a poor cell of monks of Tavestoke. Sum caulle this Trescaw; it is the biggest of the islettes, in cumpace 6 miles or more.

S. Agnes Isle so caullid of a chapel theryn.

The Isle of S. Agnes was desolated by this chaunce in recenti hominum memoria. The hole numbre of V. housoldes that were yn this isle cam to a mariage or a fest in S. Mary Isle, and going homewarde were al drownid.

Saynet Lides Isle wher yn tymes past at her sepulchre was gret superstition.

Few men be glad to inhabite these islettes, for al the plenty, for robbers by sea that take their catail by force. The robbers be Frenchmen and Spaniardes.

One Danvers a gentilman of Wilshir whos chief house at Daundsey, and Whitington, a gentilman of Glocestreshire be owners of Scylley; but they have scant 40 marks (£26 13s. 4d.) by yere of rentes and commodities of it.

In the biggest isle (cawled St. Nicholas Isle) of the Scylleys ys a lytle pyle or fortres, and a paroch chyrche that a monke of Tavestoke yn peace doth serve as a membre of Tavestoke Abbay. Ther be yn that paroch about LX howseholdes. The ground of this isle berith exceeding corn; insomuch that if a man do but cast corn where hogges have rotid it wyl cum up.

Ther is a nother cawled Inisschawe, that ys to say the Isle of Elder, by cause yt berith stynkkyng elders. Ther be wild bores or swyne.

Ther is one isle of the Scylleys cawled Rat Isle, yn which be so many rattes that yf horse, or any other lyving beast be brought thyther, they devore him. Ther is a nother cawled Bovy Isle.'

The notes appear to have been written down on a hurried visit or possibly from hearsay.

* * * * *

By the 16th century the priory was run down and the monks were keen to leave Scilly to obtain posts as parish priests perhaps on the mainland, where life would be less troubled. With the dissolution of all the larger monasteries in 1539, Tavistock Abbey became Crown property, but the islands are not mentioned in the records, although £6,000 was expended by Edward VI (1547-1553) on fortification, of which little trace remains. But there may have been repairs to Tresco Castle (later called King Charles' Castle) first built about 1540 in the north of Tresco to command the channel there, and a start to building a fort at which is now called Harry's Walls on St Mary's to command St Mary's harbour, both buildings being badly sited for their purpose.

Then, Thomas Seymour, Lord Admiral and brother of the Duke of Somerset, the Protector to the boy King Edward VI (1547-53), bought Scilly in 1547. He had married Catherine Parr – the sixth wife and widow of Henry VIII – and he made deals with pirates and even – once Catherine Parr had died – plotted to marry the young Princess Elizabeth. Seymour allowed the islands to become a pirate base according to the bill of attainder brought against him in 1549, in which he was accused of entering into relations with pirates and 'to have gotten into his hands the strong and dangerous isles of Scilly where he might have a safe refuge if anything for his demerits should he attempted against him'. For this, and the other matters, he was attainted and beheaded, and the islands reverted to the Crown (5th March, 1549).

CHAPTER V – THE GODOLPHINS, THE CIVIL WARS and SCILLY'S DEFENCES

By Elizabeth's reign the connection of the Godolphin family with Scilly had been well established. William Godolphin and later Thomas Godolphin had been military governors of Scilly; then, in 1570, Elizabeth leased the islands to Francis (afterwards Sir Francis) Godolphin for thirty-eight years, on condition that he defended them and paid a yearly rental of £10 to the Receiver of the Duchy. Subsequent leases were granted to the Godolphin-Osborne family (at £20 a year in 1609), and for some 250 years (except during the Interregnum) they were the owners of the islands. Thereafter, for a further 31 years from 1800, the islands were leased to the heir of the Godolphins, the Duke of Leeds, who in 1831 decided to give up the lease, causing Scilly to revert once again to the Crown.

In May 1593, Queen Elizabeth ordered Star Castle to be built on St Mary's at the expense of the Crown, partly as a precaution against a further descent from Spain and partly as a protection from pirates and privateers. The Spaniards had a base at Brest, from whence issued the four galleys which raided Mousehole and Penzance in 1595, and there was good reason to anticipate that Spain might use Scilly as a base from which to launch an invasion of the mainland. The war with Spain continued until 1604, and several further Spanish invasion fleets were planned but never reached England's shores. But the danger from Spain helps to explain Elizabeth's anxiety to fortify Scilly. It is on record that Philip of Spain had instructed his Admiral Menandez, as early as 1574, to seize the Isles of Scilly and establish a base there; but plague broke out in the fleet, the Admiral dying of it, and the scheme was abandoned.

The rendezvous of the Armada of 1588 was Scilly, and there are many references in the State Papers regarding Spain's intentions towards the islands. The following extract from the General Orders issued by the Duke of Medina Sidonia, C. in C. of the Spanish Armada, is of interest:

The Garrison Gateway was of Elizabethan construction but was rebuilt by Master Gunner Abraham Tovey who had his initials writ large put upon them. Above these – though smaller – are G R (for George Rex, the king in 1742 being George II), the date of the rebuilding 1742, and F G, the initials of the governor, Francis Godolphin. Tovey then added the bell-tower.

'May, 1588 ... on leaving Cape Finisterre the course will be to the Scilly Isles, and ships must try to sight the Islands from the South, if ships get separated from the Armada they are to continue on the course. If on arrival there the Armada is behind them, they will cruise off the place until the Armada appears ...'

As a consequence of the Menandez episode, the attention of Elizabeth and her advisers was directed to Scilly, and Francis Godolphin was ordered to conduct an enquiry. In the Calendar of State Papers (Eliz. I add: 1579) his report is given, and some details are of special interest as showing the condition of the isles at that time.

1) The rent of £20 is paid to the Queen for the islands, and she is at no charge, except that she sometimes grants an allowance for powder.
2) As to Abbey lands, Treskawe Island belonged to Tavistock Abbey, and Chris. Coplestone can shew writings for Brear Island. Mr Fortescue for Agnes Isles, and the heirs of Mr Whittington and Mr Danvers for others. No ancient rents were paid except puffins or like small value,
3) King Edward VI built two clock houses [blockhouses] in St Mary's Isle and began a fort and a house, and two clockhouses on Treskawe, their charge, with that of the garrison, cost £6,000.
4) Lord Admiral Seymour not only had the Abbey lands, but all the Islands, buying the interests of others.
5) Since the Islands came into King Edward's possession, 80 tenements have been erected and laborious inclosures of rough land made.
6) There are now not a hundred men, but more women and children; the tillable ground does not find half of them bread. Only the two islands wherein are fortifications are inhabited two others are habitable for 20 persons. There are good roads [anchorages] and convenient harbours, and it would he mischievous for the enemy to take them; but I could not defend them in war, without help.

In the Calendar of State Papers appears the following:
'Aug. 9th, 1587. The Council to Sir George Carey. Report of a

Entrances to Powder House and Detention Cell on the Garrison

fleet of 120 sail having been seen off the Isles of Scilly, supposed to be Spaniards.

June 23rd, 1588. Information by Sir Francis Godolphin. Of the discovery of the Spanish fleet off the Scilly Islands. Nine sail of great ships between Scilly and Ushant, their sails all crossed over with a red cross. English boats chased and fired at.

July 6th, 1588. Lord Adm. Howard to Walsygham ... Part of the Spanish fleet has been discovered off the Scilly Islands, but they had been dispersed by the stormy weather.'

The Spanish Armada was defeated in 1588 and, with the historians' hindsight, the defeat can be seen to mark the beginning of the decline of Spanish power. But to contemporaries, Spain was still the greatest power on earth and her fleets 'marvellously strong'. A further armada was expected to be launched against England's shores and had to be prepared for. In 1593, Queen Elizabeth, usually so indecisive, finally made up her mind and Sir Francis Godolphin received a letter dated 9th May, 1593, containing the following orders:

'Having resolved upon fortifying St Mary's Island according to a

41

plan which will be brought to him, order will be given that £400, the estimated charge, be delivered to him of the revenue of that County [Cornwall] as required for keeping such fort and two other sconces. During the summer a lieutenant, three gunners and twenty-six soldiers are appointed, whose wages will amount to £1 1s 10d a day or £30 11s 4d a month, but think only ten soldiers are necessary in winter.

He is to see that some of the inhabitants of St Mary's assist the said retinue if required; has ordered according to his request four iron demi-culverins to be sent, authorises him to send two minions of brass, which are in his custody in Cornwall; he will order powder and bullets for the pieces, and matches, muskets, pikes, and halberts for the Garrison. He is to undertake the building of the fort, with advice of Robert Adams, and to choose the persons to guard it, using circumspection for avoiding superfluous charges.

Upon knowing from him in what part of Cornwall, next to the Isles, some convenient number may be put in readiness to resort to the Isle upon any great necessity, order shall be given therefor.'

The building of Star Castle is a very good and characteristic example of how well Queen Elizabeth was served by her subjects, and how parsimonious was her administration in the matter of rewards. Speed was essential – threatening Spanish vessels were frequently seen near the coast – and Robert Adams must have been a genius, since the whole building, commenced in June 1593, was completed by December 1594. Not only was the work well and truly done, but he found time to incorporate certain decorations, and never for one instant did he fail to preserve those superb proportions that distinguished the best architecture of the period. He received, for his services, 13s 4d a day. Up to December, 1594, the cost had reached £958 11s 2d, of which only £450 had been paid, and although approved at the time, the extra expenditure incurred by Sir Francis was not paid until 24th November 1603 – nine years after its presentation.

The following is taken from the Calendar of State Papers. Domestic – Elizabeth VCCXLV.72:

'August 6th, 1593.
Sir Fras. Godolphin to Lord Burghley. Adams is well deserving,

The entrance to Star Castle as it was in 1989. Conservation struggles with commercialism as a notice – as suitable as could be designed – necessarily reveals its modern use but tends to overawe the 16th century gateway. Above the portal are the initials ER for Elizabeth Regina – Elizabeth I who ruled England 1558 until 1603 – below which is the date 1593 when construction was begun. At the base on either side of the tunnel entrance are, on one side, FG for Francis Godolphin, Governor of Scilly; and, on the other side, RA for Robert Adam, the designer and building supervisor. Robert Adam also built a fort on Plymouth Hoe and rebuilt Pendennis Castle at Falmouth.

In the 1930s, when only a discreet but scarcely observable notice was fixed to the wall where the lamps are now, crowds of visitors would enter the hotel asking if they could 'look at the old ruin'; others called it 'the Star and Castle' and asked where the bars were – in those years the hotel had only a table licence.

for besides his perfect skill in numbers and measures, he is very provident in saving, and no less painful in attending; the work considered, so much has seldom been performed at such small charge, and with so few hands in so short a time.'

[This sentence from Sir Francis Godolphin's report is reminiscent of Winston Churchill's speech in 1940 on the nation's debt to the pilots of RAF Fighter Command for winning the Battle of Britain.]

This is one of two lead water tanks which now stand uselessly but decoratively on either side of the entrance to the Church of St Mary the Virgin in Hugh Town. They were made in London by Hazekiah Walker and were originally placed by the Powder House at the Garrison Gate filled with water to put out any fire that might endanger that building. They bear the date 1727 (when they were made) as well as an impressive Royal Monogram and the crest of the old Board of Ordnance, which was the predecessor of the Royal Army Ordnance Corps. Probably in George II's reign, they were taken to Star Castle and positioned on either side of the building in the inner moat, where water from the roof could fill them (as is shown in the photograph). In 1933, when Star Castle ceased to be the administrative centre and home of the Duchy agent and became a hotel, the Prince Wales – as Duke of Cornwall – had the tanks taken to his Fort Belvedere, from whence after the Abdication they were restored by George VI to Scilly – but not to Star Castle – in 1938.

Star Castle was built during 1593 and 1594 on the high rocky peninsula joined to the main part of St Mary's by a sandy isthmus on which Hugh Town now stands. Some of the stones from Ennor Castle are believed to have been used in its construction, and many of the inhabitants of Old Town moved for greater protection as near to the new fortress as possible. The quay at Hugh Town, which was later extended, was built in 1601 and Hugh Town has been the metropolis and main port of the islands ever since.

Star Castle takes its name from its unusual design in the form of an eight pointed star. Certain of its salients recall the walled cities of Flanders. The two-storied residence, which conforms to the general stellar plan, is surrounded by an eighteen-foot granite curtain wall on which are ramparts with numerous embrasures for muskets and cannon. On the ramparts are also four small rooms in each of which a captain of the garrison was lodged, each being privileged to dine at the Governor's table. Over the entrance are the initials ER (Elizabeth Regina) and below are RA (probably Robert Adams but possibly Sir Ramfrye Arundel), and FG (Francis Godolphin). The arched entrance which could be closed by a portcullis, is surmounted by a bell tower, and there is an embrasure for a cannon to command the approach. Close alongside is a sally-port leading to the dry moat which surrounds the castle. The original roof was of thatch.

Carew says: 'Sir Francis Godolphin reduced the place to a more defensible plight, and by his invention and purce bettered his plot and allowance, and therein so tempered strength with delight and both with use, as it serveth for a sure Hold and commodious Dwelling.'

Lead water tank in inner moat at Star Castle before 1933

In the Calendar of State Papers there are notes by Sir Francis Godolphin on the importance of keeping the Isles of Scilly:

'Scilly lies 30 miles from the Land's End of Cornwall WSW, being the nearest port of Her Majesty's dominions towards Spain. It is as an inn by which ships trading Westerly or Southerly are to pass and return, whereby it both succours and secures our traffic, and no other place can so aptly permit or restrain the traffic of Ireland and the north of Scotland with France and Spain. The enemy may soon make it impregnable and use it as a rendezvous with his Navy, a citadel or scourge against the realm ... proving a more hurtful neighbour in the West than Dunkirk is in the East. Neither Falmouth nor Plymouth which have the country's strength always ready to reinforce their garrisons, deserve so strong a guard as Scilly, for those isles cannot be reinforced, being so far distant from the main. In the reign of her Majesty's brother, they were kept by my father against the French with a guard of 150 men when Falmouth had but 10. I will offer £500 towards the charges needful for the fortification if Her Majesty would grant me such further term in those Isles as she did to my uncle ...'

In 1637, it was reported that the garrison at Star Castle consisted of twenty-five men, with twenty-five more sent from the mainland for six months in the year. But at the same time the islanders could not muster more than thirty persons able to carry arms. In 1642 the garrison in Scilly had increased to 165 men and the cost of maintenance to £261 a month.

The first distinguished visitor to Star Castle was Prince Charles, afterwards Charles I, who, together with his and his father's favourite, George Villiers, Duke of Buckingham, and Captain Henry Mainwaring, landed in Scilly in September, 1623, and stayed for four nights. They were returning from Spain after an unsuccessful and unpopular attempt to arrange a marriage between Charles and the Spanish Infanta. It is not clear why the ships put into Scilly, but there would appear to have been some discord on board the ship of a nature which determined the Prince that he would land.

The following account is taken from the Navy Records:

'On Sunday, September 21, a Council of War was held on the *Prince Royal* [flagship], at which the possibility of landing the Prince on one of the Isles of Scilly in a ketch was discussed. For this purpose several pilots had put off from the islands, but by the time they reached the flagship, the idea had been postponed. However, after supper the matter was again debated, and beyond expectation, order was given to make ready the longboat and to

46

Star Castle from the sea in the 1930s, with the White House of Master Gunner Abraham Tovey visible in the foreground.

call the ketch, and the Prince made choice of the company that were to accompany him to the shore.

About one of the clock after midnight, with great danger to his Highness' person and to the Duke of Buckingham, they were put into our longboat, which was veered astern by a long warp, where the ketch, laying the longboat on board, and the sea going somewhat high, they entered the ketch disorderly, without regard to any, but everyone shifting for himself.

Being all shipped, the ketch was so overburdened as she could make but little way so that after we had taken farewell with a discharge of a volley of our great ordinance, we tacked into the sea.

After six hours' buffeting the ketch succeeded in making St Mary's Island where the Prince and his retinue landed. The flagship being now for the time bereft of the services of her Captain and also the Master, Walter Whiting, the Earl of Rutland, Commander of the Fleet, held a council on board to decide what course it would be advisable to take. After serious consultation with two pilots of the island it was agreed that the *Prince Royal* might go into the roadstead without danger.

We came to anchor in the best of the roadstead about two of

47

the clock afternoon, the Prince and all his train standing upon the lower point of the land, and welcomed us in as we passed close by, with much expression of joy and heaving up their hats.'

The writer of this record indicates very clearly that this visit, 'beyond expectation' and involving a stormy and dangerous six hours' voyage in an overburdened ketch at one o'clock in the morning, was not encouraged by the naval experts, but he does not state what motive induced the Prince to visit the islands in such a hurry and in such an unceremonious manner. On leaving Star Castle the Prince gave Sir Francis Godolphin 'a chayne of gold to the value of £50 and many other large giftes'.

The family of Godolphin suffered tragedy in October, 1636. The Egmont papers contain the following letter: 'Edmund Percival to Sir Phillip Percival. I advise you to send no cattle over to Ireland whilst the Turks are so busy, lest both your cattle and your gentlemen should suffer, there having been a multitude of passengers taken this summer. Sir Francis Godolphin and his lady, and his servants, and his brother Captain Godolphin and his wife, going to the Isles of Scilly some three or four leagues off the shore, were taken by the Turks, and one of the Turks attempting to abuse the Captain's wife, he presently ran him through whereupon they cut him in a hundred pieces, and they carried Sir Francis and the rest away captives. God of his mercy send us some relief'.

In 1635 no fewer than twenty sail of 'Turkish' men-of-war were reported off Scilly. They were intercepting the fishing fleet on its return from Newfoundland, and many complaints of such happenings are recorded in the State Papers of the period. These pirates (Turks, Moors, Algerians, and the Sallee Rovers) were not finally suppressed until 1816 when Sir Edward Pellew, with British and Dutch ships, bombarded and destroyed the town of Algiers.

There are in existence fragments of letters written by a Francis Godolphin, of the family of Sir Francis (and probably father of the famous Sydney Godolphin) bearing the date 1643 (i.e. during the Civil War):

'From Francis Godolphin to John Rogers.
    For your coming over and making up your books, if it were not for displeasing somebody that I never will if I can help it, I should be very glad of seeing you, and the place is worth your

Once a serving hatch

Permanently – if a little ignominiously – stuck into a wall built as a modern extension to Garrison House, is this fragment, which was once a serving hatch. It is alleged to be of considerable antiquity.

seeing too; indeed I like it, much better than I did expect, though I must confess I came much the more willingly hither because I was not well at ease where I was ... There has noe ship come in hither since Jack went, but a Falmouth warrier, which received a broadside from one of the Parl. ships the day before.

I conceive there can be no possibility of peace. Our God be merciful to us ... to come hither, considering how glad I am at all hours to have you by me, and the novelty of the place for a few days would entertain you contentedly enough, and more than a few would tire you ten times more than Compton did. There are also some things about this place, I doe not mean the fortification, but the grounds, wherein your judgement, having viewed it, would be of use to me.

I would also that you should see my patience, for this place, in respect of an Absolute want of all welcome company is a strange change to me.

Yet a very honest man, borne here, may live very happily as

49

The flight of Prince Charles (later Charles II) from Pendennis Castle at Falmouth to Scilly in 1646 resulted in the Prince staying six weeks at Star Castle, and he is said to have used this black, oak chair during his stay. Eventually, he and his retinue made their escape to the Channel Islands and then to France. Later, the chair was used at Masonic ceremonies, and in 1933, together with the two lead water tanks, was taken by the Prince of Wales to his home at Fort Belvedere. George VI returned the chair to Scilly in 1938, and it is now in the Town Hall and used by the Chairman of the Isles of Scilly Council at formal Council meetings.

many doe, that would not change for twice so much a year in Cornwall. For all this, I would by noe means be guilty of drawing you hither if it in any dislike your best friend. We have seen noe doubtful ship upon the coast a great while ...

I have received a warrant from the King to carry over two-hundred men more, for the safeguard of the port at Scilly for the summer; the estates of divers delinquents, as the Lord Robartes, both Trevills, Bosawen, Sergnt Aubin, and Erisey appointed to be sold ... out of which £600 is, in the first place, to be paid to me, for provision of a magasin of victualles at Scilly.'

The years 1642-6 saw the struggle between Charles I and Parliament. In 1646, while the Parliamentary army, under General Fairfax, had taken Bodmin, the Prince of Wales (afterwards Charles II) accompanied by Lord Culpeper and Sir Edward Hyde, left Pendennis Castle, reached St Michael's Mount and was carried from there via Sennen by the *Phoenix* to Scilly on 2nd March 1646.

The Prince wished to keep his foot on English soil to the last, and sent Lord Culpeper, two days after he landed, to acquaint the Queen (in France) 'with the wants and incommodities of the place'. Star Castle had been considered a position of great strength, but did not, in this respect, answer their expectations. Lords Capel and Hopton were unable, owing to contrary winds, to sail from St Michael's Mount to join them for upwards of a month, but when they did they brought a 'trumpet' from Fairfax, bearing a letter from Parliament, requesting the Prince to come and 'reside in such a place and with such council and attendants as the Parliament should think fit'. The Prince refused and observed that he had remained in Scilly because he wished to be among his people, but that as in six weeks he had not received more than one day's victual from the mainland, he would be compelled to depart.

Prince Charles's Chair

Prince Charles' reasons for going to Scilly – and for leaving it are given by Hyde (Lord Clarendon) in his *History of the Rebellion*, as follows:

'Because Jersey was so near to France, and so might give the greater umbrage, and that Scilly was a part of Cornwall, and was by them all conceived a place of unquestionable strength, the public resolution was for Scilly, it being in their power, when they were at sea, to go to Jersey, if the wind was fair for one and cross to the other. So the resolution being imparted to no more that night than was of absolute necessity (for we apprehended clamour from the army, from the country, and from that garrison in whose power the prince was), the next morning, being Monday the second of March, after the news was come that the army was retiring from Bodmin, and the enemy marching furiously after, and thereby men were sufficiently awakened with the apprehension of the prince's safety; the governor and his son were called into the council and made acquainted with the prince's resolution, 'that night to embark himself for Scilly, being a part of Cornwall, from whence, by such aids and relief as he hoped he should procure from France and foreign parts, he should be best able to relieve them.' And accordingly that night about ten of the clock he put himself on board; and on Wednesday in the afternoon arrived safe in Scilly.

... The prince stayed in the Isle of Scilly from Wednesday the 4th of March till Thursday the 16th of April, the wind having continued so contrary that the Lords Capel and Hopton came not to him from Cornwall till the Saturday before; at which time likewise arrived a trumpeter from Sir Thomas Fairfax, with such a message from the parliament to the prince as might well be called a summons, rather than an invitation; yet it was well it came not to Pendennis, where it would have found a party among the prince's servants. The next morning, being Sunday, a fleet of about twenty-seven or twenty-eight sail of ships encompassed the island; but within three or four hours, by a very notable tempest which continued two days, they were dispersed. Upon this, and a clear determination of the weakness of the place if it should be attacked by any considerable strength (which both by the message and the attendants of it they had reason to apprehend), together with the extreme scarcity of provisions in that island, which had not been, in the six weeks the prince stayed there, supplied with victual for two days out of Cornwall, neither had there been any returns from France upon the Lord Colepepper's application to the Queen, which returns would every day grow more difficult by the season of the year, his highness inclined to remove to Jersey.

...After consideration of the probability that the rebels would make some attempt upon his highness there, and the impossibility of resisting such an attempt in the condition the island then stood, it was by his highness with great earnestness proposed, and by the whole council (except the Earl of Berkshire) unanimously advised, that the opportunity should be then laid hold on, whilst the rebels' ships were scattered, and that his highness should embark for Jersey; which he did accordingly on Thursday; and on the next day, being the 17th of April, with a prosperous wind, landed at Jersey.'

On the day after the arrival of the 'trumpet', a Parliamentary fleet of twenty-seven ships encompassed the islands, but, a heavy gale setting in on that rocky coast, in two hours the vessels all dispersed. In Lady Fanshawe's memoirs there is an account of her adventures in connection with the Prince's expedition to Scilly:

'Five days after, the Prince and all his council embark themselves in a ship called the *Phoenix* for the Isles of Scilly. They went from the Land's End, and so did we; being accompanied with many gentlemen of that country, among whom was Sir Francis Basset, Governor of the Mount, an honest gentleman, and so were all his family, and in particular we receive great civility from them. But we left our house and furniture with Captain Bluett who promised to keep them until such time as we could dispose of them but when we sent he said he had been plundered of them, notwithstanding it was well known he lost nothing of his own. At that time this loss went deep with us, for we lost to the value of £200 and more, but, as the proverb says, 'an evil chance seldom comes alone', we having put all our present estate into two trunks; and carried them aboard with us in a ship commanded by Sir Nicholas Crispe (whose skill and honesty the master and seamen had no opinion of) my husband was forced to appease a mutiny, which his miscarriage caused, and taking out money to pay the seamen, that night following they broke open one of our trunks and took out a bag of £60, and a quantity of gold lace with our best clothes and linen, with all my combs, gloves and ribbons, which amounted to £300 more. The next

This exit under the ramparts of Star Castle clearly reveals where the portcullis (an iron grill to prevent intruders) was lowered by a mechanism housed in the building on the ramparts above. The slots carrying the side edges of the grill are clear, as are the holes in the granite slab at the base into which fitted the iron prongs of the portcullis.

day, after being pillaged, and extremely sick and big with child, I was set on shore almost dead, in the Island of Scilly. When we had got to our quarters near the Castle where the Prince lay, I went immediately to bed, which was so vile that my footman ever lay in a better, and we but three in the whole house, which consisted of four rooms or rather, partitions, two low rooms and two little lofts with a ladder to go up; in one of these they kept dried fish, which was their trade, and in this my husband's two clerks lay. One there was for my sister, and one for myself, and one amongst the rest of the servants; but when I waked in the morning I was so cold, I knew not what to do, but the daylight discovered that my bed was near swimming in the sea, which the owner told us it never did so but at spring-tide. With this we were destitute of clothes; and meat and fuel for half the Court to serve them a month, was not to be had in the whole Island, and truly we begged our daily bread of God; for we thought every meal our last. The council sent for provisions to France, which served us, but they were bad and little of them; then after three weeks and odd days we set sail for the Isle of Jersey, where we safely arrived, praise be God, beyond the belief of all the beholders from that Island, for the pilot not knowing the way into the harbour, sailed over the rocks, but being spring-tide, and by chance high water, God be praised, His Highness and all of us come safe ashore through so great a danger.'

The Prince fretted and fumed at Star Castle for six weeks (4th March to 16th April, 1646) daily fearing the arrival of the Parliament ships and doubtful of withstanding an attack. On April 17th he embarked for the Channel Islands.

From the summer of 1646 till the autumn of 1648, the 1st Civil War being over, Scilly was in the hands of a Parliamentary garrison. But the Scillonians grew to dislike troops billeted on them because they received no compensation for the boarding. So, in September 1648, one Sunday morning when the Governor of Scilly, Colonel Buller, and his principal officers were in church, many of the troops

Exit from Star Castle

of the garrison mutinied because they were in arrears of pay, and declared with some of the island people for the Royalist cause.

Poor Colonel Buller and his officers were dragged to Star Castle by their hair, robbed of their money, clothes and arms, and threatened with being sent to 'lie and rot' in the Castle dungeons, if they did not declare for the King.

Prince Charles took advantage of this opportunity and sent the 20-year-old Sir John Grenville to Scilly as Governor to organise the rebels and make of Scilly a base for privateers. Sir John arrived in February 1649 and, as Charles I had been executed on 30th January, his first act was to declare his son King as Charles II. Lord Hopton also came to Scilly with twenty ships, and Sir John Grenville held the islands for the Royalists for the following two and a half years until 1651, Scilly being the last foothold of the Cavaliers in England. The Royalists fitted out frigates which sailed from Scilly to harass Parliamentary shipping passing to or from the English, Irish, and Bristol Channels. Strategically, Scilly was well placed for this and Parliament became increasingly alarmed by the Royalist strength in Scilly. The Calendar of State Papers of 1648 reports the proceedings of a Committee of both Houses of Parliament:

'To write to the Committee of Cornwall and the Governor of Plymouth and to Sir Hardress Waller, to take care to regain the Island of Scilly before it be further strengthened or the Castle victualed. To notify to Lord General [Fairfax] the revolt of Scilly ...'

What happened to Colonel Buller (above) seems nearly to have occurred later to Grenville. Scillonians, helped by some disaffected soldiers, planned a similar sort of rising in April, 1650, against the royalist occupation; but Grenville got wind of the plot and nipped it in the bud almost on the day it was planned to take place. In a letter to Sir Edward Nicholas of February 23, 1649, Grenville had already revealed some of his difficulties with Scillonians; he wrote that he had 'endeavoured to regulate these people into some better condition and order, and have already brought them a little more conformable to the advancement of His Majesty's service; and I hope every day they will know more duty and obedience ...' It appears from all this that the Scillonians were not pleased to be occupied by either Roundhead or Cavalier forces, which is understandable as much of the burden of supporting them all was expected to be borne by the Islanders.

But while Sir John Grenville was doing what he conceived was his duty by his king, that monarch was reported to have endeavoured to pledge the islands as security for a loan of £50,000 from merchants in Amsterdam – an example of how loyalty was looked upon as due from subjects to sovereign, not the other way about.

Reinforcements came in 1649 when Prince Rupert sent a large number of soldiers from Ireland to aid the garrison, declaring that he would make of Scilly 'a second Venice'.

Whitlock, in his *Memorials*, quotes the following:

> 'Letters, 26 June 1649, mention that a Frigate of Sir John Granville, Governor of Scilly, with two Bras Guns, 24 Muskets and 24 Oars, coming near Swansea, the Governor of Cardiff sent out Boats, pursued the Frigate from Creek to Creek, and at length took her, and the men, except the Capt. and some few, who got ashore.
>
> Letters (6 March 1650) of several ships taken by Pyrates of Scilly and Jersey. Letters of 15 March of the want of Frigates on the Western Coast to keep in the Jersey and Scilly Pirates, and of their taking several Merchantmen, and none of the Parliament Frigates to help them. Letters of 19 March of the Pyracies committed by those of Jersey and Scilly.'

Apparently the Royalists in Scilly were in such straits that they were forced to commandeer provisions from the ships of any nation passing near enough for the purpose. On the plea that Dutch shipping had been seized, Admiral Tromp appeared off the islands and demanded satisfaction. Unable to persuade Sir John Grenville to provide recompense for the Dutch ships pirated by the Royalist frigates in Scilly, Tromp had no option but to sail away empty handed. But he did go to Plymouth and announce that he would be willing to help Parliamentary forces subdue the Royalists in Scilly, which raised the possibility in the Government's minds that the Dutch might plan to take Scilly, although this was expressly denied by the Dutch Government who had given orders to Tromp not to do anything of offence to the English Government. In consequence of this perceived danger, and still more the clamour of the Members of Parliament who represented the merchant interests whose ships

King Charles's Castle was completed in about 1554, but the Royalists in the Civil Wars called it after their King – and the name has stuck. However, like Harry's Walls on St Mary's, the site was badly chosen for the task it was expected to perform. Sir Francis Godolphin pointed out some of the deficiencies of King Charles's Castle as early as 1600 when he wrote that, although the guns of the castle had a wide arc of fire, they were not able to prevent enemy shipping 'coming down Tresco Channel 'for as it neither discovereth the whole harbour so through the imminent height thereof can make no good shot so steep downwards, and that which is worse, is of so weak a form as it cannot he defended'. The fortification consisted of a two-storey building with two tiers of guns, and in the Civil War earthworks were dug to give to the castle more protection from landward attack – as Godolphin had suggested – but to no avail for Blake's forces found little difficulty in taking it. Yet, between its construction in about 1554, and the completion of Star Castle in 1594, it was the principal fort in Scilly and had two blockhouses to support it, one (still to be seen) at Old Grimsby, and the other believed to have occupied the site where Cromwell's Castle now stands.

There was an excavation of the site in the 1950s and many of the stones were replaced in original positions. Photograph (top) shows two of the upper embrasures of King Charles's Castle (originally it had two storeys), but which the excavators were uncertain where precisely they had originally been placed.

Photograph (bottom) shows the kitchen of the castle with its great fireplace, and a baking oven on the left side of the fireplace.

---

were suffering from the depredations of Grenville's frigates, the Government determined to send a force from Plymouth in April, 1651, to subdue Grenville and his Royal rebels. It was commanded by the estimable Robert Blake and (under him) Sir George Ayscue. [The documents following indicate that the English error of including 'Van' in Tromp's name dates back to the 17th century]

The itinerary of the expedition was as follows, according to letters quoted in Whitlock's *Memorials*:

'17 April, 1651: Letters: That Lieutenant-Colonel Clarke with nine companies of foot, set sail from Plymouth for Scilly Islands. 17 April, 1651: Letters: That Van Tromp came to Pendennis and related that he had been to Scilly to demand reparation for the Dutch ships and goods taken by them; and receiving no satisfactory answer, he had declared war on them –
[actually this was only a posture as Tromp was under orders not to do anything to offend the English Government].

Upper storey embrasures of King Charles's Castle

The kitchen fireplace of King Charles's Castle

21 April: That Van Tromp lay before Scilly and declared that he would assist the English against it.

24 April: Letters: Of the Fleet's arrival at Scilly and of the guns heard from thence.

26 April: Letters: That 2,000 of the Parliament's soldiers and seamen were landed in the little Isles on the West of Scilly, and that the Ordnance were heard thundering there many hours together.

2 May: Letters: That the Parliament's Fleet at Scilly had taken New Grimsby after 3 times being beaten off, and that they had taken 2 Irish Frigates, one of 30 and the other of 24 guns.

3rd May: That the Parliamentary soldiers had taken all the Islands except St Mary's and had taken 3 of their Frigates, killed 14 of their men, and taken 120 prisoners. That of the Parliamentary Forces, 8 were killed and 20 wounded; that they intended to send a summons to St Mary's Island, and if they refused, then attempt it.

8 May: That General Blake and Sir George Ayscue with the Fleet at Scilly intend to fall upon St Mary's Island, that the Governor thereof, Sir John Grenville, sent to them for a Treaty, which was agreed, but took no effect, and thereupon the great guns played upon St Mary's.

12 May: Letters from Sir George Ayscue of the action at Scilly, that Captain Morris behaved himself most gallantly in the storming of the Island. That the Scilly Islands are a key that opens a passage to several Nations.

30 May: That the Foot of Scilly entered at St Mary's Island [after the surrender] and those in the Castle were in great want of water.'

[The dates here are those on the letters; the fleet actually arrived in Scilly on 12th April.]

The following account, written by 'Lange', is based on one of Jos. Lereck, an officer in Colonel Clarke's land force, which was entitled *A True Account of the late Reducement of the Isles of Scilly, Published in regard to the many false and Scandalous reports touching that Service.* [see *Scilly at War* for more detail of this]

'After we of the Parliament Forces had laid at sea from Saturday, April 12th, till Thursday, the 17th, when in the morning ... we put our soldiers in boats to endeavour to make a landing on

60

Cromwell's Castle from Bryher. It was once said that some of the stones from King Charles's Castle were rolled down the hill to be set in place in Cromwell's Castle. This seems unlikely as many stones still exist at King Charles's Castle, and few of the stones that litter the sides of the steep climb up to King Charles's Castle show signs of fashioning.

Tresco; one party was to land in a sandy bay near the Fort at Old Grimsby Harbour, and the other in a more stony bay, somewhat to the westward. We had not reckoned on the strength of the tide, which was on the ebb, and some of our boats were grounded on the rocks and others carried out of their course. So orders were given for all the boats to make straight for Old Grimsby Harbour and we sheltered by a rock in the Channel until we could make a joint attack. We then moved forward, but the pilots and many of the rowers had been taken up in the West Country and were very backward in the service, misguided us, and we came to a little island called Norwithiel [Northwethel], standing in the entrance to the Harbour, and within half-a-musket shot of Tresco. The Pilots swore that it was Tresco, but Captain Bowden was doubtful of it, as none of the enemy came to oppose our landing. Some of the Companies had landed and the boats were aground but in order that the opportunity might not be lost, the rest of the boats were ordered forward. They were again misguided, and came to a rocky part of Tresco where it was difficult to land. The enemy brought down a body of musketeers, and there was hot firing on our boats from behind rocks on the shore. Our boats were at a disadvantage, being so thickly crammed with men that many could not use their muskets. Here, we endured about 70 great shot beside musketry in abundance, so that many of the boats turned helm and rowed out of range, notwithstanding the struggle of Col. Clarke and other officers. After half-an-hour we all withdrew to Norwithiel, and found that our loss was not so great as was feared. We then rowed to an adjacent Island called Teän leaving three companies on Norwithiel. We spent a very cold and comfortless night on Teän, and the next day the enemy began firing great shot at us, which fell among our tents but did no great harm. We managed to get some much needed provisions ashore from the ships which were riding at a distance, and we prepared ourselves for a second attempt.

We sent to Admiral Blake for a better supply of rowers for the boats, and he moreover sent about 200 seamen to attempt the assault with us. We resolved to storm the Enemy by night, and during the day we took careful observations of the Channel and the place of intended landing.

We drew off our men from Norwithiel in the evening, with the exception of 80 men left to amuse the enemy while we attacked, and about 11 o'clock we set forward. By the mercy of God it was very calm, so that the enemy's frigates could not come up the Channel to do us any harm, although they fired some great shot at us.

We made fires on Teän to deceive the enemy, and the smoke blew toward Tresco, which somewhat obscured our passage. Yet the enemy discovered us when we were about half way over and fired much ordnance at us, with little hurt.

The boats came up well together, and though at first forced back, we charged them so resolutely, even with clubbed muskets, that we worsted them, killed 1 captain, 14 men, took prisoners 4 captains and 167 men, the rest fleeing, and none had escaped had we been better acquainted with the Island. We had been opposed by 1,300 men – a greater strength by far than we had imagined.

Let the exceeding goodness of God to this unthankful nation, in lopping off the bough, even with terror, and giving into our hands a place stuffed with men, a greater number by many than we were, and but yesterday a curse to our Maritime Affairs, a scourge to the Merchants, though invincible for strength, and desperate to attempt so little loss in so short a time.'

Another account of the battle on Tresco although this time from a Royalist is given in a letter of 13 May 1631, which Bishop Leslie wrote to Sir Edward Nicholas of events 12th to 18th April:

'In the morning there came against these isles two great fleets, the one of English consisting of 22 ships besides many shallopps and longboats and bringing with them 2,500 land men, the other of Dutch consisting of 13 ships. They attempted the out islands lying on the north side, especially that called Tresco, on each end whereof is a harbour. The best harbour our Governor secured by two of his best frigates and other helps that they could not enter; so they discharged infinite multitude of shot. The other harbour, where it was scarce known any great ship ever ventured to come in, they gained it, being of so great a breadth that it could not be defended; and so on the 17th day they launched forth many shallopps, each having a brass piece charged with case shot in the forepart, but then were so valiantly resisted that they were forced to retreat, their Admiral being shot through and through and driven to ship his cable, one of their shallopps sunk and another so paid with small shot that she went off with two oars, all the rest dropping into the water.

But on the 18th day in the silence of the night, they having the opportunity of a great calm, came on again with all their forces, and after a long debate they overpowered our men with multitudes and strength of their pikes, having the help of seamen too, both to lead them on and to drive on their rear, and so gained the place, we having there only 400 men, which were far more than the Governor could well have spared. Of these sixscore and odd came off by the help of their boats, the rest being killed or taken prisoner.'

After the Parliamentarians had established themselves on Tresco. Admiral Blake erected a battery at Carn Near to Command Broad and Crow Sounds. This battery could reach any ship that went into, or came out from, St Mary's harbour. By taking Tresco and building this battery Blake would, in Sir George Ayscue's words, make St Mary's 'useless to the enemy' without having to invade St Mary's itself, a strategy which worked perfectly.

Thus blockaded, Sir John Grenville soon found his position untenable, since not only were his ships prevented from approaching the islands, but he was lamentably short of provisions of all kinds. A council of war was held in Star Castle by the beleaguered Calavaliers, some of whom were diehards, men who had fought long and hard for the King's cause and had everything to lose from surrender. There was a great deal of fighting talk but militarily continuing the resistance was not an option for long – supplies would soon be short and there was no hope of succour with Blake's fleet surrounding Scilly. There was thought to be an insufficient number of fully fit men to man the defences. So, on the 2nd May it was decided to treat with Blake, the truce parties meeting on Samson as neutral ground, and some hostages were exchanged. But talks broke down, and Blake then armed his three guns at Carn Near and began firing at Cavalier ships guarding St Mary's coasts and at the Garrison fortifications 3,000 yards away. Blake knew that the Royalists would soon be short of supplies, so he again invited Grenville to talks, which this time did not break down but led to a draft agreement on terms. The document of surrender was headed as follows: 'Articles agreed on this xxiii day of May, 1651, by and betweene Admirall Blake and Colonell Clerke, Commanders in chiefe of all the fforces by Sea or Land, in and about the Islands of Triscoe and Briar, of the one part, Sr. John Grenville, Knight, Governor of the Islands of St Marye's and Agnes, in Scilly, on the behalfe of his Matie., on the other pt., touching the rendition of the sd. Isles of St Marye's and Agnes, together with all the Castles, forts, fortresses, sconces and fortifications unto them belonging, to the use and behoof of the Parliam. of England as followeth ...'

It was not, however, until he had sought and obtained permission from his king, then in Holland, that Sir John Grenville finally surrendered. The conditions offered by Blake were generous. The surrendering garrison was permitted to march out, together with arms and horses, to the beat of drums and sound of trumpets, with colours displayed and 'matches lighted at both ends' – the last of the Cavaliers. They were about 1,500 men, with 'enough commissioned officers to head an army'. It is not known at what point Tromp and

Cromwell's Castle showing its position for commanding the channel between Tresco and Bryher.

his thirteen ships left the scene.

The defeated Royalist rebels were then transported to Ireland, Scotland and France, to which countries many of them originally belonged, while the Governor and some of the chief officers were taken to Plymouth, where Sir John Grenville was soon set at liberty and permitted to embark for the Continent to share the fortunes of his royal master, who later created him Earl of Bath. 'He attended the King in his greatest distresses, throughout all his disconsolate travels, in France, Flanders, Holland and the Isle of Jersey.' There is a Cornish saying to the effect that 'a Godolphin never wanted wit nor a Grenville loyalty'. One of the special provisions of the treaty was that none of the islanders should suffer, and many Royalist gentlemen, including one of the Godolphin family, remained in Scilly.

Sir John Grenville accompanied Prince Charles 'on his travels' until 1660, and, after the Restoration of the Monarchy, was created Earl of Bath and made High Steward of the Duchy of Cornwall. In 1660 the Godolphins resumed as lessees but as absentee landlords.

After this ending of the Royalist rebellion in Scilly in 1651, a strong circular tower, Cromwell's Castle, was built (on what was the site of an earlier blockhouse) to command the channel between New Grimsby and Bryher, and was manned by twenty men. The date of Cromwell's Castle has been disputed. It has been suggested (see page 233 *The Scillonion*, Vol. XXXII, No. 132 of December 1957) that the 'castle dates from the reign of Edward VI and was probably being erected in 1550'. If this is so then two points must be answered: (i) A seaman's map of about 1585 in the British Museum by Captain John Davis shows King Charles's Castle but not Cromwell's Castle. (ii) In 1600 Godolphin wished to fortify Hangman Island because the guns of King Charles's Castle were sited too high to be brought to bear on the Sound. This would not have been necessary if Cromwell's Castle had been in existence at that time.

A garrison of six hundred was at first maintained in the islands but, not long after the surrender, the military provision in Scilly appears to have been neglected, for we find a petition dated 14th May, 1658, from Lt.-Col. Joseph Hunkin, Governor of Scilly, to the Protector: 'The stores of ammunition in the garrison are decayed; there are only 77 barrels of powder left here by the enemy at the surrender of the Islands, which is now unfit for service. There is also a great want of Sakar and minion shot, there being only two shots apiece for all these guns on the islands.' He asked for 200 barrels of powder and three tons of shot so that he might be able to 'defend the Islands in case of any vicissitude of affairs'.

For a time in the 17th century, Star Castle provided a suitable place for political and other prisoners either for their own safety or to help ensure that they could not easily escape. Dr John Bastwick was the first prisoner of note known to have been confined in Star Castle. He was a persistent pamphleteer and critic of Archbishop Laud in the reign of King Charles I. His most outspoken pamphlet concluded with the words: 'From plague, pestilence and famine, from bishops, priests and deacons, good Lord deliver us.' He was sentenced by the Star Chamber in 1637 to a fine of £5,000, to be deprived of his ears (Dr Bastwick's wife stood on a stool, kissed him, placed his ears in a clean handkerchief, and took them away with her), to suffer in the pillory, and then to be confined to the Isles of Scilly. He was released in 1640 after three years' imprisonment in the islands, but died soon afterwards.

Another prisoner was the Duke of Hamilton who, in 1643, was consigned to the care of Sir Francis Godolphin at Star Castle, with

The original entrance to Cromwell's Castle before Master Gunner Abraham Tovey built the gun platform and shifted the entrance to its modern-day position.

particular instructions from the King as to his custody. In 1655, Oliver Cromwell awarded a pension of ten shillings a week to John Biddle, the celebrated Socinian (Unitarian), and sent him to the Isles of Scilly, for confinement to keep him 'out of the way of his persecutors'.

At the Restoration in 1660, King Charles II, who had himself spent six weeks at Star Castle in 1646 after fleeing from Fairfax's victorious army, sent three prominent Roundheads to be imprisoned in the Isles of Scilly. Sir John Wildman, the Anabaptist and political malcontent, described in Pepys' diary as 'a false fellow to everybody', was six years a prisoner, first in the Tower of London, then in Star Castle, and later in Pendennis Castle. Macaulay says: 'With Wildman's fanaticism was joined a tender care for his own safety, grazing the edge of treason.' He died in 1693.

Sir John Ireton, a zealous republican and brother of the famous regicide, was Lord Mayor of London in 1658. He was imprisoned in Star Castle in 1662, released later, and imprisoned again in 1685, dying in 1689.

Another Puritan prisoner was Sir Harry Vane, one of the most influential statesmen of the Commonwealth, described as a man of a noble and generous mind. He was kept a prisoner in Star Castle in the Isles of Scilly for two years but, although King Charles II had promised that his life should he spared, he had powerful enemies at court and was beheaded on Tower Hill in 1662. Samuel Pepys was told by Will Swan: 'Sir H. Vane died as much a martyr and saint as ever a man did, and the King hath lost more by that man's death than he can get again in a good while.'

One further reference to Star Castle as a place for confinement is on record when 'seven popish priests' were conveyed thither from Newgate in 1681.

Visitors of note were the Grand Duke Cosmo III and, probably, Count Lorenzo Magalotti, the latter leaving on record in his diary an account of the Duke's stay in 1669, together with a view of Star Castle as it then existed. He speaks in terms of praise of the islands and mentions that the castle and adjacent batteries were armed with '300 very beautiful iron culverins' and a garrison of 200 men at a cost to the King of about £4,000 a year.

Just inside Garrison Gateway on the wall of the Powder House is the following notice:

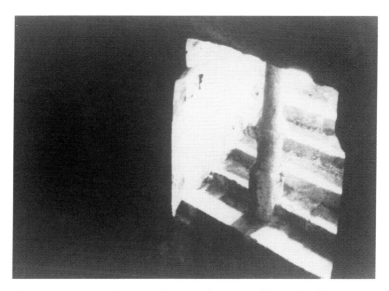

These steps were to the original exit inside Cromwell's Castle. The stairway led down to a living-room, below which was an unlit basement, and above which was another room which had a ribbed stone vault. There were six ports on the gun platform at the top of the tower.

The Garrison Walls were built in their present form between 1715 and 1746. They consist of lengths of curtain walls between artillery bastions provided with gun positions that not only command the seaways and anchorages but also the ground immediately beyond the walls. The circuit is not complete on the north west side. Within the walls were built a guardhouse and barracks, a magazine and prison, and a house for the Master Gunner. The work was carried out largely on the initiative of the then Master Gunner, Abraham Tovey, and his initials can be seen over the entrance gateway.

The walls replaced an earlier earthen breastwork of the Civil War period. They enclosed Star Castle, the fort built by Sir Francis Godolphin in 1593, and also incorporated a wall across the neck of the Hugh that had been built at the same time.

Abraham Tovey, the Master Gunner referred to in the notice above, lived in the White House on the right down the lane to Newman House, which was built in 1718 as the storehouse to the Garrison. The main building work on the Garrison was probably during the period of the war with Spain, 1739 to 1748, when not only the curtain wall around the Garrison was completed, but also the road inside the wall to service the eighteen batteries Tovey had put in. Tovey also built a seaward gun-platform on Cromwell's Castle to command the channel between Bryher and Tresco more effectively than relying on the guns on the tower's roof.

The 'prison' mentioned in the notice is presumably the small cell for the detention of wrong-doers at the entrance to the powder house, and the 'magazine' is the powder house itself. It is sunk down with high walls around it to protect it from shot. Tovey has left his initials in great prominence on the Garrison Gateway, but the road through it had to be lowered at one time to allow high vehicles through. It still will not take wide vehicles.

In 1742 the following instructions were issued by the Governor of Scilly from London where he lived:

'Orders – by the Rt. Hon Francis Earl of Godolphin, Governor and Proprietor of His Majesty's Islands of Scilly.

ORDERS TO BE OBSERVED AND OBEYED BY THE GARRISON AND ISLANDERS

1) That in the absence of the Governor and Lt. Governor, the said garrison and islanders do obey the Commanding Officer for the time being, as their Magistrate.

2) That the islanders on firing of the warning gun do forthwith repair to his Majesty's Star Castle for the defence of the said islands.

3) That the master gunner and gunners do not presume to go off St Mary's island without leave from the Commanding Officer for the time being.

4) That no islander presume to go to the main, without leave from the Commanding Officer for the time being, especially in time of war.

5) That all pilots make a report immediately to the Commanding Officer for the time being, of all ships they pilot in, with their force, and number of men, and that no pilot presume to carry any ship out without first seeking its clearance from his Majesty's Star Castle.

6) That all persons who land in any of the said islands be forthwith brought before the Commanding Officer for the time

being to be examined by him.

7) That these orders be published in the said islands, and hung up in his Majesty's Star Castle there.

GODOLPHIN.

St James', 29th May, 1742.'

After 1748 the military establishment in Scilly was again reduced. About a couple of dozen Chelsea Pensioners were used as Scilly's garrison troops in the eighteenth century, the last commander of these Invalids being Major Vigoureux (immortalised in the novel of that name by Sir Arthur Quiller Couch) and Major-General J. N. Smyth, who died in Scilly in 1838.

There was resumed military activity in Scilly, however, in the French Wars 1790–1815 when Fencibles (a sort of home guard) were mustered. Their parade ground is now a park in Hugh Town, but the road around is still called the Parade. Three towers were built on St Mary's, thought at one time to have been for defence, but now Lloyd's Tower and Buzza Tower are believed originally to have been for windmills, while Telegraph was always a signals tower.

After the ending of the Napoleonic Wars in 1815 the military establishment was again reduced and the defences decayed. In 1822 there was a Lieutenant-Governor, a master gunner, four gunners, and two or three aged sergeants; in 1857, five Invalids (His Majesty's Company of Invalids) manned the fortifications, and, by 1863, the defences of Scilly had been so run down that they were manned solely by one elderly caretaker.

In the twentieth century the Government planned to make a naval base of Scilly, and new batteries were constructed at a cost of a quarter of a million pounds as late as 1905. The guns were hoisted laboriously up Garrison Hill and mounted in the forts. They fired practice rounds using for a target a wooden post mounted on the Bow off St Agnes. But eventually the project was abandoned as too costly. The Entente Cordiale with France in 1904 had also changed Admiralty minds as to the direction of future enemies. And St Mary's Sound proved too shallow at low tides for the new dreadnoughts. Scapa Flow was developed as a naval base instead.

U-boats were often around Scilly in the First World War, and over fifty merchant ships were sunk around the islands. In 1917 a seaplane base was established at Porth Mellon but was moved to Tresco, the planes being of value as patrols to spot U-boats. The hard

The seaward gun platform of Cromwell's Castle

These two cannon on Cromwell's Castle are purely decorative. The gun carriages are new and the guns came from Portsmouth. They were lowered into their present positions by helicopter in 1971. They help to demonstrate the function of the castle, which was to serve as a means of preventing the potential Dutch enemy from using the channel between Tresco and Bryher. The gun platform was constructed by Gunner Abraham Tovey in the eighteenth century at about the time he built Garrison Gateway on St Mary's.

standings of both these bases still exist. Short 184 seaplanes and a Short Cromarty N120 flying boat were used.

In the Second World War enemy planes often attacked the islands with machine-gun fire, for there were no anti-aircraft guns at first. But from May 1941 a flight of RAF Hurricanes, fighter planes of 87 Squadron were based on St Mary's, which helped to deter enemy attacks. At first their equipment consisted of little more than 'two huts and a wind sock'; but the Hurricanes proved of value intercepting enemy reconnaissance aircraft and mine layers, and provided some cover for convoys. They operated on a 450 yard runway, and the crews were lodged in local guest houses. In 1943 units were built for RAF personnel on the south-east side of the aerodrome, and these huts developed after the war into the civilian operations and passenger reception area. They were used until 1975, when the present airport terminal building was constructed on the other side of the airport.

It is not generally realised that it was the Hurricane rather than the Spitfire which won the Battle of Britain in 1940, mainly because there were twice as many Hurricanes as Spitfires engaged. The Hurricane, although fabric-covered and slightly slower that the Spitfire, had the capacity to weather more damage and keep flying. It was preferred for the Scilly station because the aerodrome on St Mary's was short and not easy to land upon in 1941 without occasional damage, and the Hurricane was better fitted for this. The six Hurricanes performed well in Scilly, shooting down a number of enemy aircraft and deterring many others from flying in the aerial vicinity of Scilly. Only three Scillonian civilians were killed by enemy aircraft during the Second World War, all of them dying before the six Hurricanes and their pilots were posted to St Mary's – one little girl in Telegraph Tower where she was sheltering from machine-gun fire with her mother, and two young women who were in a building which was bombed and which stood on the site on The Strand on St Mary's where the dairy shop is situated. Many Scillonians left the Islands for the Mainland for the duration of hostilities, as no hotels were open and the flower industry was much restricted.

CHAPTER VI –
THE SCILLONIANS and KELPING

There is little written evidence of the lives of the inhabitants of Scilly before the 16th century, and even in Domesday Book (1086) Scilly is not mentioned. But there is good archaeological evidence that the islands were inhabited by people of the Early Bronze Age. On Halangy Down, St Mary's, and Par Beach, St Martin's, and also on St Agnes, the bases of round stone huts have been discovered; and from the surrounding middens (refuse dumps), fragments of pottery have been found similar to those found in barrows, and these help to date the inhabitants. In the middens, bones of horses, sheep, and a small breed of deer, together with stone and bone tools, stone querns for grinding corn, and innumerable shells of limpets (one of the staple articles of diet on the sea coast in those days) have been unearthed. Flint scrapers for dressing skins of animals, awls, whorls and spindles for weaving garments, stone mace-heads, and flint arrowheads have been collected in quantity.

The earliest invaders of the south-west of Britain seem to have been the Iberians, short dark-haired people. From the sixth century onwards successive waves of tall fair-haired, blue-eyed Celts penetrated to Cornwall. The antiquarian, Dr Borlase, professed to find innumerable sacrificial stones in Scilly, but the natural weathering of stone by the elements is so bizarre that human agency may be discounted. But Troutbeck supports Borlase in attributing rock basins on Scilly to the sacrificial rites of Druidism; Gilbert calls them 'supposed relics'; North considers them the work of chance; and Whitfeld on the same subject reminds us of a story: '"Here," quoth Monkbarns, waxing eloquent as he described to a guest the imaginary Roman camp, "here was the Praetorian Gate." "Praetorian here, Praetorian there," replied Edie Ochiltee, "I mind well the diggin o't it!"'. It is now generally accepted that the rock basins, including those fine examples on Peninnis, are entirely the work of nature unaided by man.

The economic prosperity of the islanders has fluctuated greatly. In past centuries the islanders have suffered much and for the most part may be said to have scratched a living only with the greatest difficulty and in the face of enormous dangers. Coastal regions were particularly susceptible to attack and, in Scilly, the elements alone were sufficient to make life hazardous.

After 2500 BC, Scilly and Cornwall were in contact with traders from Brittany, and Scilly may also have served as a port of call for the gold trade between Ireland, Spain, and the Mediterranean. After about 1400 BC this trade began to take an overland route (according to Hencken) through England across the English Channel to Europe, and then overland to the head of the Adriatic, consequently leading to some economic decline in the south-west of England. But tin mining later flourished and became the main source of trading income in Cornwall. The discovery of tin in other places, notably in Spain at the beginning of the Christian era, caused decline in the tin trade, but it revived again in the Middle Ages and continued in Cornwall until 1918, by then being considered hardly worthwhile economically to work on a large scale, though a few mines were kept operating for a time.

In the 5th century AD the Dumnonii spread over most of south-west Britain and possibly to Scilly and colonised Armorica (Brittany). This link between Cornwall and Brittany has long since disappeared; but, even later, when an Englishman was still something of a foreigner to a Cornishman, so was a Frenchman to a Breton.

The descendants of the Iberians and Celts undoubtedly mixed with the successive waves of West Britons, Saxons, Northmen, and emigrants from Scotland, Ireland, Gaul, and the Mediterranean, the geographical situation of the islands making it inevitable that a great variety of people sojourned there, some of whom remained.

Camden states, of his time (1586), that: 'The inhabitants are all newcomers, but remains show much previous habitation.' This presents a mystery connected with the islands. One may speculate exhaustively as to the reason why a population should have deserted the islands and been replaced with newcomers. It may, of course have been due to some inundation of land that would cause a widespread sense of insecurity and consequent emigration; it may have been due to some pestilence or to a raid that might have annihilated the inhabitants; or perhaps merely to hard living and the prospect of better subsistence elsewhere. Historical records do not help us, but no Scillonian today would claim descent from inhabitants of the islands before the 16th century. But, since surnames did not become widespread before the 16th century, this is hardly surprising. Some settlers are likely to have come from Cornwall, as the journey offered the shortest passage, and a few may have come from Scotland and Ireland – where low living standards may have provided the impetus – and all such people would have been squatters. Many of the existing families of Scillonians, or of Scillonians who were until recently resident in Scilly, trace their descent from the Godolphins. The Edwards, MacFarlands, Mumfords, Banfields, and Tregarthens are all connected with the Godolphin family through the marriage of Ursula, a daughter of Sir Francis Godolphin, to a Scillonian. But it was probably the popularity of the early Godolphins that resulted in a number of families leaving Cornwall for Scilly, and it is likely that this influx of highly favoured mainlanders eventually dominated the previous inhabitants, who, at that period, must have been living at subsistence level. An example of this is the story of an inhabitant of Bryher, employed in the construction of the fortifications on the Hugh, St Mary's, who rowed himself daily backwards and forwards across the two miles or so of sea and received, for his labours, the sum of 6d a week.

Since at various times a large garrison of soldiers had been kept on the islands, including Grenadier Guards and a company of the Bedford Regiment – which, tradition has it, were forgotten and left on the islands – a good deal of inter-marriage resulted, and many time-expired men, whose wives had relations on the isles, settled there. In 1669, Count Magalotti reported: 'Corn of late began to be scarce, in consequence of the increase of the population produced by marriages of the soldiers of the garrison with the islanders, but this has been remedied for some years past by forbidding them to marry.'

Each island had a generic nickname, which is now rarely used. St Mary's men were Bulldogs. Tresco men were Caterpillars (probably associated with smuggling, and files of keg-carriers as seen in the moonlight). Bryher men were Thorns, or 'lop-sided' or 'one-sided'. It is frequently averred that, whatever was done by the men of Bryher, it was aslant; that they walked askew carried their heads slightly bent sideways, held a cup or glass at an angle, and generally appeared 'one-sided'. [No evidence of this remains in the population today.]

St Martin's men were Ginnicks (etymology unknown) and at one time were remarkable for the number of them with red or sandy hair and blue eyes. They were said to be the most independent of all the different island populations. The island is supposed to have been peopled from Sennen in the 16th Century. North says that in his day St Martin's people tended to be tall and thin. St Agnes folk were called Turks and were popularly supposed to be short and thickset, with dark hair and eyes, partly as a result, it has been alleged, of inter-marriage with stranded sailors. Their speech was said to be short and crisp, and they grew long silken beards. In the 19th century the men folk of St Agnes, even more so than in the other islands, specialised in putting out quickly in their gigs to supply pilots to passing ships or to ships seeking shelter or supplies in the islands.

Tresco people according to North, were of intermediate stature between those of St Martin's and St Agnes. St Mary's people were more cosmopolitan and had no peculiarities of their own. Their main family surnames used to be Banfield, Edwards, Tregarthen, Blewett, Gibson, and Mumford. Certain surnames still predominate on the off-islands, but this is less noticeable nowadays, though St Agnes have several families named Hicks and Legg, and Tresco, Bryher, and St Martin's, have or used to have – Jenkins, Pender, Ashford and Ellis. But for over a century there has been constant and daily intercourse between the islands, and this has so weakened the special characteristics of the individual populations that the differences are now hardly perceptible. It is said, however, that the social climate on each island still varies greatly, and that the inhabitants of certain islands are exceptionally co-operative and friendly. These generalisations are transient, however, and are more likely due to the qualities of individuals who make up the island communities at any given time rather than to any particular facet of the social climate inherent in the community.

From the time when the islands were first occupied, the Scillonians had to be industrious in order to survive, tilling the soil by battling with the special enemies of agriculture on Scilly – the strong winds and burning salt spray. Yet none of this would appear to have been worth a comment by those who have left us fragmentary records, although the punishment of wrong-doers was *news* and thus received a measure of publicity. The crown leases conferred on the lessees conclusive jurisdiction in all plaints and causes – heresy, treason, matters of life and limb, with Admiralty questions excepted. Until 1827, in the reign of George IV, the clerical order had benefit of clergy, as on the mainland, and were exempt from civil punishment.

The lessee, who was termed the Lord Proprietor, created a 'Court of Twelve' to administer his affairs, and this court, by virtue of its isolation and situation, and in the absence of the lessee, soon assumed dictatorial powers. At one time it issued an order prohibiting masters of vessels from importing strangers or exporting residents, under a penalty of £10. At another time a troublesome thief was ordered to be put on board the first of His Majesty's ships of war that might call. Women were ducked at the quay head, and men and women were ordered to be whipped publicly. Paupers were deported to the mainland. Towards the end of the eighteenth century a man on St Agnes was charged with sabbath-breaking because he dug up some potatoes but, owing to his extreme poverty, the case was dismissed on his promising not to do it again. At about the same period there is a record of a woman on St Mary's who was sentenced to receive fifty lashes on her bare back for stealing a cotton shirt. But since England possessed the harshest penal code of any European country in the 18th century, and stealing five shillings or more from a shop was among several hundred other crimes punishable by death, such severe sentences must not be taken as peculiar to Scilly.

Borlase wrote that in his time (1756) the Court of Twelve 'meet once a month, hear complaints, and compose some little disputes, but rather by compromise than decision, and this is all the government they have, without calling in the Military Power ... common immoralities escape all reprehension ... so that the people are left too much to their own will ... and, as the Islands have but the Shadow of Government, the good feel not the benefit of it because 'tis but a shadow, nor the wicked the weight of it for the same reason.'

Heath, an officer of the garrison, who wrote in 1750, and must have been a wit, says: 'The spiritual court of Scilly is the ducking chair at the quay head, into which offenders (in language or morality) are put by the order of the Court of Twelve, and receive their purification in Holy or salt water. The punishments in Scilly are fines, whipping or ducking ... no venomous insects or creatures harbour these islands ... attorneys or sheriff's officers never show their face.'

He enumerates the trades exercised in Hugh Town in his time: bakers, brewers, coopers, butchers, weavers, tailors, mantua-makers, shoe-makers, sail-makers, joiners, carpenters, masons, smiths, periwig-makers, and a boat-maker. By the nature of their situation islanders develop an ability to master many trades, and it is not surprising that the Scillonians have frequently weathered economic recessions by the process of changing their means of livelihood. For instance, in 1684 the making of kelp, an alkali of value to glassmakers, soap-makers, and bleachers, was commenced, and immense quantities of seaweed were collected and burnt in kilns. This industry continued for about a hundred and fifty years and became one of the mainstays of economic life. There was also a certain amount of weaving and long-line fishing for ling, a good deal of which was dried, salted, and exported. Scilly ling was famous. Lord Nelson wrote from Toulon to a friend in Plymouth, in October, 1803, thanking him for a present of Scilly ling, which he had 'much enjoyed'.

After the Napoleonic War (1803–1815) there was widespread distress in the islands and particularly in the off-islands. The findings of a deputation sent by the Penzance magistrates in 1819 give a good illustration of the troubles of previous years. Some causes of distress in the off-islands, according to the report, were:

1) the bad harvests of the two preceding years.
2) the failure during the preceding year of the means of making kelp.
3) the decrease of employment in piloting resulting from the establishment of branch pilots, by which employment was monopolised by very few hands.
4) the failure in a considerable degree of the ling fishery.
5) the suppression of smuggling by the Preventive boat system, by the loss of which contraband trade the Islanders lost their chief means of support.

The fifth point is interesting as indicating the extent of smuggling in the islands during the 18th century. The activity became not only important to Scilly's economy but also a way of life for many of the inhabitants. The customs officers who attempted to combat it were not helped by the requirement that the officer making the charge, in any prosecution, had to pay the expense. This meant that normally only clear-cut cases were brought to book and, considering the amount of contraband, very little was, in fact, seized. The off-islands were the most favourable points for operating the traffic, and many a small boat ostensibly carrying a pilot may well also have been running contraband, An East Indiaman bound up Channel may well have parted with some of her cargo of muslin and silk for it to be hidden perhaps on an off-island. Spirits, brandy, rum, wines, and tobacco would constitute the greater part of smuggled goods.

James Silk Buckingham, MP for Sheffield (1823-27), wrote of Scilly about this time: 'Nothing could be conceived more primitive than the state of society among which we are now thrown. The town of St Mary's had a Governor, two clergymen, three doctors, two lawyers, several merchants, who were all smuggling; the rest were mere tradesmen, shopkeepers and boatmen, who lived partly by fishing, still more by smuggling and worst of all, it was said, by visiting wrecked vessels and helping themselves freely to whatever could be saved from destruction.'

Smuggling was an eighteenth century industry not only in Scilly but all round the coasts of the UK because of the high import duties and the profits to be made. Pilot cutters were in a most advantageous position to take Virginian tobacco, Indian tea, or Jamaican sugar or rum from a passing ship in exchange for piloting services or for potatoes and other farm products with no duty paid. A custom station was set up in Scilly in 1682 (often with only one exciseman) and was not effective in preventing the trade, which was a lifeblood to many islanders. The stationing of the naval cutter *Tamar* in 1784 led to the start of a decline in smuggling, and the French Wars 1792–1815 meant fewer ships calling – and a hostile coast across the Channel. The report of 1819, which talked of extreme miseries on the off-islands, also mentions the increase in population, and the ruin of kelp-making as factors bringing about the depression. Another factor was an Act of Parliament of 1790 which allowed the legal costs of cases of smuggling to be met by the Commissioners out of the sale of seizures, and allowed revenue officers to keep a small share of the proceeds for themselves. This gave the officers a financial incentive to be diligent in checking smuggling.

In consequence of the grim report of 1819, which bears witness to this distress, and its publication in *The Times* and other London newspapers, a General Committee was formed and subscriptions invited. A sum of £9,000 was collected and administered by a Resident Agent for the Committee, and it was used mainly in an attempt to establish a pilchard and mackerel fishery by means of the purchase of suitable boats, the repair of the existing ones, and the erection of storehouses.

Unfortunately, owing to misdirection or maladministration of this enterprise, or possibly to the vagaries of the pilchard which is somewhat unreliable in its habits, the expected alleviation of the islanders' conditions was not entirely successful, and the distress continued for some years, as shown in the old Scillonian saying about the islanders' staple diet:

> Scads and taties all the week
> And conger-pie on Sundays.

The off-island populations were probably the worst off and the island of Samson, which at one time had some forty or fifty inhabitants, was finally evacuated in 1855 owing to the poorness of the living and the difficulty of looking after the old people there. The war years after 1794 had seen some increased naval and military activity and interest in Scilly – with attendant economic benefits to the islanders – and a demand for potatoes, some of which it is believed, went to help feed the Duke of Wellington's army fighting the French in Spain; but the coming of peace in 1815 ended this, and some Scillonian families became destitute, reduced, it was said, to living on limpets. Some of the relief money went to purchase fishing nets, and some, it is believed, helped fund the visit of a Honiton lady who came to teach threadwork skills to Scillonian women. There were also continuing climatic troubles, such as the terrible drought of 1825.

A close observer of Scilly and of the lives of his fellow Scillonians was Robert Maybee. He was a ballad singer and poet who was born on St Mary's in 1810 and died there in 1891. In his later years he was reduced to hawking fruit and doing odd jobs about the islands, but his verses have always been treasured by Scillonians, His native charm and simplicity of character shine through the records he has left, and his record of island life has been enriched by his artless descriptions of what went on around him. He was said to have been an insignificant-looking little man with weak, blue eyes and curly hair, and he could neither read nor write. Others wrote down for him his word pictures. Here is an extract from his *Sixty-Eight Years' Experience on the Scilly Isles*, slightly amended to allow for the failings of his amanuenses.

'When I was young I many times wished I had been a scholar, that I might have written a long history of the Scilly Islands; but, being no scholar and, in fact, unable to read or write, it was useless my thinking of making a book, so I gave up all idea of it until the year 1883. I was working in Tresco at that time, and in the evenings, when I had leisure, walking round the hills and thinking of what had passed on the islands in my lifetime, I found that I could remember everything that had happened in the islands for 68 years, just as if it had occurred on that day. It then came into my mind that I would have a little book written if I could get anyone to write it for me as I told it to him, about the changes in life and trade and shipwrecks and loss of life and also some pieces of poetry of my own composition ...

I asked the master of the house at which I lodged whether he would write a little book for me in the winter evenings, and he was agreeable. The first line of this book was put to paper on 5th November, 1883, my age at that time being 74 years, I chose that day to begin my book because 50 or 60 years ago it used to be a great holiday on this island, being known as 'Ringing Tide', when all the boys were looking forward to having a day's holiday to ring the church bell.

At that time Scilly was a fine place for catching fish. There were more than four times as many men on St Mary's at that time as there are now, and they were a bigger and much stronger race of people than the present inhabitants. They did not call themselves fishermen because a living could not be made out of fishing in those days; fish would not sell, as every man on the island could get as much as he liked to go after. It made no difference what their employment was – after they left work those who had no boats to go in could go out on the rocks and catch as many fish as they could carry home every night through the summer ... Fifty years ago there were 23 public houses on St Mary's and companies in all of them every evening; at this time there are only five and you will scarce see a man belonging to the island in any one of them – that is one great change that has taken place.

I was born on 1st April 1810, on the Head of the Peninnis, at St Mary's, one of the Scilly Islands in the County of Cornwall, and that was my home till I was 42 years of age. My father was a native of the Isle of Wight, in the County of Hampshire, and came to the Scilly Islands to work the windmill that now stands on the Head of Peninnis. After the machinery was all taken out of the mill, it was fitted out for a signal station and now goes by the name of Rowet's Tower. My father had a house built about 60 yards to the east of the tower, and there he resided until the year 1834, when he died. Peninnis at that time was considered one of the pleasantest places on the island by visitors; it was a large open downs with no hedge on the west side of it till you got half-way to Buzza's Hill, and it was covered with long heath and wild flowers of various kinds which made it very pleasant in the summer time. It was about three-quarters of a mile from Hugh Town, with a footpath to it from Porthcressa close by the seashore.

The weather was different in those days to what it is now. The summers were very hot and we sometimes had calm weather for three or four weeks at a time, with a great number of small fishing boats all along the coast fishing, which made it very pleasant for travellers; and in winter time, with an easterly wind, there were a great number of ships coming in through the Sound every day, and a great many people used to go out to see them come round Peninnis Head. On the east side of Peninnis was Old Town Bay: large pilot boat, two six-oared rowing gigs and eight smaller boats belonging to Old Town were kept there, which could be manned at any time at a quarter-hour's notice, so that there was something new every day. I can remember everything that has happened on the islands since I was 5 years of age. The great battle of Waterloo was fought on the 18th June, 1815, and shortly after that, peace was proclaimed and a public dinner was held at St Mary's in the open air and the town lit up well that night. I can remember being there with my father and mother; there were big guns mounted all round the Garrison, which used to be fired on certain days in the year, such as the Queen's birthday. There were 100 soldiers in the Garrison, who used to march to church every Sunday and play the drum and fife as they marched; and a large number of men-of-war coming and going every day. The captains and officers and their boats crews would be ashore walking up and down the street, so you see there was more life in Scilly 68 years ago than there is now.

After the French War was over, the 20 or 30 invalids who had been doing garrison duty were pensioned off with a small sum of money and they all stopped on the island till they died. Peninnis at that time was one of the best places for catching fish from the rocks. The pensioners, not having much work to do, often came out to catch fish mornings and evenings – some for pleasure and some for pastime; and after that most of the ladies and gentlemen in the town used to come out for pleasure. I have known as many as 40 or 50 people to be on the different rocks fishing on a fine summer's evening, and that was carried on for many years. In those days people could catch as much fish as they wished to have by going to the rocks to get them. When I was about 8 or 9 years old I could go down to the rocks at any time of the day and catch more small whiting fish than two men can get at this time by sailing all round the islands in a boat – unless it is at a time when the fish are in. There are 11 rocks around Peninnis where we used to go fishing. I shall name them. Beginning at the west side of Peninnis, there is Carn Michael, The Chair, The Murre, Deep Water, High Jolly, Low Jolly, Louise's Rock, Humphrey's Rock, New Jolly, Westward Carn Lee and East Carn Lee, I was so much used to these rocks that I could come up over them in the darkest hours of the night, and many times, after all my company had gone, I have stayed behind myself to try to catch a conger.

Fifty years ago in Old Town there were between 40 and 50 strong able men, and they most of them got their living by labouring and fishing, piloting and making kilp. At that time, by making kilp in the summer season, men could get very good wages when it was a dry summer. The first kilp I can remember was £5 a ton, and almost every person on the island was working on it that summer. There are but three or four people on the island who can remember anything about kilp-making, so I will give you an account of how it is done. They would begin to make kilp in March month all around the island as soon as they could get any of the late drift-weed in. They most commonly used to go two families together: there were but three or four horses and carts on the island at that time and the seaweed used to be brought up in baskets by men, women and children, and every party had its own piece of ground to dry it on. The weed was spread and, if the weather was dry, in a day or two it was turned over, and when it was properly dry it was all made up in cocks, just like hay, above high-water mark where the sea could not come to it, and then the weed would be saved. After it had been in cocks for some time, and the weather being fine for burning it, they would have pits dug in the sand in the shape of a pan, quite small at the bottom and paved with small stones, and afterwards built round with single stones to a height of about two or three feet. The women would burn most of the kilp and the children would bring the weed to them while they were doing it, so that the men could do other work between times. All through the kilping season they would light up the kilp between twelve and one o'clock, and keep it burning till about eight or 9 o'clock in the evening, putting on the weed in handfuls as fast as it would consume. After the kilp was burnt, six or eight men would come with kilp rakes to strike the kiln – that is, to work the kilp up – and when it was worked up it was like so much hot lead. They might have to work up as many as eight kilns, so they would have to run from one to another till they had completed all of them. There might be 40 or 50 kilns burning around St Mary's in one day, so that each party would have to do its own work. The next morning a man would go down with a bar and raise the kilp up out of the pit; it would come out in a hard lump of about three-hundredweight: it was then broken up in handy lumps and put under the cliff, and the pit was cleaned out for burning again the next day: and so they would continue their work till August month, getting as much seaweed as they possibly could. Everyone knew his own ground for drying the seaweed just the same as going in his fields to work.

In the summer days kilp was being made on the six islands, and some days there would be as many as 100 kilns burning on the different islands. The smoke would come from the kilns as thick as it would from a steamer when new coals were put in: on a calm day the smoke would go straight up (a light smoke, almost white) and that would look grand.

There were five kilp merchants on the island; they were all shopkeepers, selling groceries and drapery, so that all the people who worked about the kilp could go and take up anything they wanted. This work was finished in the middle of August and the kilp was then all shipped off to Bristol to make glass and soap. This work was carried on till the year 1835, when the last kilp was burned on the islands. Few persons made kilp that year and it was sold for 30s per ton.

The harvest now begins. There were fine crops of grain on the island at that time and every man and woman that could reap was employed to save the harvest; the grain was all cut with the reaphook and the farmers were particular as to how it was cut, especially the barley, which was spread thin on the ground so as to cover it all over in order to get it well dried. It was all used for making bread: they would leave it on the ground for six or seven days and then bind it and make it up in round mows in the fields and leave it for three or four weeks before bringing it into the mowhay. The main thing farmers looked out for in those days was to get a good harvest and save their 12 months' bread in good condition. The grain would all be got into the mowhays by the latter part of September and then they would begin to get up the late crop of potatoes. Every man and boy would be employed, just as they are in this day, getting out the early crop: men's wages were 1s 6d a day and find themselves, or 1s 3d a day and have meat at the house of the farm they were working on. They had their choice as to which they would take: men with families would take 1s 6d a day and go to their own homes, as living was very cheap at that time. It was 3d a day for three good meals to the young men who used to have their meat where they worked, and I think they got the best of it at the end of the week.

The potatoes were of much better quality than those grown at present and were sold for 2s per bushel all the year round. Every labouring man who had no potatoes of his own would take in his winter's stock when he was digging – 30 to 40 bushels, according to the number of his family – so that they would not fall short until the next crop. This was the way the work was carried on in St Mary's until the disease got into the potatoes.

Every family on the island used to have as much fish as they could make use of in the 12 months without any cost, except the salt to save them. Every man could go and catch his own fish after finishing his day's work, whatever his employment may have been.

Every householder on the island, whether a farmer or not, kept some pigs, and a piece of ground by the house for growing potatoes to feed them. They would all have a pig to kill about Christmas-time, weighing from 16 to 18 score – pigs at that time being very large in the island; particularly about Old Town they would have them from 24 to 30 score weight, and their pork was better and sweeter than that of any of the small pigs killed in the present day. Pork was sold then for 3d per pound by the side, and sometimes less; and best cuts of beef were sold on the market for 5d per pound and other parts for less. The cattle were small, the average weight of a bullock being from 4 to 4½ cwt. The winter bullocks were all fed on potatoes with a little dry meal, and the beef was richer and had a better flavour than we get now. Veal sold for 3d, mutton for 3d to 4d per pound; young fowls for 1s per pair; eggs 3d to 4d per dozen; and fresh butter 8d per pound.

With the first strong breeze of wind we got from the east after the harvest, a great number of ships would come into the harbour. Vessels in those days were of a different class to those in use at present; they were not built to beat the wind but to sail before it, so that all the vessels that got into the Bristol Channel had to wait till the wind turned to the eastward before they could sail, bound for the South Channel; when they came to the Land's End they would all bear away for Scilly and come in a fleet. I have known as many as 200 come in one day, reaching from Giant's Castle up to the Roadstead, three and four abreast, which was a grand sight; and after that the vessels would be coming in every day, while the wind was to the eastwards.

The Roadstead, New Grimsby Harbour, Old Grimsby Harbour and St Ellen's Pool would be as full of vessels as they could hold; and these ships must have left a great deal of money in the islands, as they had to lie there till the wind shifted to the westward. If it changed on a fine day, all those vessels left the harbour on that day: that is a sight we cannot see nowadays, which is another great change that has taken place in 68 years.

When we got east wind further on in the winter it was very cold. The weather was very different 50 years ago to what it is now. We used to get a great deal of calm weather, with the sun very hot, and the hotter the summer, the colder was the winter. I have known everything frozen up for three or four weeks at a time. In cold winters there used to be a large number of wild fowl on the islands. I have run around Peninnis on a cold morning to keep myself warm and have put up as many as 20 cocks before breakfast. In some cases they may have dropped and I may have put the same bird up again, but woodcocks were very plentiful on the islands at that time and, after heavy rain, on the flat part of Peninnis where shallow pools of water would stand, I could put up hundreds of snipe every day. No person would fire at a snipe in those days, so they were never disturbed unless anyone was walking over the downs. A great quantity of wild geese and duck used to come to this spot in the winter. Many people were in the habit of walking around Peninnis to look at the vessels coming in, and some would take their guns with them and shoot a goose or duck, whichever they could fall in with. There were hundreds of lapwing and plovers on the islands, and everyone was allowed to carry a gun who could buy one, but there were not many people here then who cared for shooting.

The summer of 1824 was the finest and pleasantest I ever knew; in April, May and June we had fine, warm pleasant weather, with some showers to keep the crops growing. The stems of the potatoes were three or four feet long that summer, and there being no wind to hurt the crops, they grew as high as five feet, and in many places higher than the hedges, so that when two or three adjoining fields were in potatoes they looked like one field. When in bloom the potatoes carried a pink blossom, so that the islands looked like a flower garden.

In 1825 occurred the season which was called the famine season, when everything was dried and burnt up by the hot sun, There was some rain on the 3rd March ... [then] not a drop of rain fell on the islands till the latter part of May ... [when] it rained heavily for 1½ hours ... and after that shower not a drop of rain fell till September after the harvest was gathered in. This occurred at a time when kilp was being made on the islands and most of the people working at it; they had a chance of keeping themselves cool by wading about in the sea during the hot weather. In the middle of the day the sand was so hot that nobody could stand on it for a moment. Several wells were dried up and also all the pools where the cattle drank, except a little in the lower moors, to which they were all driven. We had to fetch our water from Piper's Hole, at the Head of Peninnis. The sun was so hot that summer that when the small pits were filled with water by the high tides, the water would be dried up and the salt left during the neap tides. I have gone down many times and scraped up 10 or 12 pounds that has been made by the sun, and you could get salt every neap tide through that summer. The hardest gale of wind that ever blew on the islands occurred on 13th February, 1833, from the westward. It was almost impossible for a man to stand on his legs, and we could not look to windward. A heavy rowing gig belonging to Tresco was up on the bank, and the force of the wind took her up in the air and the weight with which she came down broke her to pieces.

It was thought that after the kilping was done away with people would not get any employment, but about that time shipbuilding began to go ahead on the islands. Small schooners were built for the fruit trade to St Michael's and other ports and it was found to pay so well that they could not get men to build them fast enough; they had to get shipwrights from wherever they could. There were four master builders and all the young men were learning the shipwright business, which increased very fast; and shortly after that they began to build larger vessels for the Mediterranean and different parts of the world, and this trade was carried on for a great number of years. The shipowners had got some very fine vessels – large schooners, brigs and barques – trading in most parts of the world ...

The fleet of ships belonging to the Scilly Islands numbered between 60 and 70; the greater part of them were owned by the inhabitants, and it was said that they were paying thirty per cent at that time. A shipping company was got up in £10 shares and did very well, and after that another was started in £5 shares, so that every person who had any money to lay out might have a chance of getting good interest for it. I belonged to the last company that was got up, and I believe most of the people on the islands who could raise £5 or £10 belonged to it to try their luck. There was £5,100 laid out in vessels, and after they had been running two years the accounts were made up, and, owing either to bad captains or mistakes, the shares that were bought at £5 were only worth £2. Most of the small shareholders sold their shares at £2 and the company was broken up; but some of the large shareholders kept one of the vessels and ran her for a great number of years, almost bringing the shares up to £5 again.

Since that time, as fast as shipping has got up it has gone down again. At one time there were nearly 70 ships belonging to Scilly, and now there is only one little coal vessel of 100 tons belonging to the port.

It was about this time that they found out the markets for early potatoes which brought high prices for a number of years. It was almost like coining money, and it was said that at that time the island was the richest place in the world for the number of people on it. It is not only the shipping that has failed, but every trade on the island. There is scarcely any work to do now. You will see many people standing about for want of work to do, who would willingly take any work they could get for low wages.

The longest easterly wind I ever remember was in 1853; it commenced in February and lasted till the latter part of May, making between 13 and 14 weeks, with a great many strong breezes during the spring. There were nearly 100 sail of vessels lying in St Mary's Roadstead in May and there was not a day they could get to sea.

In 1854 we had a heavy storm of wind from the south-east; on the morning after the storm there was scarcely a green leaf to be seen on the island. Ten or twelve vessels were repaired on the island.

In 1855 I engaged to work on the Trinity Works to build the lighthouse on the Bishop Rock. It was a very pleasant summer and I was much pleased with my employment. The labourers and bargemen were paid off on the last day of November, but the stone-cutters, carpenters and blacksmiths were all kept on three weeks later. The stones for the building were all worked in the yard on Rat Island. Shortly after I was paid off from this work I went to St Agnes on a visit, and while on the island I met with a farmer who asked me if I would stay there and work for him all the winter. He had plenty of work for me to do till I wanted to ship on the Bishop works again, and I should lose no time as when it was not fit to work out of doors he had plenty for me to do in the barn. He offered me good wages, victuals and lodgings. There was plenty of money being got in St Agnes at that time. The farmer belonged to one of the six pilot boats, and they were at sea every day in the winter when it was fit to go, so he was all behind with his work on the farm.

I could not content myself on St Agnes, but I was there all through the shortest days of the winter; they have five meals a day on this island ... I worked on the Bishop works five years, and on St Agnes each winter of that time.'

Robert Maybee[1] refers to the kelp industry in Scilly. Kelp is the product from burning seaweed, and it is used in bleaching, and in making soap, iodine, and glass – mainly window and bottle glass.

The industry was introduced to the islands by Nance and his family, who, for several generations, lived on Tëan, which they leased for the purpose, and where the weed was most suitable. It was necessary to burn an enormous amount of seaweed to obtain a relatively small amount of kelp – about 22 tons of seaweed to produce one ton of kelp – which was worth about £4, and an average ton of kelp would yield about eight pounds of iodine. Some old kelp pits where the weed was burnt are plainly visible today on White Island off St Martin's, and on Toll's Island and elsewhere. The quays at Pendrathen and at Watermill were originally built to export the kelp produced on St Mary's.

Then, in the 1830s, the kelp industry declined rapidly, partly as a consequence of the making of synthetic iodine on the mainland, and partly because the kelp was often adulterated by sand. This decline added to the economic troubles of Scilly in the first half of the nineteenth century. At its height kelping produced a constant pall of smoke all over Scilly, with an awful stench everywhere; so the industry's disappearance at least cleared the air.

(1). For further details of Robert Maybee, reference can be made to the entry in the *New Oxford Dictionary of National Biography.*

CHAPTER VII – AUGUSTUS SMITH, SHIPBUILDING and PILOTING

In 1831 the Duke of Leeds decided he had had enough of Scilly's problems, and surrendered the lease to the Duchy who, for nearly the next three years, administered Scilly directly without any intervening lessee. A surveyor, Edward Driver, was sent over by the Duchy and his 1929 report showed an appalling state of affairs, including so many rents that had been allowed to drift into arrears by the Duke of Leeds' agents that many were now beyond recovery. The new agent which the Duchy appointed was ordered to raise rents, but this made the Duchy so unpopular at a time when the inhabitants were poverty-stricken that, by 1834, the Duchy were quite pleased to offer a lease to a suitable person in order to unburden themselves of the problems. The petition to Parliament of 13 March 1826 makes clear the sufferings of the islanders, and speaks of their 'severe distress ... which at the present time is frightfully increased from the want of employment and particularly from the very peculiar circumstances under which the Islands are held from the Crown whence result the absence of any due form of civil government and administration of law ...'

The new man who took the lease was Augustus Smith, a big, energetic and imposing figure who came from an old Hertfordshire family that had made money through banking in Lombard Street. He was born in 1804 in Harley Street, London, went to Harrow School and Christchurch, Oxford, where he graduated in 1826, but he shunned a social life in London and sought some estate where he could employ his talents to put into practice his serious ideas about self-improvement of the poor and oppressed. He heard that the Duke of Leeds was wanting to surrender the lease, so he went over to Scilly on the weekly packet boat from Penzance and talked to many in the islands including General Smythe (Lieutenant Governor), who exercised the Lord Proprietor's military authority, W.J. Johns, the son of the former agent of the Duke of Leeds, who was to become Augustus' agent, George Driver, the Duchy surveyor and agent, and

Augustus Smith, 'Emperor of Scilly'   photo Gibson, Scilly

many Scillonians, who were a little suspicious of his motives and resentful of his questions. Everywhere seemed to Augustus to be run down and everyone idle and ignorant – it was the challenge he had been seeking – and when he returned to the mainland he went immediately to see the Duchy.

The lease he signed ran from 1834 for ninety-nine years or three lives at the almost peppercorn rent of £40 a year; but Augustus had to give the Duchy £20,000 and undertake to pay the islands' clergy and to build the church and the quay on St Mary's. Coincidentally, Parliamentary legislation enabled him as proprietor to have legal powers within Scilly and to appoint JPs.

In 1834 Augustus arrived and resided in Scilly for the next 38 years till his death in 1872. He was a man perfectly suited to the needs of Scilly at that time, for the Scillonians had been struggling for years against a package of debilitating disadvantages, including the effects of the overhaul of the Pilotage Service by Trinity House in 1811, the decrease in numbers of vessels calling at Scilly following the conclusion of peace with France in 1815, the burden of the Salt Tax which fell most hardly on those least able to pay, the failure of the corn and potato crops in 1817, the continuing troubles resulting from an increase in population, the lack of reforms, absentee proprietors, and dishonest and extortionate agents. Especially unsatisfactory was the system of land tenure. This was because the law of majorats or primogeniture did not operate in Scilly; on the death of a tenant his landholding was divided up among his sons, each farm therefore becoming smaller with each generation and less able to support those who lived on it. It is not surprising therefore that one of Augustus Smith's first actions was to announce that any tenant who sub-let his land without permission would have his tenancy terminated. He then began the task of re-allotting the farm lands so as to create viable farms to ensure that each farmer had a sufficient and compact portion to support his family, and to which Augustus decreed only the farmer's eldest son should succeed. [See appendix 7 for the importance of this in Scilly's story.]

This might have resulted in more disgruntlement than in fact it did, as it could have been very hard on a tenant's other offspring, but, fortunately, Augustus could provide much building work which occupied the able-bodied unemployed. Under the terms of the lease Augustus had to build the new church and to extend the quay at Hugh Town (in 1836) and to these works was added the construction of new roads and schools, and the erection of the Lord Proprietor's new residence on Tresco. There was still a problem of overpopulation in Scilly (Tresco had 933 inhabitants in 1801 and 266 in 1871) and he dealt with this problem by drafting boys to

94

serve in ships, sending girls to the mainland to jobs such as shop assistants and domestic servants, and encouraging habits of thrift and industry among everybody in the hope that fewer people would be idle. He also used his influence with the Elder Brethren of Trinity House to try to get Scilly made a pilot-station. He even introduced deer (and rabbits of various colours) into Scilly to provide for the inhabitants.

One of his most novel ideas was the erection at King George's Battery on the Garrison of a huge air pressure indicator, consisting of two masts, each sixty feet in height with cross bars between them, on which a square black board ran in a groove. Its position indicated the position of the mercury in a barometer, and was adjusted twice a day for the information of pilots, ship captains and others who needed some weather forecast. Attached to one end of the groove was a semi-circular piece of board, which, if turned up, showed that the mercury had risen since the last adjustment, and, if turned down, showed that barometric pressure had fallen.

It was simply by virtue of his land tenure that Augustus governed Scilly and was called Lord Proprietor and could make reforms. Strictly speaking, Augustus was neither a lord nor the proprietor, but he ruled Scilly as a benevolent despot. Although inevitably making some enemies along the way, his life's work was the saving of Scilly, and, as the Rev. H.J. Whitfeld acknowledged in 1852, 'under Smith the islands passed from poverty to prosperity'. It is little wonder that he was addressed as 'My Lord', referred to as 'the Governor', while some even termed him 'the Emperor of Scilly'.

Augustus' many decrees were on the whole wise but fairly tough. For instance, he forbade young people to marry until they had a house to live in, and if they could not manage in Scilly he would pack them off to the mainland. He was also chief magistrate, and through the Select Vestry, which the islanders had set up before his arrival in Scilly and which had replaced the corrupt Court of Twelve, he was able to form a more efficient administration. Nominally, this Select Vestry was in control of the police and licensing, but as the local bobby (sergeant by courtesy, who gloried in the name of Horatio Nelson) was also game-warden and a paid employee of Augustus, in practical matters the will of the Lord Proprietor always prevailed.

At one time Augustus was crossed by John Banfield, a leading merchant on St Mary's and a man described as 'never happy except when he had something to be miserable about'. Banfield was one of a few people who held a lease direct from the Duchy, and so thought that he could defy Augustus. His offence was to build a store without asking Augustus' permission, among other matters; Augustus dealt with him by building pillars at the entrance to St Mary's quay and threatening to close the quay to Banfield's goods if he was not obeyed. One of these pillars still stands today as a monument to Augustus' autocracy.

At first Augustus lived in Hugh House on the Garrison, but in 1838 he moved to his newly-built residence called Tresco Abbey, next to the ruins of the old priory. The site was chosen partly because it did least harm to existing tenancies on Tresco, apart from necessitating the demolition of three cottages where his garden was to be, and whose old walls would provide some initial shelter. It was also a magnificent situation for a house, facing south with views over the lake. There, Augustus went to live in some style, with a butler and footman both in full livery. He was a bachelor all his life but not, it seems, a celibate, for his bedroom was next to his study from which a private winding path led away. Gossip has made much of this, but in his will he did make provision for two island women of Tresco – and their children.

Augustus also carried out the involuntary evacuation of Samson in 1855. Population figures show how numbers had declined, but do not reveal the proportion of old people to the young people who had to support them.

POPULATION OF SAMSON
1669 one family
1715 there were three men fit to carry arms
1751 two households
1794 six households
1816 forty people
1822 seven households (34 persons)
1850 three or four households
(figures from *The Scillonian*, No. 126, p. 112 and No. 208, p. 123)

Augustus did much to develop Scilly and help its inhabitants in other ways. He sowed and planted trees all around his new garden, removed rocks from Tresco Channel to help make it navigable more safely, introduced new and better varieties of potatoes to the

Entrance pillars St Mary's quay

Augustus Smith built these massive entrance pillars to the quay at St Mary's in order to win an argument he had with some St Mary's traders who would not recognise his authority as Lord Proprietor. He threatened to close off the quay and they soon came to heel.

---

farmers, inaugurated fire and postal services, planted gorse (which is wind resistant) to protect seedlings, and then elm, sycamore, oak and poplar trees. He built a bakery and stopped the wasteful cutting of turf for fuel, supplied a free steam flour mill, imported coal from Wales – handed out gratis to many elderly islanders – and helped to stop smuggling by announcing that anyone caught in this offence would be removed from his tenancy. His motto, carved in a granite stone in Tresco Abbey, was 'Thus you do not work for yourselves'. However, he wanted to ensure his name lived on, and in his will required his nephew and heir, Lieutenant Thomas Algernon Smith Dorrien to alter his surname by taking the additional surname of 'Smith' (the clumsy-sounding first 'Smith' is now used only on official documents).

Augustus was also MP for Truro, 1857-65, President of the Royal Geographical Society in Cornwall and Grandmaster of Cornish Freemasons. It was after attending a Masonic function that he died at Plymouth in 1872, his last years somewhat clouded by quarrels with the Duchy of Cornwall, who, when new officials took over the Duchy following the accession of Queen Victoria in 1837, wanted to increase his £40 a year rent. In any event Augustus arranged that he should not be buried in Scilly, but in the churchyard at St Buryan near Land's End – an impressive granite monument (whose shape Augustus had himself sketched) being afterwards erected to his memory on the top of Abbey Hill on Tresco.

However, the most pleasurable monument to his memory is not of stone but of plants – the sub-tropical garden he began around the site of the old priory ruins and his new house on Tresco. Here, many of the plants received by Augustus and his successors were brought by Scillonian sea captains when they returned from all over the world; but many more came from Kew Gardens as a consequence of Augustus' contacts with the staff there. Several botanical specimens had never previously been cultivated successfully in the open elsewhere in the UK. The equable climate, the shelter screens and high walls, the stepped site of the gardens sloping to the south and, of course, the dedicated attention of Augustus and his gardeners all helped to make his garden a success and attract visitors to see it from the mainland. At the entrance to his gardens near the East Rockery Augustus had a notice to visitors carved in slate which is still there. It warns visitors to the garden against 'scribbling nonsense and committing suchlike small nuisances', forbids children 'coming by themselves', and informs that 'chains, bars and round stones mark walks which are not to be used'. The notice ends on a friendly note: 'Enter then, if it so please you, and welcome'.

When Augustus arrived, Tresco was merely a bare windswept island without trees, only bramble, furze, broom and holly, but nothing over four feet high; when he died he left to his successor a unique, seven acre sub-tropical garden containing plants of 111 different species. Yet, arguably even more important as an achievement than this, was the encouragement he gave to education in Scilly, building new schools on all the main islands and insisting on high standards, even going into them and teaching himself. He made parents pay a penny a week for sending their children to school and tuppence if they stayed away – an effective method of reducing absences and stopping truancy, so making education in effect compulsory in Scilly forty years before it became so on the mainland. This shows in the HM Inspectors of Schools Report of 1848 which stated: 'In these islands through the active superintendence of the Proprietor, nearly all the children from two until thirteen years of age are under instruction ... in each of the islands there are schools for infants as well as for older children ... The children read nicely, write from dictation with much accuracy, replied shrewdly to questions upon Bible history and geography, and a few points in English history. Grammar was soundly taught at Agnes, and arithmetic and navigation well taught at Tresco.'

Under the new favourable government established in Scilly, and in the UK generally with the triumph of laissez-faire, the islanders began to show the enterprise and self-help (which seems always latent in the Scillonian character) to organise a rapid development of local shipbuilding. This industry started in 1774 with the construction of vessels to carry kelp to Bristol and Gloucester, but it was under Augustus that shipbuilding boomed. By 1850 there were four shipbuilding yards on St Mary's, two on Town Beach and two at Porthcressa. The ships were always owned by Scillonians and nearly always officered and skippered by Scillonians, for one project Augustus was most keen on was the teaching of navigation in the schools he built on Scilly. In 1825 there were eleven 59 ton Scillonian-built vessels registered in Scilly; the following table reveals the expansion that then took place:

WOODEN SHIPS REGISTERED IN SCILLY
In 1825 there were 11 with a total tonnage of 574
In 1838 there were 50 with a total tonnage of 3,062
In 1851 there were 59 with a total tonnage of 6,843
In 1864 there were 35 with a total tonnage of 6,148

Scillonian shipbuilders gained such confidence that one carpenter, Henry Trevellick, made his mark even in American history. He crossed the Atlantic and became a pioneer of the eight-hour-day movement, a leading figure in early American trade unionism, and an eminent orator.

Scilly's ships were small and built for uses such as bringing fruit from the Mediterranean and from the Azores. The biggest ship ever built in Scilly was the *John Banfield* of 528 tons, and some of the larger ones traded to all parts of the world. To many Scillonians the coming and going of shipping also afforded an opportunity not only to expand business on St Mary's, but also to emigrate abroad, if they wished.

The table also shows that by 1864 the industry had just about passed its peak, and by the 1880s all the boat building yards had closed. The last vessel to be built at Porthcressa was the *David Auterson*, launched on John Edward's slipway 12 September 1870. The last ship to be built on Town Beach was the 179 ton brigantine *Gleaner* in 1878, except for two very small craft in the 1880s. It was a development of technology which finished the industry in Scilly, the change from building wooden ships to bigger iron ships propelled mainly by steam in place of wind. All wood for shipbuilding in Scilly had had to be imported, but this was a small problem compared with the impossibility of Scilly competing with mainland yards building iron ships.

An attempt was made to replace shipbuilding by coal-bunkering to refuel the new steamships, but most ships were soon going up Channel without needing to stop at Scilly.

The replacement of sailing ships by steam-driven ones also saw the decline of that other occupation of Scillonians – piloting, and for much the same reasons. Sometimes Scilly was the first landfall of ships that had been at sea for many weeks, and they would welcome fresh food which the pilot cutters and gigs could bring them. An easterly wind had meant a demand for Scilly's pilots from passing sailing ships heading up the English or Bristol Channels in order that they could navigate the dangerous rocks of Scilly and take shelter in the islands to await a favourable wind from the west. Moreover, ships anchored in St Mary's Roadstead brought trade and business to the islands, for their crews came ashore and spent money, and their ships took on provisions. All this income was lost when steamships steamed by ignoring the direction of the wind, and Scilly's pilot cutters – so long part of Scilly's seascape (there had been ten in Scilly in 1846) – were eventually abandoned or broken up. Scilly was no longer a port of call after 1890, and the pest house, built on St Helen's in 1764 for isolating plague victims in ships calling at Scilly, never came to be used for that purpose.

However, there was always fishing, although the late eighteenth century had been the best years for mackerel fishing. The industry received a small fillip from the linking of the railway line from London to Penzance in 1865, and Algernon Dorrien Smith tried to encourage pilchard fishing. There was also the export to the mainland of shrimps, lobsters, crawfish and limpets, and in the nineteenth century the harbour at St Mary's was crowded with

Abbey gateways

The gateways to the old priory on Tresco are surrounded by the luxuriant growth of Tresco Abbey Gardens. Lying on the ground and serving as a paving stone immediately under the smaller archway is a tombstone which has on it the earliest writing found in Scilly, dating from about the early centuries AD. It is only a tantalising fragment which reads: 'TH FILI ... COGVI' Roughly translated, this means 'the grave of the son of ...'

These ruins are all that remain of the twelfth century Benedictine priory which, in 1114, Henry I granted by charter to the Abbot of Tavistock. All the monasteries in England were ordered by Henry VIII to be dissolved in 1539, but it is believed that Tresco Priory may have been abandoned and allowed to decay some time previous to this. It is likely that piratical attacks on Scilly had made life in Scilly unendurable even for monks.

fishing craft.

The gigs, too, became of less importance once engines began to be fitted in other boats. They had served innumerable purposes such as helping cutters carry pilots to ships requiring them, salvaging from wrecks, lighthouse relief, and even as lifeboats. The *Klondyke*, now restored, in the museum in Church Street on St Mary's, was heavier than most other gigs, and at one time was used for taking the doctor to the off-islands for emergency calls. She is rigged with sails from the old Bryher gig *Czar*. Nowadays the gigs are important once again in the life in Scilly, racing each other across St Mary's Roadstead on summer Wednesday and Friday evenings to the enjoyment of Scilly's visitors, and in May 1990 there was held in Scilly, the first international pilot gig championship races.

The international gig championships then became an annual May event in Scilly and over 70 gigs competed in 2004, with Carudon's *Mary Newman* winning the men's event for the seventh time, Scilly's newest gig *Tregarthen*, coming second. Some of the gigs date back to the 19th century – or are replicas of those that were of that age – one of the oldest being *Bonnet*, built about 1830, and still racing. Gig racing is today Scilly's most popular sport.

CHAPTER VIII – THE FLOWER INDUSTRY and THE LATER SMITHS

Augustus' successor, Algernon Dorrien Smith, arrived on Tresco to take up residence in 1874 at the age of 26, and with capital from his mother to help him. He found that in Augustus' garden, the plants had now grown so high that gales blew them down. But he noticed some trees that seemed to withstand gales and these were Monterey pines from California. Consequently, he planted above his gardens the rows of Monterey pines that are still an effective shelter screen today.

By 1887 Algernon had a son and five daughters, so the Abbey was extended and the magnificent square tower added. The Duchy granted him a 31 year extension to his lease in 1884.

He married Edith, daughter of Lady Sophia Tower who had been for long a friend of Augustus, with much correspondence passing between them. Theoretically, his power in Scilly was somewhat reduced by the formation of the Council of the Isles of Scilly in 1891 after the Local Government Act of 1888, but with himself as hereditary chairman (the Dorrien Smiths continued to be chairmen with no election till 1955), and the Select Vestry no longer of much consequence and abolished in 1929, his authority was not in fact affected. Indeed, it had been one of his plans that the council should be set up, for it gave Scilly independence from Cornwall in every aspect of its administration, and it was a council with powers almost equal to a mainland county council.

Algernon also extended St Mary's quay to nearly its present length in 1889 mainly to cope with shipping the flowers. To try to recover some of the £14,000 the extension cost him, Parliament empowered Algernon to levy a charge on those who used the quay, but there was much grousing and reluctance to pay it. That the extension was necessary can be seen from an article in the *Western Mercury* in 1894: 'On a single day ... 3760 cases weighing 16 tons were despatched from the Scilly Isles to Penzance: and another day the total was 1900 cases, weighing 9 tons 6 cwt, all containing lilies and narcissus. Mr T.A. Dorrien Smith, the Lord of the Isles, is one of the largest growers, and by one steamer alone he sent across to the mainland no fewer than 32,000 bunches of blooms.'

Augustus Smith and his successors all helped to promote the flower industry. They encouraged the islanders to plant pittosporum, veronica, escallonia and enonymus around small fields to shelter the flowers, so presenting a chequer-board appearance to much of the cultivated land in Scilly. The mainstay of the industry became the Soleil d'Or, a rich yellow narcissus with several delicate flowers on each stalk and a marvellous scent. Together with Paper White, it is one of the earliest to reach maturity. Many other varieties followed such as King Alfred and Fortune, and innumerable new varieties were developed.

The origin of some of these flowers is uncertain. It is unlikely that they were indigenous; the Scilly White may have come from the South of France, the Paper White from Italy and Spain; and others from China. Grand Monarque came from China, but may have originated somewhere in the Eastern Mediterranean; and Princeps grow wild in northern Italy and have become naturalised in Ireland. It is thought that the earliest bulbs, the Scilly Whites were obtained by the monks of St Nicholas' Priory and became naturalised on all the islands. There is a local legend that the first bulbs were given to the wife of a governor of Star Castle by a Dutch merchant captain in return for some favour received. The lady, thinking they were onions, boiled some and, not liking the taste, threw the remainder into the castle moat, where they flourished.

Scilly's flower industry developed rapidly at the end of the nineteenth century. One story of its origin – which by oft repetition has come (as so much else that is classed as history) to be accepted as fact – is that William Trevellick of Rocky Hill Farm had secretly over the years been collecting the daffodil and narcissi bulbs growing wild on the Garrison, and, in about the year 1867, he sent an experimental consignment of flowers to Covent Garden (packed in a hatbox, so the story goes) and was delighted to be sent £1 for it. However, others claim that Augustus Smith had already sent a box of flowers to Covent Garden in about 1865. From this early beginning the industry grew till daffodils and narcissi are today the islands' glory as well as providing their inhabitants with a winter livelihood.

The cultivation of flowers – planting, picking and packing – is a

A flower field: late March and the flower season nearly over, yet there are plenty of daffodils still 'bobbing their heads in sprightly dance' to engage the early visitor.

skilled process. Flower farmers – they are always called farmers – have to contend with many forms of disease to which flowers are liable, with competition from East Anglian flower growers nearer the central markets, and with the fluctuations in prices. Bulbs are expensive and much capital is required to stock even a small field. There are also unpredictable changes in the buying habits of the public, with some of the older varieties no longer being in demand. New varieties are continually being developed in the islands to meet these changing fashions. The industry also depends on the weather. A severe winter in Scilly can delay the flowers so that profits are considerably reduced; on the other hand a cold snap on the mainland can have the reverse effect and bring considerable profit to Scillonian growers.

It is fortunate that the Scillonian 'year' is spread over the seasons in such a manner that there are few labour problems. From January to March, the islanders are mainly engaged in picking and packing flowers. When the flowers are ready and the market price is satisfactory, islanders capable of lending a hand drop other business until the packed boxes are safely on board the ship or aircraft on their way to market. In May, June, and July, there is work in the

105

William Trevellick and family

A posed photograph by Alexander Gibson which became a popular postcard in its day. On the far right is William Trevellick of Rocky Hill Farm with his wife far left, and other members of his family and flower pickers behind. The blooms are 'Grand Monarques' in the glasshouse of the farm.

fields. Every three to four years the bulbs must be dug up for separation and drying. They may also be par-boiled to destroy eel-worm, or treated to protect them from the many forms of virus to which they are susceptible. Some are refrigerated and others 'warm stored' in order to accelerate their winter sleep and enable them to advance their flowering season by several days or even weeks. From March to October there is a continual flow of visitors to be catered for, perhaps three-quarters of Scilly's income now emanating from this source, with the flower industry down to around ten per cent. November seems to be the quietest month, with many Scillonians taking holidays abroad.

After the initial assignment in 1867, Mr Trevellick sent another. Other Scillonians followed Trevellick's lead including Richard Mumford of Holy Vale, Hugh Watts of Parting Carn, and W.M. Gluyas of Old Town. However, most credit for promoting the flower

New Grimsby bulb fields, Tresco

A photograph of New Grimsby, Tresco, showing typical small Scillonian bulb fields, surrounded by tall hedges to protect the flowers from high winds.

industry in Scilly belongs to Mr T.A. Dorrien Smith, as can be seen from the following statement, dated 1893, for submission to His Royal Highness the Prince of Wales on behalf of the trustees of the late Mr Augustus Smith:

'Mr Dorrien Smith ... endeavoured to improve the cultivation of early potatoes by the introduction of new seeds and fresh sorts; but owing to foreign competition, their cultivation has proved to be too hazardous and speculative for the Islanders to embark in to any considerable extent.

He next determined to introduce the cultivation of bulbs, and with this in view he spent some time in Holland, studying the system of cultivation there, and then imported by degrees large quantities of them, selling them at cost price to his tenants. This has now become a very popular and the most lucrative industry there, and in favoured and sheltered spots can be successfully carried on, and so long as the fashion of bulb flowers continues, this industry promises to be a source of considerable profit to the Islanders. But its introduction has cost Mr Dorrien Smith £10,000, expended in the purchase of bulbs, the erection of bulb and flower houses, etc.'

Mr T.A. Dorrien Smith went to the Netherlands, Belgium and the Channel Islands in the spring of 1882 and some 190 kinds of bulbs were planted on Tresco in the autumn of that year. He visited Messrs. Ware's grounds (then agricultural land) at Upper Tooting in London and also Messrs. Barr's nurseries, where many of the Incomparabilis, Barri, and Ornato hybrids, were first raised – a few of these original kinds still exist in the Abbey Gardens, but they have long since been surpassed by more popular varieties.

Between 1881 and 1886 Algernon imported large numbers of bulbs and had thirty acres of trial beds on Tresco and glasshouses for forcing experiments. At first the flowers were exported in wicker boxes, then wooden boxes were used and, after the Second World War, cardboard boxes.

In 1885 the Isles of Scilly Bulb and Flower Association was formed. Annual shows were held at St Mary's and Mr Dorrien Smith presented a silver challenge cup for the best exhibit of cut flowers. The fashion for cut flowers in English households was revived in or about the year 1873 and has been maintained ever since.

The growth of the cut-flower trade in Scilly can be seen from the following table:

1867	one box
1885	65 tons
1886	86 tons
1887	100 tons
1889	198 Ions
1896	514 tons
1901	650 tons
1904	800 tons
1924	700 tons
1931	1,061 tons

The above figures are based on 200 boxes to a ton, each containing eighteen to twenty-four bunches. Later the tonnage

Neptune Steps

Neptune Steps in Tresco Abbey Gardens – a sub-tropical scene impressive even in a black-and-white snapshot.

exported exceeded 1,200 tons, and by 1989 it was estimated as 400 tons (this included packing in cardboard boxes).

The growth of the flower trade came just in time to save the islands from destitution, for it was introduced when the early potato harvests (which had been profitable since 1838) were failing, and when shipping and shipbuilding had come to an end.

The backbone of the industry in the twentieth century has been the *Soleil d'Or* which blooms from November for six weeks or so, and is not picked in the bud. It's real name is *Tazetta aurea*, and it is indigenous to Africa and its bulbs were first brought to Scilly by French sailing ships. It grows in Scilly better than it grows anywhere else in the British Isles, although it has been known in England since James I's reign. In 1875 there were nine sorts of Narcissi growing in Scilly and exported; these were: Double Daffodil; Odorus Major; Odorus Campanelle; Scilly White; Soleil d'Or; Grand Monarque; May Lily (biflorus); Double White; and Pheasant Eye.

The flower trade in the twentieth century has served as a useful complement to the visitor trade, providing a winter livelihood for some of those who 'do the visitors' in the summer. Only during the Second World War has the trade slumped badly – there were wartime restrictions on the export of flowers. For the duration of the war the Scillonians grew vegetables instead.

* * * * *

Major Arthur Dorrien Smith succeeded his father in 1918 and, as a noted horticulturalist, was most competent to continue his predecessors' development of Tresco Abbey Gardens and support the flower industry. The Major – as he was usually called – felt he could not finance all the repairs and improvements necessary in Scilly after the First World War, so he sought a new lease just for Tresco (and for a time the uninhabited islands) which was given him in 1929 for a period of 99 years. Three of his four sons were killed during the Second World War – and two nephews – so when he died in 1955 at the age of 79 (his ashes were scattered at sea), it was his remaining son, Lieutenant-Commander Thomas Mervyn Dorrien Smith who succeeded him. The Commander – as he was usually called – had served for nineteen years in the Royal Navy. His first marriage was to Princess Tamara, daughter of Prince Michael of Russia. They divorced, and his second marriage in 1967 was to Mrs

Worthington who already had children by her previous marriage. The Commander died in 1973 at the age of sixty, and was succeeded by his son Robert Dorrien Smith, who had been a student at an agricultural college before he came to live in Scilly. He has made innumerable improvements to Tresco since taking over, together with his wife Lucy, who, among other things, started Tresco Gallery and composed the shell decoration in the Gazebo in the Mediterranean Garden of Tresco Abbey Gardens. In the years 2003/2004 alone there has been a new terminal building at Tresco Heliport, a new shop, cafe, lecture hall, and entrance to the Gardens, and the acquisition and improvement of a second superb Tresco Estate hotel on Bryher. It is true to say that Scilly today 'is not what it was' because it 'is infinitely better', preserving what was wonderful while providing good, modern facilities of a high quality.

Neptune Figurehead

At the top of the steps is the figurehead of Father Neptune from the paddlesteamer *Thames*, which was wrecked on the Western Rocks in 1841 when on passage from Dublin bound for London. The figurehead looks as if it is made of stone, but a rap on it will confirm that it is actually wooden.

Roman Altar

An interesting find on Scilly is this granite Roman altar, which was believed to have been unearthed somewhere near the bottom of Garrison Hill on St Mary's, and removed by Augustus Smith to his Tresco Abbey Gardens. On one side of the altar is a sacrificial axe carved in the stone and on the other a sacrificial dagger.

Smith Monument

The rough-hewn granite monument to Augustus Smith, designed by Augustus himself, and placed at the top of Abbey Hill where there is one of the best views in Scilly.

CHAPTER IX – WRECKS,
LIGHTHOUSES and LIFEBOATS

Methought I saw a thousand fearful wrecks;
A thousand men that fishes gnaw'd about;
Wedges of gold, great anchors, heaps of pearl,
Inestimable stones, unvalued jewels,
All scatter'd in the bottom of the sea.
– WILLIAM SHAKESPEARE (Clarence's Dream, *Richard III*)

Until about five hundred years ago the Isles of Scilly were located at the edge of the known world, but with the discovery of the mainland of North America by John and Sebastian Cabot in 1497 (Columbus reached the mainland a year later), not only was Britain and the other maritime powers of Europe eventually to become pre-eminent in the world, but the Isles of Scilly were to find themselves in the middle of shipping routes that passed either side, to the north up the Bristol and St George's Channels and to the south up the English Channel. From America the islands are the first landfall after a voyage of some three thousand miles.

This geographical location of Scilly in the Western Approaches, together with the large increase in shipping, the difficulty sailors had of calculating longitude accurately, the poor charts of those times, the failure of many captains to allow sufficiently for the Rennel Current which tends to carry ships northwards, bad compasses, the low lying nature of the islands (which at their highest point at Telegraph are only 165 ft above mean sea level) so that they do not make a clear silhouette on the skyline before ships are almost into the islands, the lack of warning lights, the numerous partly-submerged rocks and ledges, and the fact that Scilly was often the first landfall for ships after travelling great distances which could easily magnify any small errors in navigation – all these factors help to explain the large number of ships which have come to grief in Scilly, over three hundred wrecks having been recorded since the seventeenth century.

When Sir Walter Besant wrote in 1860 that 'every rock in Scilly has a shipwreck', he was exaggerating – but only just. Indeed, there is a grim local proverb from the past in Scilly that said: 'For one who dies a natural death, nine are drowned'.

Sad though the tale of these wrecks often is, to the inhabitants of Scilly at times barely scraping a living, they were looked upon as sources of succour, windfalls given them by a merciful God. So often the cruel sea was the source of the islanders' troubles, but when there was a wreck they were able to benefit from others' misfortunes. There is an apocryphal story of a significant Scillonian addition to the liturgy:

> We pray, O Lord, not that wrecks may happen,
> But that, should they happen,
> Thou wilt guide them into these islands
> For the benefit of the poor inhabitants.

But though Scillonians may have profited from wrecks with relish, there is no evidence to warrant accusations that they have at any time deliberately lured ships on to the rocks; the term 'wreckers', when it is used in Scilly, always describes those who salvage from a wreck – save anything of value from it – not those who may in any way have contributed to the wreck.

Stories of cows left to wander on the coast with lights attached to their tails to confuse ships at sea have never been substantiated. But that the islanders benefited from shipwrecks and came to regard the proceeds from them as part of their natural harvest from the sea is undeniable, and helps to explain the apparently callous objection that the islanders made when it was proposed that a lighthouse should be built in Scilly.

Where Scillonians have particularly distinguished themselves, is as life-savers from wrecks, a tradition carried on today. With no hope or expectation of reward, and solely at the dictates of humanity, Scillonians have again and again risked their lives to save others, and sometimes lost their own lives in the endeavour. Those sailors who preserved their lives often did so because of the courage shown by Scillonians, particularly in their gigs and latterly in their lifeboats.

Of all these innumerable wrecks in Scilly the worst recorded disaster occurred on the night of 22 October, 1707, when,

The Cresset from St Agnes lighthouse, now in Tresco Abbey Gardens

The coal-burning cresset from the top of St Agnes lighthouse (see the photograph on the front cover of this book) was used from 1680 until replaced by oil burners in 1790.

returning from Toulon, five large ships of the fleet of Rear Admiral Sir Cloudesley Shovell struck the Western Rocks and about 1,670 men were drowned. [When Shovell wrote his name, he sometimes varied his spelling of it, for there was not then the insistence upon spelling consistency as there is today.]

The flagship *Association* and the large ships *Eagle* and *Romney* were lost with all hands save only one man – the quartermaster. The *Phoenix*, which had been despatched with two other warships ahead of the main fleet, was badly damaged but beached between Tresco and Samson. The body of Sir Cloudesley came ashore at Porth Hellick, St Mary's, where it was buried, later to be disinterred and placed in Westminster Abbey with great honour. Henry Trelawney also lost his life in this wreck; he was the son of Bishop Trelawney, who was the hero of the Cornish song:

And shall Trelawney die?
Then twenty thousand Cornish men
Will know the reason why.

117

The tragedy was the result of poor maps and navigational techniques of the time, and lack of sun observations which had made the fleet unsure of its position.

It was strange that, on that dark and stormy night, no lookout on any of the ships saw the warning light burning in the cresset at the top of St Agnes lighthouse (the Bishop Rock lighthouse was not built and functioning until 1858). Indeed, the first intimation of the disaster to come was when the flagship, the 90-gun *Association*, a second-rate ship-of-the-line of 1,459 tons, struck the Gilstone Ledges. Sir Cloudesley Shovell, a stout man of fifty-seven and one of Britain's naval heroes of the time, managed (according to some accounts) to get away in a ship's boat, together with his treasure chest and pet greyhound, and was wrecked a second time that night, possibly – by a quirky coincidence – on the other rock in Scilly called Gilstone, which lies at the entrance to Porth Hellick, where his body was eventually buried after drowning at sea. The gruesome story of his murder by an island woman, who stole the emerald ring from his finger, is largely discounted today; but the ring was missing when his body was found, although the impression on his finger where two rings had been was clearly to be seen.

A shallow grave was made for Shovell's body on the sandy foreshore where today a rough-hewn granite monument stands to mark the spot, although it was not until 1990 that a notice explaining the reason for the monument was attached to it by the enterprise of one of Shovell's descendants. Eventually, Shovell was given a state funeral by Queen Anne. Today a memorial to Sir Cloudesley can be seen in Westminster Abbey over his tomb, but it is regarded as somewhat less than beautiful.

Of the other ships in the fleet, the 70-gun *Eagle* went down amongst the Crim Rocks between Zantman's Rock and Tearing Ledge with the loss of 500 men, the 48-gun *Romney* went down on the Crebinicks with the loss of all but one of her 365 crew, but from the fireship *Firebrand*, twenty of her crew of forty-five survived. Exact numbers are, however, open to question, as the eighteenth century press gang system of involuntary recruitment to the navy created many unwilling sailors, some of whom, having escaped a disaster with their lives, took the opportunity to desert but were included in the figures of those presumed drowned. The *Association's* normal complement is thought to have been 739, but she and other ships may also have been carrying sick and wounded from the war

Shovell's Monument

On the margin of Porth Hellick beach is this granite monument to the naval hero Sir Cloudesley Shovell, whose body was washed ashore here after the wreck of his flagship *HMS Association* on the night of 22 October, 1707. In 1990 descendants of the admiral added a plaque to the foot of the monument so that it should no longer remain unexplained. In the background is Dick's Carn better known to visitors as the Loaded Camel.

in the Mediterranean, and these were presumably also drowned and are not included in the figures.

The *Association* did not break up immediately, and salvage of her valuables was continued for many years with many islanders benefiting. However, all trace of the ship eventually vanished, and it was not until 1967 that divers rediscovered her wreck site in about ninety feet of water off the Gilstone. Quantities of seventeenth-century gold and silver coins, including Spanish pieces-of-eight, were found among rocks on the seabed. Eventually a silver plate bearing Shovell's crest was brought to the surface and this positively identified the wreck site.

All manner of goods were then salvaged. One was the admiral's pewter chamber pot which sold at Sotheby's for £270. However, when it was being cleaned, two gold coins were discovered embedded under its rim, and each of these turned out to be worth more than £300. At the same auction the silver plate bearing Sir Cloudesley's crest upon it fetched £2,100.

Diving to bring up remaining items of value from Shovell's other stricken ships has taken place since then, but, in those waters, can be hazardous. Wreck sites in Scilly are hard to locate because all but a few traces of the ships have disappeared beneath shifting sands, and the hulls of vessels are often pulled apart by the tremendous power of the surging sea and then covered by sand.

Another famous wreck was that of *HMS Colossus* on 10 December 1798, on Southward Well, a shallow reef south of Samson. She was a 3rd rate ship-of-the-line of 74-guns, and was the supply ship to Nelson's fleet at his victory at the Battle of the Nile. She was in poor seagoing condition. On her way home with sick and wounded, she put into Scilly, but in the storm her anchors dragged and she drifted on to rocks and broke up – with only one casualty. Some of her guns were taken off and it is believed that one at least is among the barrels which today serve as bollards on St Mary's quay. But what makes her wreck most notable is that among her cargo was part of the priceless collection of Etruscan vases belonging to Sir William Hamilton, British ambassador at the Court of Naples and the cuckolded husband of Emma Hamilton, Horatio Nelson's paramour. Eleven cases of vases were lost on the seabed until, in 1975, divers found many of their contents hidden in dense weed. The salvaged artefacts were sent to the British Museum where they were put on public exhibition.

One wreck which actually saved Scilly was in 1800 when two French ships full of soldiers were sent to attempt the capture of St Mary's, but one was wrecked with all on board off St Agnes and the other gave up the attempt.

The most famous nineteenth century wreck in Scilly was that of the 3,421 ton German transatlantic liner *Schiller*, which left New York bound for Hamburg (via Plymouth) on 27th April 1875 with a general cargo plus 250 bags of mail and a quantity of gold pieces. Her crew numbered just over a hundred (she was one of the largest steamers afloat at that time), and there were 59 saloon class passengers, 75 second class ones and 20 steerage class – but none were from the UK.

On the 7th May, thick fog was encountered and the ship reduced speed to four knots. Lookouts were posted all round the ship's deck – including volunteers from the passengers, the first of whom to

THE WESTERN APPROACHES

The position of Scilly in the Western Approaches; the first land fall many sailing ships saw after weeks at sea.

spot the Bishop Rock light or hear its fog bell was promised a bottle of champagne from the Captain. Then, without any warning at about ten o'clock in the evening, the ship struck the Retarrier Ledges and came to a stop. At first all seemed well as the engines reversed and pulled the ship clear, but then the heavy sea caught the vessel broadside and sent her grinding on to the rocks again. Signal guns were fired to summon assistance (one of these guns is preserved among the ships' figureheads in the Valhalla on Tresco), but one report, though heard clearly enough on shore, was misunderstood and presumed to be only the normal arrival signal of a ship approaching the islands. Scenes of panic then took place on the decks of the *Schiller* among the passengers as they began to realise what peril they were in, and Captain Thomas felt obliged to fire a revolver over their heads to try to keep order. Only two lifeboats were launched successfully, and these, carrying 26 men and one woman, reached Tresco, Of the other six lifeboats, two were crushed when the funnel collapsed on to them, two jammed in the launching gear owing to the list of the ship, one was smashed against the ship's side as it was being lowered, and one capsized into the sea. Thus over three hundred people were left on the *Schiller* that foggy night with no means of getting off and no one ashore aware of their plight.

By dawn the tragedy had become clear to those on shore, and many vessels had put out to lend assistance; but by then most of the crew and passengers had died, and the *Schiller* had broken open. The mailbags had floated off with the wind (many to come ashore on Samson and some almost to reach Penzance), and gold coins lay scattered on the seabed. A few men survived by climbing in the rigging and clinging on desperately. The *Schiller* had carried 372 people but only 37 survived the wreck. Of the 335 who were drowned that night, many of their bodies were never found. Over a hundred bodies were buried in the churchyard at Old Town in plain deal coffins painted black and laid in mass graves. There never has been a funeral like it in Scilly, with dozens of carts forming in a procession to Old Town and fresh bodies washed up on many of the beaches with every tide, many of the women passengers still in their fineries as there had been a dance in progress when the ship struck. One passenger was Louise Holzmaister, a 23-year-old newlywed who was sailing on the *Schiller* to Germany to be reunited with her millionaire husband, but whose body was never found. The huge monument in Old Town churchyard, which was erected to her

The listing *Earl of Lonsdale* and Troy Town Maze   photo Gibson, Scilly

Navigation at sea in foggy weather, without the navigational equipment available today, can play tricks on the mind. On the 8th June, 1885, the captain of the 1,543 ton steamer the *Earl of Lonsdale*, bearing cotton seed from the Mediterranean, was so sure of the open sea before him that, believing himself ten miles south of Scilly, ran into Periglis, St Agnes, at full speed. The ship was holed in many places and salvage was out of the question. By August the ship had broken in two and was a total loss. The photograph shows the ship listing to starboard and low in the water. In the foreground is Troy Town Maze, said to have been constructed originally by a St Agnes lighthouse keeper called Amor Clarke in 1729, but which may be much older; it has been carefully preserved by St Agnes folk ever since. Strictly speaking, it is a labyrinth, because a set route within it has to be followed, rather than a maze in which there is a confusing choice of turnings.

memory by her grieving young husband, is a poignant reminder of the sad events of that foggy night.

But disasters are things difficult and perhaps odious of comparison. Just before the Second World War the large aircraft carrier *Courageous* put into Scilly, and some of her crew went to a dance held at the Town Hall. Soon after the war started, the ship was sunk by U29 with many more lives lost than in the *Schiller*; yet, because it was wartime and the dead were servicemen rather than civilians, the tragedy is not remembered in quite the same way. It is now thought to have been a tactical error, foolishly advocated by Winston Churchill, for *Courageous* to have been on anti-submarine patrol at the time.

An episode involving the sinking of three ships on one day in Scilly's waters took place in the First World War. At about 7.30 am. on the 12 March, 1915, the same German U-boat U29 intercepted and set on fire off Scilly the merchant ship SS *Indian City*, and, before sinking her, permitted the crew to take to the ship's lifeboats and towed them all towards Scilly so that none of the seamen should come to any harm. Elements of courtesy and civilised behaviour of this sort still survived in the First World War at least until 1915; states might be at war and ships might be sunk, but that strong common bond between mariners of all nationalities that unites them to aid each other in distress, still survived.

The tow was ended, however, when two Royal Navy patrol boats based in Scilly put out to engage the enemy and obliged U29 to cast off the lifeboats and use her superior speed on the surface to outdistance them. About twenty rounds of ammunition were fired at U29 by the patrol boats, but all fell short so the pursuit was abandoned. Later that day U29 met another merchant ship the SS *Headlands* from Liverpool, again within sight of St Mary's, and having given the crew time to take to their lifeboats, torpedoed her. A huge explosion mixed with a cloud of black coal dust from the ship's bunkers made a dramatic sight from the shore, the watching schoolchildren of St Mary's actually cheering as if they were attending a firework display. Later, on the same day, U29 fell in with a third merchantman, the SS *Andalusian*, and after giving the crew ten minutes to clear the ship, sank her, and once again towed the crew in their lifeboats – but not towards Scilly – to hand them over later to a French schooner. Thus, in all these sinkings, no human lives were lost.

Humans are not the only ones to suffer in shipwrecks. In 1887 the steamer *Castleford* of 3,044 tons and laden with 450 head of cattle bound for London from Montreal, went ashore in fog on Great Crebawethan in the Western Rocks on 27th May. The eighteen cattlemen on the *Castleford*, who were accompanying the cattle, offered Scillonians £2 for every animal they could help rescue alive

Anchor from *Sophie*

A well-known anchor cemented into the wall at New Grimsby, Tresco, comes from a Norwegian ship, the *Sophie*, which was found drifting north of Tresco with nobody on board except a dog. Yet in the cabin a table was set for a meal which was in preparation – it was a mystery not dissimilar to the *Marie Celeste*, only with a solution. (see p.128)

---

and put safely on to the island of Annet. Unfortunately, although some were landed, the vessel broke in two and disappeared before the operation was completed, and many cattle drowned. Carcasses of steers from her holds drifted ashore for months afterwards.

Three wreck incidents illustrate how numerous have been the wrecks in Scilly. The first concerns the 2,869 ton steamer *Plympton* carrying Indian corn, which in thick fog and with foghorn blowing, ran hard on the Lethegus Rocks off St Agnes on 14 August 1909. The St Agnes lifeboat took off all the crew, and the Scillonians set about salvaging what they could – ropes, blocks, compasses, etc; but suddenly, on the flowing tide, the ship, which had seemed hard and fast on the rocks, keeled over and sank without warning, throwing Scillonian wreckers into the sea. Two men were drowned, one being trapped in the captain's cabin. Then, on the 2nd of December 1920, the 7,060 ton German steamer *Hathor* hit the same rocks and sank right on top of the *Plympton*, the remains of the two rusting ships remaining entwined together on the seabed to this day.

The second incident is that ships of the same name have been wrecked in Scilly. In 1874, the *Minnehaha*, a large four-masted sailing ship struck the Big Jolly Rock on Peninnis and was a total loss, half the crew of eighteen saving themselves by climbing up the bowsprit and jumping onto the rocks. Then, only 36 years later, the 13,443 ton transatlantic liner *Minnehaha*, carrying 66 passengers, 230 cattle and a mixed cargo ran on to Scilly Rock off Bryher. The passengers were all taken ashore in Scillonian gigs – there was salvage money paid for this service – but to lighten the ship in the hope of pulling her off the rocks, much of the cargo was unceremoniously tipped overboard into the sea so presenting the islanders of Bryher with much to retrieve. It was a remarkably varied cargo because fire in New York docks before the liner had sailed had resulted in much of the cargo from other ships being transferred to the *Minnehaha*. Most of the cattle reached the shore (about 200 of the 230 aboard) and were saved – with a little help from men from Bryher with ropes; but among the rest of the cargo floating in the sea were cash registers, Panama hats, pencils, cigarettes, Old Judge tobacco, even cars. Barrels of petroleum were also taken from the sea by Scillonian wreckers – a few of which only came to light in 1989 in an old cellar under Field House in Church Street, St Mary's. There were also some pianos tipped into the sea of which, it is said, a number later found their way to cottage homes, giving some Scillonians an undeserved reputation for musicality. Three weeks later the *Minnehaha* was refloated and sailed away, but in all Bryher's history there never was a wrecking so profitable.

The third incident was on the 25/26 October 1899, when two ships again sank on the same rock. The German ship *Erik Rickmers*, carrying rice, hit Scilly Rock in dense fog, her crew all being rescued by boats from Bryher; then, a few hours later, the French ship *Paramé*, carrying coconuts, struck the same rock, and the same boats put out from Bryher and rescued all her crew also.

Of other shipwrecks in Scilly, the 5,218 ton steel-hulled *Thomas W. Lawson* was the largest purely-sailing vessel ever built and had seven masts. In December 1907 – on Friday the 13th – she was sailing from Philadelphia for London when she was driven onto the Outer Ranneys to the west of Annet. She was carrying over two million gallons of crude oil which spilled out all around the shores of St Agnes. Only two of her crew were saved (out of 18) and she took

The steamer *Plympton* wrecked on Lethegus Rocks

down with her a St Agnes pilot who had gone on board to help. She turned turtle and broke in two, and what little remains of her two sections now lie on the seabed a quarter of a mile apart. The gig *Slippen* saved the two sailors (the captain and the engineer) from a rock called Hellweathers, and each member of the *Slippen*'s crew subsequently received a gold medal from the US Government.

In the enormous storms of November 1863 it was said that over five hundred sailing ships tried to take shelter in St Mary's Roadstead, and six of these did not survive. One was the *Friar Tuck*, which parted her cables and went on to Newford Island. She was carrying a cargo of tea from Foochow in China and, despite the efforts of preventive men, the islanders managed to acquire so much of it that little tea was needed to be purchased in Scilly for quite a while afterwards. Her monkish figurehead adorns the Valhalla in Tresco, and the Chinese geese which she was carrying went to Tresco.

Sometimes wrecks occurred without anyone in Scilly knowing that they had happened, save later when tell-tale flotsam and jetsam drifted ashore. One such wreck took place in 1875: a St Agnes girl

127

was filling a pail of water from the well at Troy Town, when she was amazed to see a half-dead man crawl out of the sea. It transpired (when he had recovered) that he was Italian and the sole survivor of a three-masted ship called the *Catherine Griffiths* which, on her maiden voyage carrying coal from Rio de Janeiro, had sunk without trace after striking Gorregan, one of the outer Western Rocks.

Another vessel, the 554 ton Norwegian barque *Sophie*, was found dismasted and wallowing in the sea north of Scilly in 1896. There was no one on board, except a dog which wagged its tail to welcome its rescuers. Down below places were laid at the saloon table, a meal was half-prepared on the stove, the ship's log was up-to-date and the stove was actually still slightly warm. Her hold was full of coal – she had come from Swansea – yet there was no sign of any of her crew. It was a second *Marie Celeste*. The rescuers towed the vessel on to the beach at New Grimsby, where the *Sophie* eventually broke up. Algernon Dorrien Smith taking her coal to warm his glasshouses and her timber for his fencing. All that is left of her today is the large anchor set into the New Grimsby sea wall, and a fiddle board in the Valhalla.

The mystery of the disappearance of her crew was solved later. *Sophie* was an old ship and, when her mast snapped, the crew thought she was breaking up and asked a passing steamer to take them off. They found themselves transported to Gibraltar. The owners laid claim to the vessel and, disappointing to the Scillonian salvagers, won their case because the dog had been left on board. So Dorrien Smith had to pay £250 for his coal and his fencing. Another derelict to sail to Scilly was a Thames barge, the *Lady Daphne*. In 1927 she became swamped in heavy seas, so the Lizard lifeboat took off her crew. But the vessel sailed on crewless and, by chance, accurately found a channel to bring herself safely inside the Isles of Scilly and run on to a beach. On board, a canary in a cage was still singing merrily.

Although her navigation aids consisted of only compass and log line, the *Scillonian* (429 tons) ran aground in Scilly just twice in her long career. On each occasion she was floated off on the next tide with little damage. The first time was in 1942 during the Second World War, when she ran aground in fog on Newford Island.

The second occasion was on the 10 September 1951 when on her normal voyage from Penzance. As it was foggy, Vic Trenwith had followed his usual practice of blowing his bugle on Peninnis when

Steer from the *Castleford* safe on Annet   photo Gibson, Scilly

he judged the *Scillonian* to be approaching – so that she would know
her position. Unfortunately, the *Scillonian* passed too far south for
the bugle to be heard, and continued on her westerly course.
Eventually, Captain Reseigh realised that he must have overshot the
entrance to St Mary's Sound, but, while turning back, the ship ran
onto Wingletang Ledges off the south point of St Agnes. Her 54
passengers had to be transferred to the Isles of Scilly Steamship
Company's launch *Kittern*, which herself then ran aground on Rat
Island as, in the gloom, she tried to find the entrance to the harbour
at Hugh Town. She lost her rudder and had to be towed in by the
lifeboat *Cunard*. The day trippers on board the *Scillonian* that day
must have felt they had had more than their fair share of adventure.
Both vessels were undamaged, and were later floated clear with the
tide with a few scratches but no great harm done.

One unlucky man was the Italian cook on board the *SS Isabo*,
which was wrecked on Scilly Rock in 1926 with the loss of six of its
crew. Nearly thirty years later, the same Italian cook was wrecked
again in Scilly with the loss of the *Mando*, which went aground on
Golden Ball Brow in 1955. He was rescued again by the same

129

lifeboat coxswain.

The largest ship to be wrecked in Scillonian waters was the 61,263 ton, Liberian registered tanker, *Torrey Canyon*, sailing from the Persian Gulf bound for Milford Haven with 119,000 tons of crude oil. On the 18th March 1967, she decided to take the shorter route between Scilly and Land's End rather than the more usual passage west of Scilly, where there was more sea room for such a large vessel to manoeuvre. At sixteen knots in broad daylight and good visibility she came to a sudden halt on the Pollard Rock in the Seven Stones reef, rupturing her starboard tanks and spilling vast quantities of oil into the sea. The red-hulled lightship stationed at the Seven Stones was clearly visible but her presence failed to prevent disaster. The oil drifted away from Scilly eastwards, fetching up on the coasts of Cornwall where thousands of sea birds died. Royal Navy Buccaneer aircraft bombed the ship and RAF Hunter jets eventually set the oil alight, watched from Scilly by the Prime Minister.

The stories of Scilly's wrecks produce some remarkable accounts of persons who have been saved in spite of the elements, but none so remarkable as that of the four men of the brig *Nerina*, of which the following is an account:

'The brig *Nerina*, of Dunkerque, sailed from that place on Saturday, the 31st October, 1840, under the command of Captain Pierre Everaert, with a cargo of oil and canvas for Marseilles: her burthen was about 114 tons; the crew consisted of seven persons, including the captain and his nephew, a boy 14 years old. At three o'clock in the afternoon of Monday, the 16th of November, they were forced to heave-to in a gale of wind at about 10 or 12 leagues south-west of the Scilly Islands. At seven o'clock of the same evening, still lying-to under their close-reefed main-top-sail and balanced reefed main-sail, a heavy sea struck the vessel and she suddenly capsized, *turning completely bottom up*.

The mate succeeded in wrenching open the trap-hatch in the cabin deck, and then he scrambled up into the vacant space and took the boy from the hands of the captain, whom he assisted to follow them. In about half an hour they were joined by Vincent and Vantaure from the forecastle. There were then five individuals closely cooped together; as they sat they were obliged

130

Graves for *SS Schiller* Victims at Old Town   photo Gibson, Scilly

Workmen are here seen preparing the graves in Old Town churchyard in 1875 for some of the 311 passengers and crew who drowned when the German transatlantic liner *SS Schiller* was wrecked in fog on the Western Rocks.

to bend their bodies for want of height above them, while the water reached as high as their waists; from which irksome position one at a time obtained some relief by stretching at full length on the barrels in the hold, squeezing himself up close to the keelson. They were able to distinguish between day and night by the light striking from above into the sea and being reflected up through the cabin skylight, and then into the lazarette through the trap-hatch in the cabin floor.

The day and night of Tuesday, the 17th, and the day of Wednesday, the 18th, passed without food, without relief, and almost without hope; but still each encouraged the others, when neither could hold out hope to himself, endeavouring to assuage the pangs of hunger by chewing the bark stripped off from the hoops of the casks. Want of fresh air threatening them with death by suffocation, the mate worked almost incessantly for two days and one night in endeavouring, with his knife, to cut a hole through the hull. Happily, the knife broke before he had succeeded in accomplishing his object, the result of which must have proved fatal, as the confined air alone preserved the vessel in a sufficiently buoyant state.

In the dead of night of Wednesday, the 18th, the vessel suddenly struck heavily. Another hour or two of long suffering succeeded, when they were rejoiced to see by the dawning of the day of Thursday, the 19th, that the vessel was fast on rocks, one of which projected up through the skylight. The captain then went down into the cabin and found that the quarter of the ship was stoved and, looking through the opening, he called out to his companions above, 'Grâce à Dieu, mes enfants, nous sommes sauves! Je vois un homme à terre.' Immediately after this the man approached and put in his hand, which the captain seized, almost as much to the terror of the poor man as to the intense delight of the captain. Several people of the neighbourhood were soon assembled; the side of the ship was cut open and the poor fellows were liberated from a floating sepulchre after an entombment of three days and three nights in the mighty deep.'

* * * * *

To reduce the dangers of the rocks of Scilly to shipping, the Master Wardens of the Guild or Brotherhood of the most Glorious and Undividable Trinity and of St Clement, in the Parish Church of Deptford Strand, in the County of Kent, were granted by Letters Patent of King Charles II, dated 24th May, 1680 (32 Charles II), power and licence to erect and maintain one or more lighthouses upon any of the islands and to receive such allowance for maintenance of the same 'as should be thought fit and reasonable according to law'. Many trading companies, including the East India Company, had been calling for a light in Scilly, and as Heath, writing in 1750, pointed out: 'More wrecks of ships are sent in here (St Agnes) by the sea than to any other of the Scilly Islands ...' adding – in recognition that if wrecks were one man's disaster they could also often be another man's blessing – '... which make the inhabitants of it some amends for their forlorness of abode'.

So it was the highest point of this island of St Agnes – the most exposed island – that was chosen as the site of the Scilly light in 1680. It was the second to be built in Cornwall (after the Lizard,

The Valhalla

The Valhalla in Tresco Gardens is a building erected in the 1860s by Augustus Smith to house his collection of figureheads and other relics from ships. Most of the items were restored in the 1960s and date from nineteenth century shipwrecks which occurred in and around Scilly. The collection is now owned and looked after by the National Maritime Museum.

This gun, salvaged from the seabed, stands at the entrance to the Valhalla. It is a French 18-pounder, manufactured about 1665. It was being carried by *HMS Association* as a prize of war – probably taken at the Siege of Toulon – and went down with the *Association* when Admiral Shovell's flagship was wrecked in 1707.

1619) and one of the oldest in Britain. (The Romans had a lighthouse at Dover – its tower still stands in Dover Castle's grounds – and one on a square tower at Tynemouth. In modern times a lighthouse was built at Dungeness in 1615, but the Eddystone light not until 1698.)

The lighthouse on St Agnes was built 74 ft to the vane above the ground and 138 ft above mean high water. It was painted white to serve as a day mark, a function which it still serves. Borlase, writing in 1756, described it as 'the greatest ornament on this Island', which seems rather to damn it with faint praise for little else could reasonably be described as ornamental on St Agnes in his time.

The lighthouse was constructed under the direction of Captain Hugh Till and Captain Symon Bayly, the first light being from a coal fire lit in an iron brazier inside the lantern, which often burned brightly, but could fade to scarcely more than a glimmer if imperfectly attended. So much depended on the diligence of the keeper. As Heath remarked: 'I've known it scarcely perceivable in the night at the island of St Mary's...' and he suspected that, before his time, the fire may have been allowed to go out or not to have been lit at all on occasion. When in distress, St Agnes folk were said to turn to St Warna, who was thought to be of help in sending them wrecks to relieve their suffering; but it may be that a carelessly-fuelled brazier answered such prayers with more efficacy than simple invocation.

Coal for the light was brought to St Agnes once a year, though in 1764 the collier was wrecked on suitably-named Burnt Island. A limitation of a coal-fired light was that it was difficult to distinguish it from other lights. So, in 1790, the coal-burning cresset was replaced (it is now preserved in Tresco Abbey Gardens) by copper oil lamps with twenty-one revolving reflections. It is impossible to say how many ships were saved from shipwreck over its 230 year operation but, in 1757, a ship carrying Benjamin Franklin was heading for possible disaster on Scilly and was able to alter course in time on seeing 'the Scilly light' – and Franklin did much to encourage lighthouse construction in the USA when he returned there.

One problem was the collection of dues from passing ships, for such exactions were strongly opposed, and stringent measures had to be taken with many ships in order to enforce payment. The net revenue derived by Trinity House from the St Agnes light was £1,765 17s 1d in 1805, rising to £3,191 9s 11d in 1815.

St Agnes is the oldest light in Scilly but the most famous is the Bishop on one of the outermost rocks in the archipelago. Like the Wolf Rock, this rock is small and covered by the sea at high spring tide before the lighthouse was built upon it. The lighthouse was designed by James Walker and built by the Douglass family of engineers (several generations of the Douglass family contributed to lighthouse construction in Scilly). The first structure they built was of wrought and cast iron, open at the base to permit the sea to pass through. But this proved a mistake because, on 5 February, 1850, a

The Chieftain figurehead

This outstanding figurehead is from *The Chieftain*, a sailing vessel thought to have been built and, later, wrecked in Scilly.

135

storm swept away the entire structure. Fortunately, this was prior to completion so no keepers were living in it. The second structure put up was of granite, and the workmen securing the lowest stone blocks by means of iron pegs into the rocks often had to put up with being swept off the rock by waves. A waiting boat always rescued them, and, indeed, in all the building of the lighthouse – hazardous though much of it was – no person died nor was anyone seriously injured.

The granite came from Lamorna and other Cornish quarries, and the stones were fashioned on Rat Island. They were taken to Rosevear where the workmen lived in huts, the ruins of one of which being still clearly apparent. In rough weather the workmen were sometimes cut off from St Mary's, even on occasion being reduced to eating limpets. It was not a comfortable life, though they did grow vegetables on Rosevear, and surprisingly, they actually held some sort of a dance on the island before the end, inviting all in Scilly to it.

The Bishop Rock lighthouse (116 ft above high water) was first lit on 1st September, 1858, and was described by Prince Albert as 'a triumph of engineering skill and perseverance'. It was certainly that, but it did not prevent all wrecks, and one vessel, the 2,867 ton four-masted *Falkland* bound for Falmouth, was actually wrecked on the lighthouse itself. On 22 June 1901 a south west gale had broken her stays and sent the *Falkland* broadside on to the rock; her mainyard hit the tower of the lighthouse, and the ship overturned – drowning the Captain and five others.

The tower is entirely solid to forty-five feet above the rock and is thus built on an opposite policy to the original wrought-iron structure. Even above 45 ft the circular walls are nearly five foot thick, tapering to about two feet near the top. The report of inspectors visiting the lighthouse in 1859 described it as 'magnificent, and perhaps the most exposed in the world'. There is considerable depth of sea immediately around the Bishop, and in storms much damage is likely inside the lighthouse, the vibration causing shelves to empty of crockery. Waves can reach right up the lighthouse. In fact, after one storm in this century, a fisherman's net was actually found dangling from an outside aerial seventy feet up, and one storm wrenched the fog bell near the top of the tower away from its mounts.

This explains why, in 1882, a cylindrical base was built around

The *Schiller*'s signal gun

One of two signal guns from the liner *Schiller*, which were fired to summon assistance when the ship ran on the rocks, but whose reports were misunderstood, so leading to disaster.

the bottom of the lighthouse, an outer casing constructed, and the height raised a further 36 ft to its present 175 ft – the tallest lighthouse in the British Isles. It has successfully withstood everything the sea has thrown against it since – although a storm in 1925 did succeed in damaging its glass and extinguishing the light – a graceful and stately tower of delicate proportions yet, by reason of its weight, conveying the strength required to combat the roughest seas, Its light is a group of two white flashes every fifteen seconds which, in clear weather conditions, can be seen at a distance of 42 miles. When visibility is poor, an electric fog signal gives two blasts every ninety seconds. Once the Bishop Rock lighthouse was built, the St Agnes light was no longer of such importance, though it continued until it was finally extinguished when the automatic Peninnis light was installed in 1911.

Even after the construction of St Agnes light and the Bishop Rock lighthouse, Scilly's northern shores remained unlit. So, along with the extensions to the Bishop in 1887, the Douglass family of engineers built a 63 ft white-painted tower on the 180 ft top of three-acre Round Island. Formerly, large colonies of puffins had nested on Round Island, but the workmen found their eggs were edible and human presence stopped the birds returning. For many years Round Island light had an attractive ruby colour, but it is now a simple white light. With most lighthouses becoming automatic, servicing is by helicopter with occasional help from the Trinity House flagship *Patricia* and the reserve ship *Stella*, whose main work is looking after buoys, lifting any that need repair and taking them to Blackwall on the Thames. There is a saying in Scilly that when one of the Trinity House vessels comes into the Roadstead, bad weather will follow. There are rational grounds for believing this because, in rough seas, servicing buoys is impossible, so that ships do seek shelter within the islands while awaiting calmer conditions. In this connection, the Trinity House National Lighthouse Centre opened at Penzance in 1990 and is well worth visiting.

All the lighthouses on land serve also as daymarks, but, Thomas Ekins, the first steward of the Godolphins, erected a daymark without a light to aid ships approaching Scilly from the east. This is a twenty-foot-high, hollow tower with an internal staircase, on St Martin's Head. It was described by Abraham Tovey, approvingly, as 'a steeple built for a landmark' and by Jessie Mothersole, disapprovingly, as 'quite the most hideous object to be seen in Scilly'. It was completed in 1683 as Borlase recorded, and not in 1637 as inscribed on it or 1687 as Troutbeck and Woodley state. It was originally white-painted, but could thus be confused with St Agnes lighthouse; so, after a ship was wrecked nearby in 1830, its colour was changed, and in 1891 given its present rather dramatic alternate red and white bands. Nearby can be traced foundations of huts used by soldiers when the daymark was also a signal station during the French wars (1793–1815).

Seven nautical miles, roughly north-east of St Martin's Head, is a large submerged reef known as the Seven Stones, once supposed to have been part of the fabled land of Lyonesse. In 1841 a lightship was anchored there, but she and her successors have on several occasions broken moorings, and, having no engines, have drifted away. The row of cottages on Tresco under the Old Blockhouse at New Grimsby were built originally for the lightship crew and their families. They are notable as all their windows are facing inland away from the sea, whereas today the fashion is for sea views with picture windows – probably the first of which in Scilly was

Bishop Rock lighthouse – the helicopter pad was added in 1976 and somewhat spoils the clean lines. For the position of many of the wrecks mentioned in this chapter, please see the folding-map at the end of *The Isles of Scilly Standard Guidebook*

constructed in Garrison House in 1960.

As many as eight light beams can be distinguished on a clear night in Scilly from Telegraph tower, but radar and navigation services are now more effective than such a multiplicity of warnings in ensuring safe passage for ships passing Scilly.

Although there was a lifeboat in Scilly as early as 1837, the first one of note was the *Henry Dundas* stationed on St Mary's from 1874. There was also a lifeboat on St Agnes, and in 1903 the slipway there was lengthened to be the longest in the UK. But in 1919 the first motor lifeboat, the *Elsie*, was stationed at St Mary's, and this led to the closure of the St Agnes station in 1920. The *Elsie* was succeeded by the *Cunard* in 1932 and the *Cunard* by the *Guy and Clare Hunter* in 1955, the last lifeboat which could be launched down the slipway. Then, in 1981 an Arun class boat, the *Robert Edgar*, took over, with a speed of eighteen knots she made the *Guy and Clare Hunter*'s eight knots seem very slow, but she was too big to go in the lifeboat house. Over 650 lives have been saved by the crews of Scilly's lifeboats – all volunteers, they have always held themselves in readiness in all weathers to put out to answer a signal from a ship in distress. The traditional firing of two rockets to summon the crew to the station is still made, although effectively most of the crew are today called up by telephone. By 2004, the lifeboat on Station was *The Whiteheads*, 7 knots faster than *Robert Edgar*.

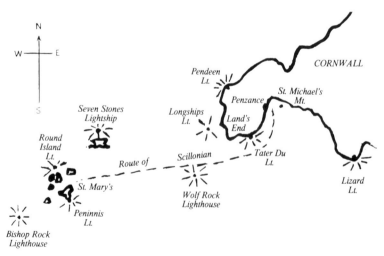

Map of the location of the lighthouses around Scilly

CHAPTER X –
SCILLONIAN LIFE and CUSTOMS

In Scilly, as elsewhere, the growth in this century of the scientific attitude, and the success of modern education in fostering it, have been steadily destroying the vast system of folklore and superstition by which people used to live. But, in Scilly, as in most sea-faring communities, the remnants of omens and charms still linger tenaciously, if sometimes ludicrously, particularly those connected with the sea and ships. It is said, for instance, to be difficult to persuade a Scillonian to change the name of his boat, however inappropriate the name may be, because doing so might bring bad luck to the boat and to those who sailed in her. In the days of wind power there used to be a whole series of taboos connected with boats, but the greater safety afforded by the internal combustion engine has played its part in ending them. For example, it was advisable, when at sea, never to mention any land animal, especially a rabbit; nor to count fish as they were being hauled aboard; nor to whistle unless it was calm – 'there is wind enough!' A gale was thought to be inevitable if a parson was aboard, and if the dinghy had to be turned, this had always to be done in a clockwise direction.

Among the customs that survive is that of crowning the May Queen on May Day, followed by song and dance around the maypole erected in the Park in the centre of Hugh Town. The Queen, attended by her maids, used to parade colourfully through the town. In olden times, the blowing of May whistles (cut from alder or sycamore branches) and cow-horns added to the fun. May Day was a general holiday and fishing boats from Newlyn would come over and the fishermen join in the singing and merriment. In the morning children walked to selected farms where they were given a round of bread, thick cream, and black treacle. (A round of bread, in Scilly, is equivalent to a slice of bread, whereas a slice is equal to half-a-slice on the mainland.) Today's festivals include an August carnival when the Carnival Queen leads a procession of decorated vehicles and comic set pieces. There is also, in some years, a regatta

Dancing round the Maypole in the park, Hugh Town, in the 19th Century

including water sports, with traditional diversions such as 'walking the greasy pole'. Jessie Mothersole, writing in 1910, says how charming and friendly the Scillonian children always are: 'They used to crowd round sometimes when I was painting, but they never got in the way. Occasionally, they would plant themselves in the middle distance under the impression that my eye was like a photographic lens, and that so long as they came within the field of vision they must infallibly appear in the picture!' She quotes Heath's statement that in Scilly 'there are no robbers, housebreakers or highwaymen', and adds 'for there is no real poverty, and no one who has not got a character to lose.'

In previous centuries, harvest festivals, termed 'Nicla Thies', occurred after the last of the grain had been gathered, and they were accompanied by much feasting. On the near approach of Christmas, the Goose-dancers (a survival of Morris-dancers), Merry Maskers, or Guise-dancers made their appearance. Maidens dressed up as men, sometimes in ship captains' uniforms, and men in women's costumes would parade through the town. Some of the men and women would dress in parti-coloured costumes, 'half of one colour to the right and left, or above and below', says Heath. The

The post-office, Hugh Town

An unusual building in Hugh Street showing what could be done with granite in 1897, the confident year of Queen Victoria's golden jubilee. Algernon Dorrien Smith seems to have been fond of chunky granite blocks, for the style is found also in the Town Hall (1889) and in extensions he had made to Tresco Abbey. Possibly the most gracious family house in Hugh Town is Lemon Hall (stuccoed regency, circa 1820) – its name the result of a Mr Lemon marrying a Miss Hall.

children would blacken their faces or don hideous masks. On Shrove Tuesday the boys had a right to throw stones in the evening against the doors of dwelling houses. They could be bought off with pancakes or money. This night was called 'Gravel-night' and the stones, which were collected from the beaches, were about the size of small marbles. The custom of going limpeting on Good Friday, according to Jessie Mothersole, still continued in 1904. In addition to limpets, the islanders collected winkles and a kind of rockling called 'whistlers'. They are said to be very tasty and are found under beach stones. On Good Friday, young and old made a point of releasing paper boats on the water. The origin of this custom is unknown, but it may have been a votive offering to the gods of the sea. In addition to paper boats, there were regular model-boat racing competitions. None of this survives today.

143

Gathering seaweed from the shore on a Scilly ass for kelping or for fertilising
the bulb fields.   photo Gibson, Scilly

An annual fair was held in the Park in Hugh Town on Whit-
Monday. Midsummer Night was 'Tar Barrel Night' when blazing
torches were carried and bonfires set going. Tar barrels, stove in at
the tops and alight, were carried in procession on men's heads. The
flames would leap up eight or more feet and molten tar fall on the
bearers who had to choose their moments for dropping their loads.
On the 5th November the boys of St Mary's had a holiday called
'Ringing Tide', part of which day they spent in ringing the church
bells. Trips to Penzance were rare, but Whit-Monday was the great
excursion day and, in 1914, cost 3s 6d return. An annual daylong
picnic of school children to Samson is still maintained. Islanders on
St Mary's are still great picnickers, and Pelistry Bay, St Mary's, is well
patronised by them on fine Sundays in the summer.

Of legends, that of the so-called 'Saint' Warna is the most
persistent. St Warna was supposed to have been an Irish saint who
landed in a coracle in St Warna's Cove, St Agnes, and possessed the
power of attracting ships to their doom. The people of St Agnes were
said to propitiate the 'Saint', and invoke her aid during poor
wrecking seasons by dropping pins into her 'well' on the day after

Tresco Abbey Gardens

It is worth a trip to Scilly if only to see the sub-tropical gardens on Tresco. Begun by Augustus Smith after 1835, they have been assiduously maintained and extended by the Dorrien Smith family ever since. Apart from the great variety of exotic plants, what makes the gardens almost unique is the number of plants from different climes and different regions growing in close proximity. The climate in the gardens is just warm enough for one, just wet enough for another, just dry enough for a third and just cold enough for a fourth. It is said that the gardens deserve to be visited every month, for their appearance changes as the varieties of plants mature and flower at different times.

Twelfth Day. Others claim that St Warna is a corruption of *Santa Juana*, a Spanish ship said to have been wrecked there.

Of fancies, it is said that a cat lying in front of the fire with its tail turned to the north is an indication of a gale of wind. The granite in Hugh Town is claimed to possess the property of glistening early in the morning in advance of fine weather, whereas, when it is dull, a storm may be expected.

Dancing is often mentioned in the records, but only one dance, the Phoebe (Phoebe was the Moon Goddess), seems to have any local flavour, which it shares with West Cornwall:

145

Cannot you dance the Phoebe,
Don't you see how my shoulders shake,
Don't you see what pains I take,
Cannot you dance the Phoebe?

Of superstition, we are informed by Whitfeld (1852) that Tresco 'swarmed' with witches, and Heath (1750) says that it cannot be expected that these islands should be quite free of delusions. Fairies are said to have frequented Buzza Hill on St Mary's, but haunted houses, giants and apparitions, so feared in Scilly (as by children all over Britain before the 20th century), are now 'all charmed, cast in a spell or conjur'd out of the islands'.

Of medical practice in his time, Heath says:

> 'For Want of *Male* Practitioners in Physic, the few *Diseases*, and Hurts, in these healthful Islands have, for these many Years last past, been remedied by a Society of *skilful Aunts*, constituting a Sort of College of *physicians* in *Scilly*, of which *Aunt Sarah* is the Head or *President* ... When they assemble upon a woeful, desperate, or doubtful case, they resign the Patient to *God* and *Nature*, while the attending *Doctress*, provides a warm Room, a Nurse, and fit Necessaries, which co-operate with uncommon Success. Common Diseases here, not proceeding from *Luxury* or *Laziness* and *Intemperance*, are cured by one of the subordinate Practitioners with a few *Simples*, without calling in the Assistance and Judgement of a second or third *Graduate*.
>
> 'They have some disguised *Nostrums* and *Specifiks*, the true Secrets of which Compositions are deposited with their President.
>
> 'As to the President, Mrs Sarah Jenkins, (commonly called *Aunt Sarah*) being a Person of singular Skill and Circumstance, she does many Acts of Charity and Benevolence to the Poor-Distressed; to which the rest of the younger *Sisterhood*, who are not a little amiable, contribute their Parts. The President is remarkable for her venerable *long Beard*, which some imagine operates miraculously to the Benefit of those who stroke it.'

Heath was the first chronicler to pay any special attention to the Scillonian people as such, excusing himself, somewhat patronisingly, by saying: 'I consider that the little Oddities in the

King Edward VII

photo Gibson, Scilly

King Edward VII visited Scilly three times, the last being in 1902. In this photograph his pony and trap (the same trap that had carried Queen Victoria in 1847) is seen descending the hill from Star Castle. The King is showing remarkable prescience in acknowledging the cameraman recording for posterity's unseen millions, rather than the cap-waving duo to his left.

Customs and Manners of the lower Class of People are not without both Amusement and Instruction ... Truth appears in its native Simplicity, unadorned with meretricious Embellishments, and beautiful in its own Nakedness ... Honour, Justice, and every social Virtue is exercised among them in the strictest Punctuality, though there is never a Lawyer, and but one Clergyman, in all the Islands.'

Of the products of the soil, Woodley said that wheat, barley, potatoes and pillas were grown – pillas were wild oats – and, of the cattle, he says that they were black and small, and in the off-islands were fed in a great measure on seaweed. Horses, he adds, were small and generally poor; 'their chief food is the furze which they find on the hills, and which they carefully bruise with the forehoof before manducation; yet I have been assured that both cows and horses, by

147

The Prince of Wales as Duke of Cornwall visited Scilly in 1921 in a destroyer, and again in 1933, only this time by flying-boat from 204 Squadron based at Mount Batten. His aircraft was accompanied by three other Supermarine Southampton's and by a destroyer *HMS Broke* – 'in case he fell out', as one Scillonian wag put it. Looking down upon the islands as his aircraft approached them on a cloudy morning, the Prince is said to have remarked that the islands 'looked like cow pats in the sea'.

The Prince chose to have lunch at Star Castle as he had done before on his 1921 visit when the Castle was the home of the Duchy agent. Upon hearing that the Castle was being converted into a hotel, he decided to go there, and therefore became the first guest.

In this photo the Prince is being greeted on the steps of Star Castle by the owners, Mr & Mrs E.L. Bowley.

---

custom, acquire such a relish for these peculiar and piquant articles of food, that they pine when deprived of them'.

An interesting fishing procedure, which used to be employed at low tides on St Martin's Flats and around Samson, is that of clapping the hands. The cockles, lying under the wet sand, respond to the claps by closing their shells sharply, thus emitting a small jet of water upwards and disclosing their location.

An old manuscript, dated 1695, mentions the following curious custom: 'In all these Islands they take a sort of fish about a foot in length, by angling upon the shore. This they called the 'Whistling Fish' and giving it that name because they whistle whilst they take it, this fish rarely taking the bait unless they doe, for whereas if the anglers whistle and make a vocal noise (which they usually do alternately) they bite very freely.'

The manuscript continues: 'In the Islands of St Martin and St Mary they have a sort of bituminous earth in great plenty. They use it for fire and indeed burnes very well only it emits a sulphurous smell. 'Tis the only fewell they have, there being no coal nor any trees, not soe much as a shrubb, except brambles, furzes, broom and holly; and these never grow above four foot high ...'

Of the customs of the mid-eighteenth century, Heath tells us of the proverb 'Aways a feast or a famine in Scilly', and that they had a very plentiful feast after harvest time called 'Nickla Thise'. Heath summarises the detached and independent nature of the islands in his time in the following paragraph: 'As there is no Islander a Freeholder in *Scilly*, so no Person has a Vote there for choosing Members of Parliament, nor are these Islands represented by any;

The Prince of Wales climbing Star Castle steps in 1933

The upper lounge at Star Castle where the Prince of Wales had luncheon 23 May, 1933.

Lunch was held in this upstairs sitting-room at Star Castle with the Prince, Mrs Dorrien Smith and Mrs Bowley being present. The rest of the party ate outside in the landing area. The Prince sat on the couch on the left of this photograph and finished his lunch with an apple, whose core he inadvertently let slip to the floor. It was not picked up – it being impolite in the thirties for royalty to trespass upon the role of servants.

The Prince showed real charm to everyone except perhaps to the pompous, one of whom attempted an unscheduled speech of welcome as the Prince emerged from the lounge after lunch; but the Prince only listened to this for a moment before continuing his way down the stairs followed by everyone else.

which shew that they are no Part of the County, or County-Jurisdiction of *Cornwall*; but are distinct from both, under a separate Government ... Here is no Prison for the Confinement of Offenders, which shews, that the People live upright enough not to require any, or that the Place is a Confinement of itself.'

Of burials, Heath says: 'When an Islander dies, some Friends sit up the first Night with the dead Body, where it is a Custom with them to feast cheerfully during the Time. The next Day ... Mourners ... express very great Concern for the Loss of their Friend, whom they lament *is no more to be seen*. A Funeral Sermon, when desired on the Occasion, is preached by the *Chaplain*, who is well paid for his

150

Lower lounge at Star Castle, c 1935

When Star Castle became a hotel in 1933, the ground floor was almost an empty area used for games. But in 1934 the back kitchens were fitted with Aga cookers set in the magnificent fireplace where oxen could be roasted whole, and the front area made into a lounge, with seats converted from barrels, and a dining-room behind the far curtains.

Performance, and claims by the Right of his Office a *Scarf*".

Of matrimony, Heath says that fifty years before his time banns were called and the chaplain was paid five shillings, or not above half-a-guinea – or he would take what he could get. 'Soldiers and Persons, at that Time, not in Circumstances to pay for being joined, either joined themselves, or were joined *gratis,* i.e. they were joined by Vows, or taking one another's Word, which was binding as long as they could agree. And this sort of *conscientious Binding* was observed to hold as fast, and be as good a Security of their future Felicity, as if the Parties had been tied together with the sacred shreds of Matrimony.'

Woodley, in 1822, seems to have nurtured a few grievances against the islanders; he complains of the difficulty of obtaining labour, particularly domestic, 'because the women preferred kelping or knitting', and he comments unfavourably on the finery (straw

151

hats and flying ribands) displayed on Sundays, which he thinks 'ludicrous' by contrast with the week-day lack of shoes and stockings. He also speaks of the exorbitant charges 'for any little service', but subsequent writers refute this statement and suggest that the islanders had a special price for the Rev G. Woodley. One observation he makes is revealing: 'There is an affected degree of independence amongst the Islanders, which even the pressure of poverty and affliction is unable to subdue.' This independence he refers to as 'this sort of Spanish feeling'.

The military and ecclesiastical history of the islands up to the eighteenth century gives us very little information regarding the inhabitants, who were ruled by the abbots and military governors and by the stewards of the absentee landlords. From the time of Elizabeth to 1831, when the islands reverted to the Duchy, tenure of the stewards was often short, so there was little encouragement for them to accumulate family fortunes in buildings or farmland in Scilly.

After the dissolution of the monasteries in 1539, the ecclesiastical administration of the islands was somewhat anomalous, and it was not until 1836 that the islands were declared by Act of Parliament to be within the jurisdiction of the Bishop of Exeter. In the year 1660 the church at Old Town, St Mary's, was reconstructed on the site of an older Norman structure, and when this fell into decay, the new church at Hugh Town was built and completed in 1838. It was provided by Augustus Smith with seating in a form rather like that of the chapel of an Oxford college. On Tresco there was a small church whose origin is uncertain, but which existed in 1798. It was enlarged in 1824 and again in 1835, and finally replaced by the present church in 1879. It was built as a monument to Augustus Smith and was dedicated in 1882. Bryher had its church in 1742, and it was enlarged in 1928. The church on St Martin's was enlarged in 1790 and restored early in the nineteenth century. A church on St Agnes was erected sometime in the sixteenth or seventeenth century, but it was destroyed in a gale. In the eighteenth century a second church was constructed by the inhabitants of St Agnes from the proceeds of wreck and salvage. This also was destroyed and the present church was erected early in the nineteenth century, and its roof has since been renewed.

The oldest Anglican church on Scilly is that at Old Town which today is a fragment of a large cruciform building dating back to the

The Prince of Wales leaving Star Castle in 1933 photo Gibson. Scilly

Before he left the Prince signed the Visitors' Book as the hotel's first guest, and the rest of the Royal Party did likewise – but on a separate page. The photograph shows the Prince (in beret) and his companions leaving Star Castle after lunch. He is accompanied by Earl Fortescue, Major McCormick (Duchy secretary), Mr P. Kingsley (assistant secretary), and by Captain Stanier, the Duchy Steward on Scilly – all of whom wore the fashionable plus-fours of the period. The Prince also promoted the wearing of the beret in Britain in the 1930s.

But it was not only matters sartorial which engaged him. The Prince was something of an authority on the growing of rhododendrums and he also took a personal interest in Scilly's flower cultivation and marketing. Following his tour of the UK's distressed areas in 1929, he arranged for some unemployed miners and their families to be settled in Scilly and to be shown how to grow and market flowers. In the same year he promoted improved packaging for Scilly's flowers, after he had visited Covent Garden and noticed how battered and bruised appeared the blooms from Scilly compared with those from France, which were wrapped in tissue and protected by cardboard.

twelfth century, but with the shift of population to Hugh Town, a new church was planned. It was designed and largely paid for by Augustus Smith (who had to do so under the terms of his lease, and to pay the clergy stipends). The parish rector lived in a house on the site of the present Bishop and Wolf public house, but moved to a commodious residence with a large garden next to the church when that became vacant.

There has been an Anglican clergyman on St Mary's since 1662, but in Heath's time (1744) he did not receive institution, induction, or visitation from the Bishop, but held his appointment from the Lord Proprietor. The off-islands had curates only from 1842, previous to which date they were served mainly by laymen. The Society for Promoting Christian Knowledge founded 'The Scilly Mission' in 1765, and continued to supply missionaries to the off-islands until 1842 both for religious instruction and secular education, and established a charity school on each of the main inhabited islands between 1765 and 1774.

A Roman Catholic church was built in Hugh Town, St Mary's, in 1840 and dedicated to St Martin. In 1844 the Baptist Society came to Scilly, and flourished until the late 1940s, when its activities ceased owing to controversy amongst its members. The Bible Christian Society established itself in 1821, and in the following year numbered 144 adherents. Chapels were constructed on St Mary's in 1823, and on St Agnes in 1832. In 1827 Mr William O'Bryan visited Scilly, and the members of the Society afterwards became known as Bryanites. The United Methodist Society, the United Free Church, and the Methodist New Connexion amalgamated in 1907 to form the United Methodist Society; and the final union of Wesleyan Methodist Church, the Primitive Methodist Church, and the United Methodist Church, was formally sealed in 1932.

Woodley, speaking of religion in his time (1822), says that the Scillonians' behaviour at church was decent and exemplary: 'They pay such attention to the external duties of religion that in St Mary's and Tresco, where dissenters have established themselves, many of the people, halting between two opinions, repair to the meeting-house in the morning, to Church in the forenoons and afternoons, and again to the Meeting in the evening.' Sundays were so very crowded with services of one kind and another that the Sunday School had, at one time, to be held on Saturday afternoons.

Rowet's Tower, Peninnis – all that is left of the windmill (later, a signal tower) which once stood near the end of King Edward's Road, Peninnis, but had to be dismantled in the 1960s when it became unsafe. There is a circle of stones, the corn grinding stone in the centre, and the foundation stone with the date of erection 1726 and the initials of the Governor, Francis Godolphin.

John Wesley visited Scilly in 1743 in a boat borrowed from the Mayor of St Ives. In rough seas the voyage took seven hours, his party keeping their peckers up by singing hymns the way over. Wesley landed and preached on St Mary's, but it is not perhaps surprising after such a voyage, that he pronounced Scilly to be 'a dreary, barren place'. Later, in 1788, the Wesleyan Methodist Society was established in Scilly, and, in 1792, the membership reached 150. The original chapel was erected in 1790 and replaced in 1828. There were Wesleyan chapels on three of the islands in the 19th century. The present Methodist Church in Hugh Town was built in 1900.

* * * * *

Of royalty who have visited the islands, the earliest record (apart from the doubtful conquest by Athelstan in AD 927) is the possible one of Olaf Tryggvessön, King of Norway, followed by Svein Ashlifarson, King of Orkney and Caithness in AD 1115. Others

View from Star Castle looking eastwards over Hugh Town

were: Charles I, when Prince of Wales in 1623; his son, Prince Charles (afterwards Charles II); and Queen Victoria, with Prince Albert and the Prince of Wales, in 1847.

This visit of Queen Victoria's on August 13th was unexpected. The Royal Family was en route in the royal yacht *Victoria and Albert* from the Isle of Wight to their Scottish home at Balmoral, when fog in the English Channel persuaded them to put in to Scilly. There were six ships in the royal convoy, but the islands were not seen in the mist until quite close. The royal convoy then anchored in St Mary's Roadstead and was given a royal salute from the Garrison. Mr Augustus Smith welcomed the royal party on the quay, and lines of Scillonians cheered the visitors as they drove through Hugh Town in Augustus Smith's pony carriage and up to Star Castle. The Queen and Prince Albert, together with Lady Jocelyn and Prince Leiningen, who were in attendance, spent time on the ramparts of Star Castle admiring the views. Queen Victoria later wrote in her diary (13.8.1847) 'The extensive view of the islands and rocks is very beautiful'.

On the return drive down the hill from Star Castle, the coachman mistook the way. After passing through Garrison Gateway, instead of turning right into Garrison Lane, he started to descend the very

156

Ramparts of Star Castle – The photograph shows the ramparts of Star Castle in 1935. Close observers will notice two ex-windmill towers in the far distance; on the left is Buzza Tower, originally a Corsican tower, then a windmill and finally converted with seats to commemorate the visit to Scilly of King Edward VII in 1902. On the right, and only just in view, is the tower at the end of the road leading to Peninnis, which was built as a mill by Godolphin in 1726 but became unsafe and was demolished about 1960. The boy in the foreground gives an indication of the age of the photograph because he is wearing his school blazer even when on holiday – not considered 'cool' in 2004 – in this instance that of Mount House School, a preparatory school then in Plymouth and now at Tavistock where, in 1990, the son of at least one of Scilly's residents also attended.

steep hill immediately before him alongside Tregarthen's Hotel. One of the horses stumbled and alarmed the Queen – she was only 28, but it is said that the Queen's nerves had been shaken by a recent attempt on her life – so she insisted upon alighting and completing the journey to the quay on foot.

On the royal yacht that evening, Queen Victoria made the following entry in her diary:

'We started at four and reached the Scilly Islands at three in the afternoon; it had been very rough. The numerous little rocky islands, in the midst of which we are lying, are very curious.

157

'St Mary's, the principal island, has a little town, a church, and a small harbour. Exactly opposite, on the isle of Tresco, is Mr Smith's house; he has the lease of all the islands from the Duchy of Cornwall. Farther to the left is St Agnes, with a lighthouse and innumerable rocks.

'Albert (who, as well as Charles, has been unwell, while I suffered much) went with Charles and Bertie to see one of the islands. The children recovered from their sea-sickness directly. When Albert and the others returned, soon after five, we went with our ladies and gentlemen in the barge across the harbour – when, blue as the sea was, it was still rather rough – and landed at a little pier on St Mary's. The harbour, surmounted by the old fort of the Star Castle, reminded me of the harbour of St Helier.

'We got into a pony carriage belonging to Mr Smith, with Charles and Lady Jocelyn, and drove through the place, which looks like a small fishing town, and then round the fortifications of the castle, where there is a very pretty walk overhanging the sea; the rock being covered with fern and heath and furze.

'The extensive view of the islands and rocks around is very beautiful. The town is built upon a very narrow strip of land, with a small bay on either side. We got out at the old castle, which bears the date of one of the Edwards. The view from the battlements is very fine. We returned the same way we went, a little before seven.'

This was almost an accurate account but seems lacking in a little enthusiasm, particularly from one who in her letters was given to underlining many words for emphasis. On the other hand Victoria was never a good sailor and she may not have recovered entirely from the voyage of the previous day.

During the evening bonfires, torches and fireworks celebrated the great occasion, and the next morning the ships sailed away.

Prince Edward was a young boy in 1847 and is said to have been taken to one of the off-islands while the Queen and Prince Albert landed on St Mary's. Prince Edward, as Prince of Wales, came again in 1865 and his third visit was as King in 1902. The later King George V came when he was a young midshipman.

Between the wars Edward VII's grandson and namesake visited Scilly as Prince of Wales on two occasions – in 1921 and 1933 – before he became King as Edward VIII in 1936, and later, after his

Armorel's Cottage, Samson

In the Victorian novel *Armorel of Lyonesse* by Sir Walter Besant, which did something to popularise Scilly in the nineteenth century, an unsophisticated island girl Armorel Rosevean, saves artist Roland Lee's boat from shipwreck; but before leaving Samson he inspires Armorel to better herself and see the world. Armorel comes into money, leaves Scilly and becomes an elegant lady. Later, she meets Roland Lee again, who is now in reduced circumstances; it is her turn to inspire him, and – naturally – they fall in love, return to Samson and live happily ever after.

This ruined cottage – last inhabited in 1855 when residents of Samson were all evacuated on the instructions of Augustus Smith because they could no longer care properly for themselves – is the one which has been ascribed to Armorel by the novelist.

---

abdication and marriage to Mrs Simpson, Duke of Windsor.

Since the Second World War, many members of the Royal Family have visited Scilly – sometimes officially, more often privately – staying at Prince Charles' two-bedroomed bungalow Tamarisk, next door to Hugh House on the Garrison, which the Prince (as Duke of Cornwall) took over in 1966. There, they have been able to holiday without attracting public scrutiny – the islanders loyally respecting their privacy and not drawing undue attention to their presence in the islands.

CHAPTER XI – TRANSPORT and SERVICES

The extent of Scilly's isolation for much of its history is sometimes overlooked in this era of instant communication. For instance, it was said that Queen Elizabeth I had been on the throne for several months in 1558 before anyone in Scilly was aware of the death of her predecessor 'Bloody Mary'. Even by the eighteenth century, transport to Scilly was irregular and mostly by open boats sailing once a month or so, and Borlase commented in 1752 of 'seventeen weeks without any provisions' to Scilly. The journey was hazardous in many ways; one early sailing packet to Scilly, the *Lord Howe*, was totally wrecked on Kennel Reef near Mousehole on 27 June 1819, the captain and crew having gone below to enjoy a meal, leaving only a young boy at the helm. The first mail coach did not reach down the West Country to Penzance regularly till 1820, so Scilly's isolation was to be expected. Then, in the early years of the 19th century, there began a weekly service to Scilly from Penzance, operated by brothers called Tregarthen, and from 1837 Captain Frank Tregarthen (who owned a hotel on St Mary's which still bears his name) began a service which lasted 36 years – and he also carried the Royal Mail. But the biggest advance came after the railway reached Penzance in 1859. The recently-established Scilly Isles Steam Navigation Company started a service by a steamer called the *Little Western* in 1858 three times a week from Penzance. This ship replaced the cutter *Ariadne* which had made the Penzance run for many years and whose journeys under sail were often long and uncomfortable.

This more frequent, faster and reliable contact with the mainland did something to improve life in Scilly, if only by ensuring the possibility of more regular supplies of fresh food. In 1871 the West Cornwall Railway Company's Scottish built 144 ton paddle-steamer *Earl of Arran* was also running excursions from Penzance but was wrecked on Nornour in 1872. This ship had been built in 1860, originally for work on the River Clyde. The story goes that, on her voyage from Penzance carrying 92 passengers and mail for the islands, her skipper, Captain Deacon, had been persuaded by an

From biplane to no wings at all. The 7-seater De Havilland Dragon Rapide is replaced by the 32-seater Sikorsky S61 helicopter in 1964.   photo Gibson, Scilly

islander called Stephen Woodcock that he could save time on the journey by sailing through English Island Neck. The result was that the *Earl of Arran* struck rocks on Irishman's Ledge and only avoided immediate sinking by beaching. Today only her huge iron boiler can be seen at low water lying on the rocks to the west of Nornour – a cautionary reminder to mariners who would take short cuts in Scilly.

The same year the *Little Western* was also wrecked and this disaster ended the Isles of Scilly Company. The packet service was continued by the West Cornwall Railway Company till 1904 with their small but graceful ship *Lady of the Isles*, which still acted as relief boat in the 1930s when the *Scillonian* went for her winter refit. In 1889 the West Cornwall Railway Company had another vessel, the *Lyonnesse*, but went bankrupt in 1907, and this vessel was bought and operated by a Penzance man, John Banfield, until he sold up in 1917. For the rest of the war years supplies to Scilly were maintained by Government vessels, but it became clear to Scillonians that what they needed once the war was over was their

161

Lowenva: the holiday bungalow of Lady Wilson on St Mary's

An accompaniment of fame is often a diminution of privacy. In the case of Lord and Lady Wilson, their bungalow Lowenva (photographed here) became an object of curiosity to holidaymakers in the 1960s when Lord Wilson was Prime Minister. Many expressed surprise that it was so small, for there was still the idea in that decade that anyone prominent in public life was sure to live in an opulent dwelling, even apparently when on holiday. (Many other famous people holiday regularly in Scilly, but the most infamous to have done so in the last hundred years was probably Dr Crippen. His doing so led to his undoing. After murdering his wife, Crippen, in disguise, attempted to escape to Canada; but a fellow passenger – a sea captain who had also holidayed in Scilly – recognised Crippen and alerted the Captain of the liner *Montrose* on which they were travelling. Upon disembarking in Canada, Crippen was arrested, tried in England, and executed on 23 November, 1910.)

own link with the mainland.

Thus was the Isles of Scilly Steamship Company formed in 1920 (with £20,000 raised mainly in the islands by selling five shilling shares) and it ran its own vessel, the *Peninnis*, which it had been able to purchase for £7,000. In 1926 the Company bought a new ship, the *Scillonian*, which serviced the islands for nearly thirty years – including throughout the Second World War – for much of this time under its famous master, Captain Reseigh.

162

Coronation Shelter, the Strand, Hugh Town, St Mary's

This practical, if distinctly spartan, shelter on the Strand, Hugh Town, has seats on all four sides, providing shelter from winds from all directions, if not a good view.

The notice on its wall proudly reads:

'This shelter was erected in 1954 to commemorate the coronation of Her Majesty Queen Elizabeth II by the Council of the Isles of Scilly ...' a claim which tends to promote grins among the more literate passers-by.

In 1956 this first *Scillonian* was replaced by a larger and faster ship also called *Scillonian,* and she was joined from 1965 by a second vessel, the *Queen of the Isles.* This additional vessel eventually proved a commercial mistake. The early sixties had been boom years for passengers and, despite the *Scillonian's* 600 passenger licensed capacity, there had been occasions when intending passengers had been so numerous that some had had to be left on the quayside at Penzance. But in 1964 British European Airways had replaced their 7-seater De Havilland Dragon Rapide biplanes flying from Land's End Aerodrome with 32-seater Sikorsky S61 helicopters flying from the new heliport at Eastern Green. Penzance, and there were not enough passengers after 1964 to fill all the accommodation in the helicopters and two ships. So, in 1968, the *Queen of the Isles* was given charter work, and in 1970 sold and went to the Pacific as the

The Monk's Cowl, Peninnis

The granite rocks of Scilly, carved naturally over immense periods of time by the action of wind, rain and sea, impress with their awesome grandeur. Many have assumed shapes which, to the more imaginative, look like something recognisable, and have earned suitable names such as Pulpit Rock, the Loaded Camel, the Tuskless Elephant, and the Kettle and Pans. This photograph shows a heavy sea on the Inner Head of Peninnis, with the curved crest or tuft on top of the outermost rock known as the Monk's Cowl from a fancied resemblance to a hooded head.

Olohava. A new *Scillonian* (this time given a number as well as a name, viz. Scillonian III) was built for the Company at Appledore and came into service in 1977 to replace the older ship. *Scillonian III* is just over a thousand tons and is fitted with stabilisers and comfortable seating which makes the 42-mile crossing from Penzance a much more pleasant journey in rough weather than was endured by many passengers in her predecessors. On the first *Scillonian* there had been a feeling that cargo was more important than passengers – though two stewards were often kept busy supplying metal sick pans to the distressed; but it was possible then – as a passenger – to walk most of the ship and even stand on deck right up in the prow looking down at the *Scillonian* bow slicing the water. On *Scillonian III* cargo and passengers are kept separate, with

The *Springfield*

The motor launch *Springfield* (one 15 h.p. engine) was licensed to carry twelve passengers, and was operated by Vernon Thompson for many years taking visitors on trips from St Mary's around to the other islands.

The taut tow-rope astern of the *Springfield* indicates that a punt is being towed for landing at low water on islands such as St Martin's, Bryher and Samson. In high summer, the limitation of only carrying twelve passengers was circumvented on occasions by towing one or more barges overflowing with visitors.

---

passengers important, but they are restricted from perambulating forward of the bridge.

In 1989 the £1 million, interest-free loan from the government to help pay the cost of building *Scillonian III* was paid off, and the Isles of Scilly Steamship Company then bought a Norwegian freighter, the *Gry Maritha*, to supplement *Scillonian III*'s freight work in summer and substitute for her in winter – she can carry over twice the cargo of *Scillonian III* and therefore make fewer trips so saving costs. But, also in 1989, competition appeared; the Fair Island Trading Company started a twice-weekly freighter service by the MV. *Busant* from Falmouth to Scilly, supplemented by a 42 ft. seatruck named the *Fair Islander*, which delivered cargo from the *Busant* to the off-islands. Meanwhile the Isles of Scilly Steamship Company's launches, which had previously served the off-islands

Scilly has number of natural but intriguing caves, mainly on the off-islands, of which the longest is Piper's Hole on Tresco. It has the reputation of having been a tin adit, a smuggler's hideout and a mermaid's home, but is in reality a natural fissure carved by escaping water. It has an unpretentious entrance but, after one has penetrated a few yards, a fresh water lake bars further exploration. In the past, enterprising Tresco men kept a punt on the lake, and for a fee would ferry visitors across to the sandy beach on the other side of the lake to explore the furthermost recesses – all in the light of well-placed candles to impart that feeling of magic which is curiously present in a damp seaside cave.

---

with goods, had been reduced to one – the *Gugh* – because the Company found that it was uneconomic for them to run two boats. Indeed, for years, the inter-island service had been run at a loss.

But the main challenge to the passenger transport of the Isles of Scilly Steamship Company over the last half century has come from the development of air transport – aircraft at first landing on the golf course.

The nine-hole golf course on St Mary's was constructed in 1904 by Scillonians in their spare time with the encouragement of T.A. Dorrien Smith, the Lord Proprietor. They cleared an area of Carn Morval Down, which had been covered in gorse and granite outcrops, and by 1908 the scratch score for the nine holes was forty. The first plane to land on the course was a De Havilland Gypsy Moth in 1929.

During the First World War the Local Defence Volunteer Corps used the golf course for manoeuvres, but when the air service started to Scilly on 15th September, 1937, Captain Olley's Channel Air Ferries rented the 5th and 7th fairways of the golf course to use as landing strips – golfers being obliged to cease play when a plane wanted to land. A warning bell was tolled when this was about to occur.

During the Second World War, gun emplacements were built on the course edges, but little golf was played in wartime. The clubhouse has magnificent views and from the second tee almost all the islands can be seen. The fairways are wide but, owing to scanty topsoil, the greens tend to be hard and run fast, with heavy penalties for overshooting.

The success of the air service persuaded the Duchy prior to the Second World War to begin the construction in 1938 of an airport on the high ground above Old Town, which was used by a flight of

166

Piper's Hole, Tresco

A Cornish stile, Peninnis – an impassable barrier for the cattle which used to graze the headland.

Storm demolishes lighthouse

The Victorians put small lighthouses at the ends of many of the quays in this country. This one was washed away by the storms early in 1990. Storms of great magnitude have been recorded in other years (1744, 1813, 1820, 1850, 1854, 1924, 1925, and 1962) but, understandably, it is the more recent which are remembered best and seem the worst; one in 1703 completely swept away the Eddystone lighthouse.

Hurricane fighter aircraft from 1941, while De Havilland biplanes kept up flights to Scilly for most of the war. British European Airways took over these flights from 1947 and operated them with Dragon Rapides until 1964, when they were replaced by helicopters. Some other entrepreneurs also started air lines to Scilly: Mayflower Air Services lasted from 1961 to 1963, and Scillonia Airways (1964) and Westward Airways also had short existences. But Brymon Airways was successful, flying planes from Newquay and Plymouth from 1972, and connecting with flights from Heathrow. In 1987, Skybus Ltd., which is owned by the Isles of Scilly Steamship Company, started a service from Land's End Aerodrome to St Mary's using nine-seater Britten-Norman Islander aircraft – so in 1990 there were three well-established airlines operating to Scilly successfully and in competition (BIH had taken over from BEA), and in the winter the services have been used to carry early flowers as

169

Island School

The main entrance to the Isles of Scilly School, the coeducational, comprehensive secondary school on St Mary's taking pupils to the school-leaving age – and surely the only School in the UK guarded by an old cannon dredged up from the seabed.

well as passengers. The post has come by air to Scilly since 1967. In 2004 British International operate the helicopter service.

All these services to Scilly have a good record of conveying passengers safely, although one Dragon, on its way to Scilly in the Second World War with a family of five on board, was shot down by a Heinkel III. But there has been one tragic accident since then: after nineteen years of faultless operation, a helicopter, approaching Scilly on July 16th, 1983, in fog, flew into the sea. The lifeboat rushed to the spot and, despite the misty conditions, the coxswain, Matt Lethbridge, located and picked up six survivors of the twenty-six people who had been on board.

Semaphore arms built in 1814 on the old tower at the highest point of St Mary's (165 ft above mean sea level) were once the only direct means of communication with the mainland and account for the building's present name – Telegraph Tower. But, in 1901, Marconi did some experiments there – he had previously, in 1898, heard wireless signals at Telegraph Tower, which had been

A ruined flower field at Porth Minick after the gales of the early months of 1990; the large size of some of the boulders strewn over the field testifies to the awesome power of the sea. Yet, if the sea governs much in Scilly, it has nowhere near the destructive capability of man. In the words of Lord Byron:

Roll on, thou deep and dark-blue Ocean roll!
Ten thousand fleets sweep over thee in vain;
Man marks the earth with ruin, his control
Stops with the shore; upon the watery plain
The wrecks are all thy deed, nor doth remain
A shadow of man's ravage.

---

transmitted from Porthcurno, over 30 miles away – and the coastguards erected a mast and have occupied the tower ever since 1902. From the observation room a constant watch was maintained for many years over shipping, assisted since the Second World War by the use of a mounted pair of powerful binoculars, captured from the Germans. Since 1982 the post has not been permanently manned except in periods of bad weather, since radio communication and satellite navigation (Falmouth is the coastguard centre) has largely replaced visual watch. Good terrestrial television reception came to Scilly in 1969 with the building of a mast at Telegraph.

Before the Second World War when there was a permanent watch

171

Hugh Town harbour

Boats nestle for shelter close up behind the old quay at Hugh Town in the winter, though most are hauled up on dry land until April. The foreshore now has an abundance of windows overlooking the Pool from flats, guesthouses and hotels.

at Telegraph, a black ball used to be hoisted on the mast when the *Scillonian* had left Penzance and was on her way to Scilly. This ball was dropped down the mast when the *Scillonian* was almost within the islands, so informing the hotels and guesthouses when to put the lunch on.

There was a post office of sorts in Hugh Town by 1804, but the present remarkable building in Hugh Street was constructed in 1897 under the aegis of Dorrien Smith, with daily deliveries of local mail being organised by 1909. In 1869 a telegraph cable was laid between Deep Point and the mainland, and inter-island cables in 1893–94, thus messages by Morse code could be relayed. From 1938 short-wave wireless has carried telephone calls to the mainland, but it was not until 1968 that all the islands had Subscriber Trunk Dialling with, from 1972, three hundred simultaneous telephone calls to the mainland being possible. From 1987 calls to Penzance were charged only at the 'A' rate, so enabling islanders to have convenient communication with the mainland.

172

Tennyson's garden

The small, sunny garden of Tregarthen's Hotel where Alfred Lord Tennyson is reputed to have sat and composed his poem *Enoch Arden*.

The first proper roads in Scilly were built by Augustus Smith and there was no more than perhaps one 'infernal combustion vehicle' on each of the off-islands till the Second World War. But, as everywhere else, vehicles increased, and before the Second World War a sign on the roadside as it rose from Porthmellon announced a speed limit in Hugh Town of 15 mph, although this is now no longer operative.

A voluntary road tax (£1 a wheel) to pay for road upkeep was begun in 1947 and most gravel lanes tar-macadamed by 1951. By 1965, St Agnes folk, in a remarkable spirit of self help, completed a six-foot-wide cement road from Porth Conger to Periglis, working voluntarily in the winter months. St Martin's men followed with a highway from their new quay linking their three towns which was completed in 1969, and Bryher and Tresco also concreted their roads. Driving tests were introduced on St Mary's in 1966 and the Road Fund Tax began in 1971, although for the first year it only applied to motorists who drove into Hugh Town where roads were owned by the Council of the Isles of Scilly. The nine miles or so of roads in the country areas of St Mary's are owned by the Duchy of Cornwall and therefore, strictly speaking, private roads. Disposal of old vehicles was for many years on the old rubbish dump at Porth Minick, where, even today rusting back-axles still litter the beach. When this dump was closed, vehicles were tipped unceremoniously into the sea at Deep Point, where there is a resemblance to a cliff and allegedly some deep sea water. In 1988 this environmentally unacceptable practice was stopped, and islanders became obliged to dispose of their old vehicles either by breaking them up themselves or by paying for their transport to dumps on the mainland.

There used to be an old Scillonian who would sit on each sunny day on a bench in the Strand of St Mary's, watching the boats in the harbour and enjoying conversing with visitors passing by. He was often asked what the residents of Scilly were like to live amongst. He always replied by asking his questioners how they found the people they at present lived amongst on the mainland; to those who answered that their neighbourhood at home consisted of unfriendly and mean people, as well as to those who answered that the people of their home town were helpful and charming, he would deliver the same reply – that they would find exactly the same among the people of Scilly.

CHAPTER XII – OTHER DEVELOPMENTS
of the 20TH CENTURY

The Godolphins established charity schools in Scilly in the eighteenth century, and the Society for the Promotion of Christian Knowledge also promoted education, so that each inhabited island had a school. But it was Augustus Smith who rebuilt the schools and charged parents a penny a week for sending children to them and tuppence a week if they stayed away, thus, in effect, helping to make education compulsory in Scilly. On St Mary's the present Church Hall was an infants' school, the girls' school was the present Catholic Church, and the boys were sent to the old buildings at Carn Thomas.

The Council of the Isles of Scilly became the local education authority under the Education Act of 1902, and in 1906 both the infants and the girls were absorbed into the enlarged school at Carn Thomas. The Education Act of 1944 laid down that secondary education was to be provided for all and that children should he educated 'according to their age, ability and aptitude'. This meant that children, who as a result of the 11-plus exam, were selected as suitable for a grammar school education, had to be sent to boarding school on the mainland at Council expense. A new secondary modern school was built in 1965 on St Mary's on the other side of the road from Carn Thomas (which became the primary school). In 1968 the Secondary Modern School became a comprehensive school, and this saved the Council the expense of funding secondary pupils following academic courses on the mainland. In 1990 there were still primary schools on four of the inhabited islands despite falling numbers of off-island children over the years. Bryher school was closed in 1972, and so Bryher children between the ages of five and eleven have to journey by launch each day to Tresco at Council expense. Tresco primary school has about twenty children from the two islands, and St Martin's and St Agnes schools have about five or six pupils each. The largest primary school in Scilly is Carn Gwarvel on St Mary's, whose new buildings were opened by Prince Charles in

The old quay at Hugh Town, built at the end of the reign of the first Elizabeth in about 1601, and a fine example of drystone walling.

1977 and which has about a hundred pupils. At the age of eleven, pupils transfer to the Isles of Scilly School, which also has about a hundred pupils and provides mixed, comprehensive secondary education to the school-leaving age, with transfers to mainland sixth-forms and technical colleges afterwards. Off-island secondary pupils numbering twenty to thirty are accommodated as weekly boarders in the School Boarding House, Mundesley, next to Godolphin House. The Secretary of State for Education (Mrs Margaret Thatcher) visited the school on 31 March 1973, and, although it was Saturday, the pupils all came into class so that she could see the school functioning. It is little wonder that the Minister was impressed by the 'pleasant relationships and general atmosphere of the school.' She then visited the three pupils of St Agnes School – and watched the Grand National with them.

By 2004 the schools in Scilly had been federated because the educational provision was costly, the first LEA school in the UK in five 'bases' taking children from age five to the school leaving age. The schools are administered by the local education authority, which consists of all twenty-one councillors (who sit as independents without party labels) and four co-opted members.

Old Trinity House cottages

These four Trinity House cottages were built for the families of lighthousemen. Now that the lighthouses are automatic, two of the cottages are let by the Council and the other two are managed by a housing association.

Before the seventeenth century, Old Town was the principal settlement on St Mary's, protected by a castle sited in a rock pile north of the settlement; but, with the building of Star Castle in 1593 and the later fortifications on the Garrison, the population seems gradually to have drifted to Hugh Town, which afforded greater security. There were practically no houses east of the Parade until after 1850, and the main street in Hugh Town (named Hugh Street) was merely an untidy collection of thatched-roof cottages until after the First World War, when the Duchy of Cornwall rebuilt all the houses in the street in its present neat form. 24 council houses were constructed on a site at Porthcressa (1949–51) and much private and speculative housing was constructed around Hugh Town at about this period and, in the 50s and 60s, some – but not all – blending well with Scilly's traditional materials. But a new local authority old people's home constructed in a prominent position to overlook the Park (and called Park House) is of especial

Garrison tennis court

The sheltered tennis court on the Garrison, and hardly recognisable as such after the storms early in 1990 – except for the net-wire still stretched tight across the middle.

note, enabling Scillonians in old age to remain in comfort in Scilly when they can no longer be cared for by their relations. It was visited by Queen Elizabeth, the Queen Mother, in 1987. Houses were also built on the off-islands, and on Tresco many buildings were converted by the Dorrien Smiths to holiday homes in the 1970s, and some to timeshare cottages in the 1980s.

But shortage of water from wells and bore holes has restricted much building in Scilly, for the use of water has increased yearly. Since the 1950s a reservoir on Buzza Hill has supplied piped water to nearly all Hugh Town from wells on the Lower and Higher Moors. However, most of this supply emanates from the bore holes on the Higher Moors on St Mary's, where there is a pumping station and a treatment works, supplemented by a supply of seawater from a desalination plant at Mount Todden since 1992. The water is then pumped to Telegraph Reservoir and then flows by a gravity main down to Porthloo and on to Hugh Town, where there are two further reservoirs to which it is sent at Buzza Hill and on the Garrison. The

Garrison Hill, too steep for her carriage, QueenVictoria thought, so she got out and walked.

water from Buzza Hill serves both Hugh Town and Old Town, while Tresco and Bryher have had their own mains water supply since 1969. The Duchy of Cornwall constructed mains sewerage in 1938 (previously some drains which were not connected to cess pits emptied on to beaches), and the sewage is pumped up to Morning Point, where a current takes most of the outflow away from the islands.

The disposal of rubbish has been an increasing problem in recent years. Historically the sea was the dump for all rubbish, and the sizeable tides in Scilly kept the beaches clean. The dump at Tolman was instituted after the First World War when household collections started, with infills of quarries and other controlled tipping used after the Second World War. The Council of the Isles of Scilly installed a German-made incinerator in the Lower Moors inland from Porthmellon in 1969, but fears that it may contaminate groundwater have led to proposals for alternative means of disposal. In 2002 an exhaust gas facility was installed at Porth Mellon helping in the recycling of waste products.

There were no doctors in Scilly in the eighteenth century, except for an occasional surgeon for the personnel on the Garrison. The

179

One of two sally ports under the Garrison Walls. This one is still much in use and serves as a quick way down to Little Porth.

present hospital on St Mary's was started in 1938 – all previous patients being sent for hospitalisation on the mainland. The National Health Service was founded in 1948 and this brought much improved services (as in the rest of the UK) with, in Scilly, two doctors and a dentist from 1950, together with nurses, and a new medical launch in 2004.

The order of Rechabites with their motto 'Peace and Plenty, the reward of Temperance' were once prominent in Hugh Town – their name now preserved for the slipway towards the eastern end of Town Beach.

There was no museum in Scilly till the opening of the building in Church Street in 1967, except that the Gibson family of photographers kept a large collection of items dating back three generations at Lyonesse Studio opposite, and which are now mostly in the present museum.

Electricity came to Scilly in 1931 but was very expensively produced by a generator under Buzza Hill, and in the early days the electricity was turned off at midnight to conserve power. Two big advances came when the inhabited off-islands were all linked to St Mary's by undersea cable in 1985, and in 1989 when mainland

180

Lloyd's Tower

Lloyd's Signal Tower, built on the highest point of the Garrison, was later called Bailey's Tower and is now part of a private house.

Woolpack Battery

Cannon and Woolpack Battery on the Garrison. Before the Second World War many old cannon were rusting away here, but since then only the two largest have survived, painted black and presented with spanking new gun carriages. They are believed to be 32-pounders from *HMS Colossus* and therefore probably helped Nelson win the Battle of the Nile in 1798.

electricity (at the lower mainland prices) came to Scilly by means of a 36 mile undersea cable laid from Sennen near Land's End to Porthcressa – the longest such cable in the UK.

* * * * *

Tourism in Scilly – today Scilly's most important industry – started in earnest after 1859, when the railway reached Penzance and trippers could sail across and admire Augustus Smith's sub-tropical garden on Tresco.

There were small lodgings in Scilly in the 19th century, such as Gahan Hotel, where now the post office is, but the main hotel on St Mary's was Tregarthen's owned by Captain Frank Tregarthen of the *Ariadne*, which plied between St Mary's and Penzance 'wind and weather permitting'. Captain Tregarthen had what surely must be every hotelier's dream: not only did three of his six daughters (Ann,

Outside Woolpack Battery

Woolpack Battery – one of the best positions for commanding the channel between the Hugh and the Gugh. The defences of three eras decay here: the oldest, from the eighteenth century, looks set to last longest, the massive granite curtain wall around most of the Hugh being particularly impressive at this point; while the searchlight house on the right of the photograph (built about 1900 for a 'range-finding defensive electric light'), still has the runways which carried its moveable iron screen, but is suffering from a bad attack of rust. The Second World War machine-gun post set in a corner of the massive eighteenth century walls looks somehow the feeblest of the three.

Jane and Mary) run the hotel for him, but none of his guests could leave his hotel and return to Penzance unless and until he decided to take them. In 1860, one guest, Alfred, Lord Tennyson, wrote part of *Enoch Arden* while sitting in the garden.

Hugh House on the Garrison had at one time been the Garrison Officers' Mess. It became a hotel in 1869 run by the Holgate family, but after the hotel closed (it was flats for a time before becoming the Duchy offices several years after the Second World War), a new hotel opened in 1891 on what had been one of the shipyards on Town Beach. It was run by Bertie Mumford, and was named Holgates Hotel. It closed during the Second World War, but was re-opened after the war under its new owner Group Captain E.J. Burling, who had once been Lawrence of Arabia's commanding officer at Mount Batten.

In 1964 Burling grew tired of visitors and closed the hotel (though, to his annoyance, the local authority still charged him rates as a hotel for a time rather than as a private house). In 1970 he gave Holgates to Cheshire Homes, but the building proved uneconomic to repair and was demolished a few years after Burling died in 1974.

The Poynter family from Cambridgeshire opened the Atlantic Hotel in 1908 in what had formerly been an inn next to the Custom House, and a saloon was built out over the beach in 1927 and became the dining-room in 1953.

The only other pre-war hotels were Springfields, which Mrs Ivy Roberts developed from a guest house in Church Street (it is now flats), and Star Castle Hotel which was converted into a hotel in 1933. But it is since the war, and since the Duchy gave up many of the freeholds in 1949, that tourism in Scilly has blossomed, with almost half the houses taking guests. The Island Hotel opened on Tresco in 1960. Hell Bay followed soon after on Bryher, with, in 1989, St Martin's Hotel, which won an award for its sympathetically-designed roofscape. Today, guesthouses and self-service flats have proliferated.

Pleasure boating now plays a major role in Scilly's tourist industry because of the natural history interests and the wide variety of trips among the many islands. It started with Albert Poynter's two boats *White Hope* and *White Heather* in the 1920s, joined by Vernon Thompson's *Visitor* (and, from 1933, the *Springfield*) with several others following. Two of the old pleasure launches took part in the British Army's evacuation from Dunkirk in 1940 – the *Commodore* of Bryher and the *Southern Queen*. The *Southern Queen* was built in 1927 and operated out of Folkestone before the Second World War, and sometimes was used as an escort for swimmers making cross-channel attempts. Her most notorious voyage was to take the traitor William Joyce (Lord Haw Haw) across the Channel, where he broadcast German propaganda to Britain during the war. In 1958 a co-operative association of boatmen was formed, and by 2004 there were about ten large launches operating from St Mary's in the summer, each carrying eighty or more passengers, whereas the original boats were limited to taking twelve people. In addition,

Two lead tanks

The two lead tanks now stand as useless sentinels outside the parish church. The diminutive tree in the foreground was planted by Prince Charles in 1989.

there are now boats operating from each of the inhabited off-islands, for boat trips are one of the best and – to many visitors – most unexpected of pleasures. Scilly specialises in quiet, unsophisticated amusements, and the question 'What is there to do in Scilly?' is only asked by visitors unaccustomed to any but organised holidays and artificial activities. Given reasonable weather everyone can relax in Scilly, while actively exploring somewhere different each day. In the words of William Blake:

Look on the rising sun: there God does live,
And gives His light, and gives His heart away,
And flowers and trees and beasts and men receive
Comfort in morning, joy in the noonday.

Board of Ordnance crest

A close up of the impressive crest of the old Board of Ordnance set on one of the lead water tanks now outside the parish church on St Mary's.

APPENDIX 1

PLACE NAMES AND DIALECT

It is uncertain how Scilly came by its name. In AD 400 Sulpicious Severus writes of the island of Sylicancis off the coast of Britain, and the Vikings called the islands Syllorgar. In old records Scilly is variously referred to as Sulla (a pre-Roman water goddess), Sullye, Sulli, Sulley and Sully (sun islands) – the 'c' not appearing regularly until the 16th century. Count Magalotti, writing in 1669, says: 'These islands, by modern geographers, are called the Sorlings ...' Leland used Scylley, but his account was not in print till 1710. At any rate the archipelago is not named after Scilly Rock off Bryher – rather the other way around; Scilly Rock seems to have acquired its name because it was tall and the first of Scilly to be visible to ships approaching the islands from the north-west. Today, Scilly gives its name to divers other places, 'Scilly Isles' being the name of a small atoll on the Society Islands in the South Pacific – and probably named by Captain Cook in tribute to a Scillonian member of his crew who had died during one of his voyages – and a busy traffic island at the Esher end of the Kingston bypass. There is also a hamlet called Scilly near Kinsale in Eire where some fishermen from Scilly are believed to have settled to escape Augustus Smith's taxation and land reforms.

Before the 16th century, the language in Scilly was the Celtic dialect of Cornwall. It survives in place-names such as *Agnes*, *Tresco*, *Bryher*, *Annet*, *Ganilly*; and in names of many rocks. *Mên* (rock) occurs in *Men-a-vaur*, *Menawethan*, *Mincarlo*, *Muncoy*, *Melledgan*, *Tolman*, etc. The Cornish word for a bay or inlet is *porth*, as in *Porthcressa* and *Porthmellon* (Mill-Bay) where an early mill stood. There are many variations: *Per Conger*, *Pelistry*, and *Periglis* or *Priglis* (Church Bay); and the common word *par* (inlet). Some of the Celtic names are intelligible: *Tresco* is *tre* (farm) and *scaw* (elderbushes); *Bryher* is *bre* (hill) and *har* (big): *Innisidgen* is *Innis-i-Geon* (John's Island); and in *Rosevear* and *Rosevean*, *vear* means 'big', *vean* 'little', and *Rose* something like 'high waste land'. Many are hopelessly corrupted: a Bryher man will say *Elzwilzick* for the island that modern maps call *Illiswilgig*; but old maps have *Inaswittick*, so that the first part was *innis* (island). The meanings of *Agnes*, *Annet*, *Ennor* (the old name of St Mary's), and most other Celtic names, are unknown. In Celtic names the defining word usually comes second and is accented, e.g. *Carn Néar, Porth Héllick* (Willow Bay), and *Peninnis* (island head). Contrast English names like *Húgh Town, Búzza Hill* (from the surname Bosow), and *Bánt's Carn*. It has been suggested that Samson got its name from its figure-eight shape, the Norse word *Sammans-on* meaning 'joined-up'.

Celtic died out in Cornwall in the eighteenth century. In Scilly, where fresh garrisons and settlers were constantly coming from England, it was given up earlier, and visitors were often surprised at the good English spoken by Scillonians. Some features of Cornish English are found: *Where's he to? Over to Bryher; He do belong* (or *he belongs) to be early*, meaning '*he is usually early*'. A *Troy-Town* or *High-Goal* is a 'confusion' or 'mess'. Some English words have unusual meanings: *nothing rash* (of the weather), 'nothing violent'; *to be frightened*, 'to be surprised'; *to be jealous of*, 'to distrust'. In Scilly the ordinary rowing boat is called a *punt*. Common words connected with fish or fishing are: *corb* (or *carb*), the floating box in which live lobsters, crawfish, and crab are stored; *wra-pot*, a close-meshed lobster-pot baited for wrasse; *hector*, the in-shore crab; *garlops*, the blennies that small boys fish for. Less common are: *gerricks*, garfish; *whistler* and *pettifox*, kinds of rockling. Of sea birds *merrick* is the tern; *cockathoden*, the shearwater. A *ledge* is a patch of rocks that is usually submerged. On land, field-walls of loose stone are called *hedges*; green hedges, which are recent, are *fences*. The general name for daffodils is *lilies*; but a grower names varieties exactly, e.g. *Fortune*, and shortens long names, e.g. *Sols* for Soleil d'Or, *Mags* for Magnificence. Bulbs are usually called *roots*; the roots of plants are *mores, vore* means 'furrow'; *teal*, 'to plant'.

Today some prefer to call 'St Agnes' simply 'Agnes', believing that the island has no right to the saintly prefix. The Davis map of Scilly of 1585 calls the island merely 'Agnes'. However, John Leland, writing 1534 to 1543, calls it 'S. Agnes' and says it is 'so caullid of a Chapel theryn'. In the 12th century, the island was 'Hagenes' (enes = island, hag = apart?), which seems appropriate as it was the first of the present-day off-islands to become separated in prehistoric times by the rising sea. Its consort 'Gugh' is a corruption of the Middle Cornish *geow* meaning field or enclosure.

In *Archaeologia Cambrensis*, the journal of the Cambrian Archaeological Association, (Vol 9, 3rd series, 1863) is a paper by E.

Norris entitled *Some Names of Places in Scilly*. It was read to an Association meeting in Truro on 29 August 1862. In it Norris quotes Borlase's remark that there are 'few British names on the islands' which Borlase attributes to the influx of people from the mainland in the 16th century, who found it 'easier to call the lands after the names of the occupiers (newcomers), than to retain the more uncouth, and, to the vulgar, insignificant old names'. Norris points out that Borlase's remark is puzzling because a look at the Great Admiralty Chart of Scilly of 1792 indicates that more than half of the names there are of British origin.

On the subject of the origin of the name of Scilly itself Norris dismisses the idea that it derives from the Celtic *Sylly* (a conger eel) because, although there are conger eels in Scilly's waters, they are in no way peculiar to Scilly. Norris also rejects the notion that the name Scilly derives from *Scylly* (separate) because islands are usually separated from some nearby mainland and the word is unlikely to have been sufficiently distinctive to have become a proper name. However, Norris points out that there is a verb *Skoly* (or *Skuly*), which means 'to scatter', and a word set which means 'a distant view', and it may be that folk on the mainland applied a form of these words to the scattered islands as they observed them from a distance at Land's End.

Some of Norris's other suggestions as to the Celtic derivation of names in Scilly are given below:

Priglis (Periglis, St Agnes)	= church port
Porthloo (St Mary's)	= port of the pond
Men-a-vaur	= great stone
Rosevear (Western Rocks)	= much vegetation
Rosevean (Western Rocks)	= little vegetation (vear = great, vean = small, rose = vegetation)
Peninnis (St Mary's)	= island headland (pen = headland, innis = island)
Biggal (there are many in Scilly)	= shepherd i.e. a rock marking shoals
Carrickstarne (a rock off Peninnis)	= a saddle rock

APPENDIX 2

POPULATION AND AREA

Estimated population figures of residents in the Isles of Scilly have been compiled from various sources as follows:

Date	Population*
1551	250
1571	300
1720	822
1744	1,400
1793	2,000
1814	2,313
1821	2,614
1841	2,788
1881	2,044
1901	2,288
1932	1,631
1951	1,900
1956	1,840
1961	1,800
1964	1,890
1965	1,950
1981	1,860
1990	1,875
1991	2,030

*Figures exclude the military (stationed in Scilly until the mid-nineteenth century). The 1991 figure was obtained from census returns after adjustments had been made. The 1990 figure is an estimate of the resident population based on the electoral role.

Lawlessness (or possibly disease) led to depopulation of the islands by the sixteenth century, and Godolphin wrote in 1579 that only two were then inhabited, St Mary's and Tresco. Newcomers took the place of previous inhabitants so that no one in Scilly today traces his family back before the 18th century. Borlase, writing in 1752, says that Godolphin brought into Scilly a number of new people, so that 'all notice of the old inhabitants was soon lost'.

191

Hectares	Acreage		Population				
			1841	1901	1961	1981	1990
1,604	3,963	Isles of Scilly	2,582*	2,092*	2,288*	1,860	1,875
629	1,554	St Mary's	1536	1,355	1,736	1,488	1,500
297	735	Tresco	430	331	283	156	130
237	586	St Martin's and White Island	214	175	118	91	110
148	365	St Agnes and the Gugh	243	134	85	62	70
133	327	Bryher and Gweal	121	97	66	63	65
39	95	Samson	29	nil	nil	nil	nil
21	53	Annet	—	—	—	—	—
20	49	St Helen's	—	—	—	—	—
16	40	Teän	—	—	—	—	—
64	159	Other islands	—	—	—	—	—
		Military	9	—	—	—	—

*Population according to census returns. The population figures are not, therefore, a true record of the resident population. The method of completing the returns varied over the years. In 1841, approximately 215 absent seamen were not included; in 1881 crews of fishing vessels at sea were allocated to the islands to which the vessels belonged, and 276 crew members of vessels in harbour were also included (presumably under St Mary's). The increasing number of visitors (approx. 400 in 1961 returns) also tends to make comparisons of population figures misleading.

APPENDIX 3

THE ISLANDS OF SCILLY (56 in all)
Leland in 1542 estimated 140 islands that grew grass in Scilly, but he was perhaps including many rocks with little more than lichen. Much depends on how an island is defined.

The following is a list of islands of the Isles of Scilly; the definition of an island – for the purpose of this list – being land surrounded by water at high tide, supporting a variety of land vegetation at all times, and locally acknowledged as an island.

Annet
Bryher
Burnt Island

Mincarlo
Newford Island
Nornour

192

Castle Bryher
Crow Island
Crump Island
Foreman's Island
Great Arthur
Great Ganilly
Great Ganinick
Great Innisvouls
Green Island (off Samson)
Green Island (off Tresco)
The Gugh
Guther's Island
Gweal
Hangman Island
Hedge Rock
Illiswilgig
Innisidgen
Little Arthur
Little Ganilly
Little Ganinick
Little Innisvouls
Men-a-vaur
Menawethan
Merrick Island (New Grimsby)
Merrick Island (Stony Porth)

Northwethel
Old Man
Outer Colvel Rock
Peashopper Island
Pednbrose
Pernagie
Plumb Island (off St Martin's)
Plumb Island (off Tresco)
Puffin Island
Rosevean
Rosevear
Round Island
St Agnes (or Agnes)
St Helen's
St Martin's
St Mary's
Samson
Shipman Head
Taylor's Island
Teän
Tins Walbert
Toll's Island
Tresco
White Island (off St Martin's)
White Island (off Samson)

(Hanjague has insufficient vegetation to qualify as an island in this list)

Confusion has sometimes arisen in Scilly because, although the area is small, there has been some duplication of place names. For instance, there are two Logan Rocks, two Piper's Holes, two Gilstone Rocks, five rocks named Biggal and as many as twelve Round Rocks. Here is a list of the principal ones:

1.	Barrel of Butter	———— NW. of Agnes
	Barrel of Butter	———— off Garrison, St Mary's
2.	Biggal	———— of Gorregan
	Biggal	———— of Great Arthur
	Biggal	———— of Melledgan
	Biggal	———— of Mincarlo
	Biggal	———— of Wras
3.	Black Rock	———— NW. of St Martin's
	Black Rock	———— Western Rocks
	Black Rock	———— Norrard Rocks
4.	Buccabu	———— to the south-west of Samson

	Buccabu	—	to the south-east of Annet
5.	The Cove	—	Agnes
	The Cove	—	St Martin's
6.	Cow and Calf	—	off Agnes
	Cow and Calf	—	off Taylor's Island
7.	Crow Island	—	off Bryher
	Crow Island	—	Old Grimsby
8.	East Porth	—	Samson
	East Porth	—	Teän
9.	Eastward Ledge	—	off Round Island
	Eastward Ledge	—	off Scilly Rock
10.	Fennel	—	off W. of Agnes
	Fennel	—	Porthcressa, St Mary's
11.	Flat Ledge	—	off Annet
	Flat Ledge	—	off Bishop Rock
	Flat Ledge	—	off Illiswilgig
	Flat Ledge	—	off N.E. St Martin's
	Flat Ledge	—	Western Rocks
12.	Gilstone	—	off St Mary's
	Gilstone	—	Western Rocks
13.	Green Island	—	off Samson
	Green Island	—	off Tresco
14.	Gun Hill	—	St Martin's
	Gun Hill	—	Tresco
15.	Higher Town	—	Agnes
	Higher Town	—	St Martin's
16.	Jacky's Rock	—	off Maiden Bower
	Jacky's Rock	—	Western Rocks
17.	Little Ledge	—	off N.E. of St Martin's
	Little Ledge	—	off N.W. of St Martin's
	Little Ledge	—	St Mary's Sound
18.	Long Point	—	Agnes
	Long Point	—	Tresco
19.	Lower Town	—	Agnes
	Lower Town	—	St Martin's
20.	The Mare	—	off Agnes
	The Mare	—	Crow Sound
21.	Merrick Island	—	off W. of Bryher
	Merrick Island	—	Tresco Channel
22.	Middle Town	—	Agnes
	Middle Town	—	St Martin's
23.	Murr Rock	—	off Maiden Bower
	Murr Rock	—	off N. of St Martin's
	Murr Rock	—	off Scilly Rock

24.	Peaked Rock	—————— Crim Rocks
	Peaked Rock	—————— off SW. of Samson
25.	Piper's Hole	—————— St Mary's
	Piper's Hole	—————— Tresco
26.	Plumb Island	—————— off St Martin's
	Plumb Island	—————— off Tresco
27.	Pollard	—————— off Peninnis, St Mary's
	Pollard	—————— Seven Stones
	Pollard	—————— off N. Teän
28.	Round Rock	—————— off N. Agnes
	Round Rock	—————— Eastern Isles
	Round Rock	—————— off E. The Gugh
	Round Rock	—————— off S.E. Norwethel
	Round Rock	—————— Norrard Rocks
	Round Rock	—— —————— off N. St Martin's
	Round Rock	—————— off N.W. St Martin's
	Round Rock	—————— Crow Sound
	Round Rock	—————— off S.E. Tresco
	Round Rock	—————— Western Rocks
	Round Rock	—————— Western Rocks (north)
	Round Rock	—————— Porth Coose (Agnes)
29.	Seal Rock	—————— Great Ganilly
	Seal Rock	—————— off Melledgan
	Seal Rock	—————— Norrard Rocks
	Seal Rock	—————— off S.E. of Guther's Island
30.	Shag Rocks	—————— off W. Annet
	Shag Rocks	—————— Eastern Isles
31.	Stony Porth	—————— Bryher (west)
	Stony Porth	—————— Porthcressa, St Mary's
	Stony Porth	—————— St Martin's (north)
	Stony Porth	—————— White Island (St Martin's)
32.	Tearing Ledge	—————— Bishop Rock
	Tearing Ledge	—————— Crim Rocks
	Tearing Ledge	—————— off N.E. of St Martin's
	Tearing Ledge	—————— Western Rocks
33.	West Porth	—————— Samson
	West Porth	—————— Teän
34.	Westward Ledge	—————— off Maiden Bower
	Westward Ledge	—————— off Round Island
	Westward Ledge	—————— off Scilly Rock
35.	White Island	—————— off St Martin's
	White Island	—————— off Samson
36.	Wrass	—————— off N. of St Mary's
	Wrass	—————— Porthcressa, St Mary's

APPENDIX 4

THE GOVERNORS OF SCILLY

1570-1608	Sir Francis Godolphin (1534-1608)
1608-1613	Sir William Godolphin (1565-1613)
1613-1619	John Godolphin (1577-1619). Captain of Scilly
1619-1624	—
1624-1626	Sir Francis Godolphin (1578-1637)
1626-1647	Sir Francis Godolphin (1605-1667) – the third one
1647-1648	Colonel Joseph Buller
1648-1651	Sir John Grenville (afterwards Earl of Bath)
1651-1660	Lieut. Colonel Joseph Hunkin
1660-1667	Sir Francis Godolphin (1605-1667) – the third one again
1667-1680	Sir William Godolphin (1640-1710)
1680-1682	William Godolphin (1659-1682)
1682-1689	Francis Godolphin (1661-1702)
1689-1700	Sidney, 1st Earl of Godolphin (1645-1712)
1700-1732	Colonel Sidney Godolphin (1651-1732)
1733-1766	Francis, 2nd Earl of Godolphin and 1st Baron Godolphin of Helston (1678-1766)
1766-1785	Francis, 2nd Baron Godolphin of Helston (1706-1785)
1785-1799	Francis Osborne, 5th Duke of Leeds (1751-1799)
1800-1831	George Osborne, 6th Duke of Leeds (1775-1838)
1831-1834	Duchy of Cornwall direct rule
1834-1872	Augustus Smith
1872-1918	Thomas Algernon Dorrien Smith
1918-1920	Major Arthur Algernon Dorrien Smith, who surrendered the lease for a new one (1929)

Below is an abstract from the lease granted to Sidney, Lord Godolphin, for 99 years from 1698, which gives an indication of the powers and responsibilities of the proprietors of Scilly in the period to 1831:

'1. Grant of the Islands of Scilly with mines of Tin, Lead and Coals and all profits of the same, and full powers to dig, work and mine in the Premises.

2. The Moiety of all Ship-wreck to be divided between the said Sidney, Lord Godolphin, and the King; such time as the office of Lord High Admiral shall be conferred on any person or persons, then the said Ship-wreck to be divided between the Lord High Admiral for the time being, and the said Lord Godolphin.

3. The grant of full power and jurisdiction to hear, examine and finally determine all plaints, suits, matters, actions, controversies, contentions and demands moved or depending between party and party, now or at any time hereafter inhabiting the said Isles.

4. To receive yearly at the King's price, one last of Gunpowder, paying ready money for the same.

5. The Lessee to have power to take up and press his tenants, tinners and servants to serve the King under his command within the Islands.

6. The Lessee not to alienate or dispose of the Estate for the term granted without the special licence and consent of His Majesty; nor to bequeath it to any of his daughters, unless she be married and her husband meet to defend the Islands; nor to any other children within age, but only to such as shall be of years fit for their defence.

7. Lord Godolphin to pay His Majesty the yearly rental of £40 at the Feast of St Michael into the hands of the Receiver for the Duchy of Cornwall.'

Leases on similar terms were granted to Sidney Godolphin's successors:

(1) to the Marquis of Carmarthen, the 5th Duke of Leeds and son of Mary Godolphin and Thomas Osborne (the 4th Duke of Leeds), and granted 1785/6.

(2) to the 6th Duke of Leeds, granted 1800 ... it ran until surrendered in 1831.

APPENDIX 5

A SHORT CHRONOLOGICAL SUMMARY

AD

380   The Emperor Maximus banished Bishops Instantius and Tiberianus to Silia Insula for heresy.

400-1100   Christian hermits; probably on all the main islands. The best known was St Elidius, who gave his name to St Helen's and was Bishop of Llandaff in the sixth century. He stayed with St Sampson, the Bishop of Dol in Brittany, to whom Samson is thought by some to be dedicated.

800-1570   Scilly was used as a base for pirates on occasions.

c.990   An old saga relates that the Viking, Olaf Tryggvessön, King of Norway, came to Scilly with nearly a hundred ships and, during his stay, was converted to Christianity. The legend is that Olaf took with him from Scilly 'priests and other learned men' and introduced Christianity to Norway and Iceland, but all this is speculative.

1114   Henry I granted Tresco and neighbouring islands to the Abbey of Tavistock, and a Benedictine priory dedicated to St Nicholas was established on Tresco.

1248   Dreux de Barrentine was sent by Henry III to be Governor of the Isles of Scilly.

1306   Ranulph Blancminster established by Edward I at Ennor Castle, St Mary's.

1337   The Isles of Scilly were included in the Duchy of Cornwall and given to the Black Prince.

1342   'Sack' of Scilly by Welsh troops.

1484   Value of Scilly, in peace time, forty shillings; in war, nothing.

1539   The larger monasteries, including Tavistock, were dissolved.

c.1540   Leland's description of the islands. Castle Ennor neglected and the islands became a prey to marauders.

1549   Bill of Attainder against Lord Seymour.

1571   Queen Elizabeth leased the islands to Francis Godolphin.

1593-4   Star Castle was constructed on the Hugh (Hoe) to prevent the islands being used as a base by Spain which was at war with England until 1604.

1623	Prince Charles, afterwards Charles I, stayed on St Mary's for four days.
1637-81	Star Castle used as a prison for various offenders – Dr Bastwick (1637), John Biddle (1655), and 'seven popish priests' (1681).
1646	Prince Charles, afterwards Charles II, and his suite, with Lords Hopton, Capel, Colepeper and Sir Edward Hyde, took refuge for six weeks at Star Castle after the retreat through Cornwall. They escaped to the island of Jersey, and the Isles of Scilly surrendered to Parliament.
1648-51	Rebellion of Scilly, which, in the hands of the Royalists under Sir John Grenville, became a dangerous nest of privateers; passing ships were plundered, regardless of nationality.
1651	The Dutch Admiral Tromp arrived off Scilly with twelve men-of-war, but was forestalled by Admiral Blake with a Parliamentary fleet. To put down the Royalist rebellion in Scilly the Parliamentary army landed on Tresco and its batteries at Carn Near commanded St Mary's Roadstead. Subsequently, lacking supplies, Sir John Grenville with 'officers enough to head an army' surrendered – the last Royalist stronghold to surrender in England.
1651-60	Lieutenant-Colonel Joseph Hunkin, a Cornishman, became Governor of Scilly until the Restoration of the Monarchy in 1660, when Sir Francis Godolphin resumed the Lord Proprietorship.
1660-74	In the wars against the Dutch (1st 1652-54, 2nd 1664-67, 3rd 1672-74) there was concern that the Dutch might attempt to seize Scilly, but only one attack took place – a raid on St Agnes in August 1666. After the 2nd Dutch War, most military personnel were withdrawn from the islands, and military control in Scilly, which had existed since 1547, ended, leaving the islanders largely to their own devices, especially as proprietorial interest in Scilly by the Godolphins declined.

1684	Kelp-ash making began in Scilly. (Kelp is an alkali of value to glass makers, soap manufacturers, and bleachers – it was obtained by burning seaweed).
1707	Four ships of the fleet under the command of Sir Cloudesley Shovell (*Association, Eagle, Romney, Firebrand*) wrecked on the Western Rocks; over 1,600 men were lost.
1720-1870	Scilly was the home of many pilots who boarded vessels on passage for the Irish Sea and the Bristol and English Channels and on ships taking shelter in Scilly.
1744	The Hugh was surrounded with immensely strong fortifications and bastions; the Garrison gateway is of this period.
1742-1834	Very poor living for inhabitants in this period (fishing, smuggling, and kelp-making, mainly).
1834	Augustus Smith obtained lease of the islands from the Duchy of Cornwall and became Lord Proprietor. The prosperity of the islands dates from the arrival of this energetic and far-seeing Hertfordshire squire. Augustus Smith built a house (Tresco Abbey) near the site of the old priory on Tresco, and laid out the Abbey Gardens. He also built schools and made education in effect compulsory.
1835-71	Shipbuilding was an important industry. The Scillonians not only made sailing vessels, but manned and owned them. At one time there were four shipbuilding yards on St Mary's, and the harbour was often full of vessels.
1849	First Bishop Rock lighthouse under construction.
1855	Samson evacuated by order of Augustus Smith, probably because the inhabitants were too old to man the fishing boats and support themselves.
1858	The Bishop Rock lighthouse was rebuilt – the original one was destroyed in a gale in 1850 before it was completed.
c. 1867	The start of the flower industry. The original bulbs are said to have been introduced by the Benedictine monks, but Scilly Whites may have been indigenous. It was not until the fashion for buying cut-flowers developed in mid-Victorian times that an experimental

	hat-box of flowers was despatched from Scilly to Covent Garden.
1869	Telegraph company formed by some Scillonians to lay the first cable to the mainland.
1872	Augustus Smith died and was succeeded by his nephew, Lieut. T. Algernon Smith-Dorrien, who added his uncle's name to his own.
1875	*Schiller* wrecked on Retarrier Ledges.
1891	A new system of local government was inaugurated.
1900-04	Strong gun emplacements were constructed on the Hugh. The work was abandoned after a quarter of a million pounds had been spent on a plan to make the islands a naval base. The Anglo-French Entente of 1904 made the base less necessary, and the new dreadnought battleships drew too much water for safe navigation in St Mary's Sound at low tides.
1910	Atlantic liner *Minnehaha*, 13,400 tons, stuck on Scilly Rock but was later refloated.
1914-18	During the U-boat campaign in the First World War the islands, being situated near the main shipping lanes, assumed strategic importance. A seaplane base was established on St Mary's at Porthmellon, and on Tresco from 1917.
1918	Major A.A. Dorrien Smith, DSO, succeeded his father, Lieut. T. Algernon Dorrien Smith.
1937	First air service to Scilly. Landings were on the golf course.
1939-45	Following the fall of France in the Second World War, Scilly was heavily manned and fortified, and received frequent attention from enemy aircraft. The islands were the recipients of much machine-gun fire and about two hundred bombs. A flight of Hurricanes and some air-sea rescue launches were stationed at St Mary's. The islands became a centre of activity against hostile submarines – one of which was claimed by the Western Rocks, and another by the Wolf Rock.
1954	Income tax was introduced to Scilly for the first time.
1955	On the death of Major A.A. Dorrien Smith, his son, Lt.-Cdr. T.M. Dorrien Smith RN (retd), succeeded to the lease of Tresco.

1964	Biplanes replaced by helicopters. This was the first scheduled helicopter service to be operated in Britain.
1966	A new secondary school was opened on St Mary's.
1973	Robert A. Dorrien Smith took over the lease of Tresco.
1977	*Scillonian III* came into service.
1983	Tresco heliport was opened.
1985	The inhabited off-islands received mains electricity – linked to St Mary's by undersea cable.
1987	Skybus service was begun, flying from Land's End Aerodrome, St Just, to St Mary's airport.
1987	The Duchy of Cornwall leased the uninhabited islands and untenanted land to the Isles of Scilly Environmental Trust (now the Wildlife Trust) for a hundred years at a peppercorn rent.
1989	Tom Gentry in the 110ft aluminium-hulled *Gentry Eagle* covered the traditional Blue Riband transatlantic race course of over 3,000 miles from Ambrose Light off New York to Bishop Rock Lighthouse off Scilly in 62 hours and 7 minutes, an average speed of 55 mph – and 18 hours less than Richard Branson had taken in 1986 in *Virgin Atlantic Challenger*. [The Blue Riband is held by the liner *United States*.]
1989	Mainland electricity (with its lower prices) came to Scilly by means of a 36 mile undersea cable from near St Just.
1989	*Gri Maritha* came into service.
1990/91	A lengthened runway was agreed for St Mary's airport, enabling larger aircraft to land in Scilly, and direct services from major cities to be possible.
1990	The two policemen in Scilly (4 in summer) took delivery of a new police boat – a 19ft Orkney Fastliner aptly called the *Peeler* – although, with relatively few offences committed, Scilly must be regarded as a particularly law-abiding place.
1990	The Australian-built sea catamaran *Great Britain* covered the Blue Riband course 2 hours and 40 minutes faster than the record holder, the American liner *United States*, had done in 1952.
1991	Airport runway extended, improving landing safety.
1992	Water desalination plant built on St Mary's, alleviating

the island's water supply problems.

1994   St. Mary's quay strengthened and extended, and given an additional flight of steps.

(Readers are recommended to see the chronological survey in the latest edition of the *Isles of Scilly Standard Guidebook* for the years after 1994).

APPENDIX 6

AESOP

Having referred to Aesop in the text on p. 6, three of his fables have been included here for interest, since few people nowadays have time or inclination normally to savour of their delights. They are based in small part on renderings by T. James (1856) and Berwick (1882).

Fables are a means of conveying truths in the form of allegories but, like parables, the senses of the fables differ from the literal meanings of the words used to convey them; yet, the meanings behind the fables are meant to be obvious and to encapsulate for humans useful moral lessons. With Aesop – who was born a slave about 600 BC, lived in Athens, and eventually secured his freedom because he was recognised by his master as a genius – creatures of the wild take the place of humans in his stories as a way of conveying lessons in an acceptable and inoffensive manner. Little is known for certain about Aesop's character, but it was said that he was a particularly nice man who delivered his fables orally, leaving it to others to write them down, his collections today being thought to include many that did not actually originate with him. He has been compared in some ways to Dean Swift, but having a delicacy and wit absent in the dean, yet showing almost as much Christian spirit.

Aesop's death seems especially sad. Delphians are said to have surreptitiously planted golden religious vessels in his luggage, then sent messengers to search for them and, upon their discovery, condemned Aesop for theft and sacrilege, and contrived to push him over a cliff edge, the fall killing him. The moral of his ending would seem to be that even the best of men can arouse the worst of actions in others.

(1) The fable of: *The Crow and the Pitcher*, by Aesop

A crow flew down to a large pitcher he had spied on the ground, hoping there might be water to drink in it. He found that there was, indeed, water in the pitcher, but that it was near the bottom, and that the vessel was too heavy to tip on its side, and too tall for his head to reach down to the water within it. However, on the ground nearby were some small pebbles and, taking each in turn in his beak, he dropped them one by one into the pitcher, until, little by little, the water level in the pitcher was caused to rise to near the brim, which thus enabled him at last to quench his thirst.

The moral of the story is that however daunting or beyond one's strength a problem task may seem, calm thought may often suggest a means of solving it, necessity being the mother of invention.

(2) The fable of: *The Fox and the Crow*, by Aesop

One day, a handsome crow came across a piece of cheese and, taking it up in her beak, she perched proudly with it high on the branch of a tree. Just then, a fox came by and, spotting the crow above with the lump of cheese in her beak, he coveted the dainty morsel and promptly devised a cunning plan to obtain it. 'O Crow', said the wily fox, 'how bright are thy wings, how beautiful are thine eyes, and your breast feathers are like those of an eagle.' 'But what a shame', he added sorrowfully, 'that you do not have a melodious voice to match.'

The crow was delighted at the fox's initial praises and, as regards the reservation regarding her voice, she decided to surprise the fox by uttering her distinctive *caw* to show him she had a voice after all; but the moment her beak opened, the cheese fell out, and was caught by the waiting fox below, who quickly swallowed it whole, 'Aha!' said the fox triumphantly, 'I said I admired your beauty, but I have little respect for your brains.'

The fable is a warning to be cautious of anyone giving you excessive flattery, behind which may lurk a hidden and less pleasant agenda; however, some may discern another and less desirable lesson from the story – perhaps overlooked by Aesop – a recognition that most people in varying degrees are prone to susceptibility to flattery, and that exploiting this is often a successful means to getting what you want.

(3) The fable of: *The Shepherd-Boy and the Wolf*, by Aesop

Most people have heard the fable of the Shepherd-Boy who, for his own amusement, used to cry 'Wolf! Wolf!' and enjoy the sight of the people of his village running to his aid. But there never was a wolf, and the villagers grew tired of his silly pranks, with the result that when the day came that there really was a wolf attacking his flock of sheep, and he cried out 'Wolf Wolf!' in hope of assistance, nobody believed him and nobody came. The moral of the fable is that a person who has fooled others with untruths is subsequently less likely to be believed even when he does speak the truth, so reinforcing that honesty is the best policy.

APPENDIX 7

AUGUSTUS SMITH AND UNEMPLOYMENT

By Queen Victoria's long reign, 1837-1901, the Industrial Revolution had produced new prosperity among Britain's upper and middle classes, with some beneficial trickle-down effects on the lower classes. But there were also long hours and hard work in up-country factories and coal-mines, matched in Cornwall by similar conditions in tin-mines. However, Scilly never had any mines, just four shipbuilding yards in the 19th century at Hugh Town. Moreover, Scilly was blessed with Augustus Smith, his dictatorial schemes often objected to at the time, but whose educational reforms were most helpful, for he insisted on all children attending school, so improving their job opportunities. He even taught some aspects of marine navigation himself – and this helped lead to employment on ships being obtained later by many Scillonian lads, a proportion eventually becoming masters.

But it was Augustus Smith's landholding reforms in Scilly which were his greatest achievement (see p. 94 for details). They were deeply resented by those obliged – by economic necessity and Augustus' insistence – to leave Scilly for the mainland; yet, by means of the changes, Augustus solved Scilly's unemployment (or over-employment) problems, or, more cynically, displaced the problems to the mainland. The long term beneficial effect of this was to re-arrange Scilly's farms into compact, economically viable units able to produce enough for the tenant farmer and his family and more besides. This meant, *inter alia*, that when the early-flower industry took off, the farms were such as could adapt to cater for the new crops, and for about 50 years the new industry became a principal source of income in the Islands.

By the start of the 21st century, flower-growing accounted for something like 8% of the Islands' income, although this palls in comparison with tourism, which, with related trades, was, by the same date, estimated to have represented something like 85% of Scilly's income. Fortuitously, the two industries complemented one another, in that one offered mainly winter employment, the other a summer one. Thus, in contrast to the great hardships Scillonians suffered after the end of the Napoleonic Wars, since the time of Augustus and his reforms, although most Scillonians remained poor, they never suffered as extensively from the worst effects of unemployment as did much of the rest of Britain, and so avoided much of the bitterness that still lingers in the minds of some elderly on the mainland.

One of Stanley Baldwin's announcements when he first became prime minister in 1923 was 'We intend to do some thinking'. The principal subject upon which this cerebral activity was to be focused was unemployment, seen then as the most important problem in home affairs, and one upon which, throughout the 1920s, more time was spent discussing in Parliament than on any other subject. Yet, until the late 1880s, unemployment, though large, had hardly figured at all in Britain as a political or economic issue or even as a problem, being comfortably assumed by the better-off – and endured by the larger numbers of worse-off – as inevitable, a permanent feature of society rather like poverty itself.

But that acceptance changed in the 20th century, particularly when large numbers of servicemen returned from the First World War to flood the labour market unable to get jobs. In the 1929 election – by which time the problem was exacerbated by the world slump – Lloyd George declared that, if his party was elected to power, he would reduce unemployment 'within a year and without extra charge upon the Exchequer', down to what he termed 'normal proportions'. There is inevitably always some unemployment through people changing jobs or not finding work suitable to their qualifications or circumstances; but how Lloyd George proposed to achieve 'normality' was left suitably vague – and, anyway, in that year his party was rejected by the electorate. Some politicians favoured raising the school-leaving age from 14 to 15, which would keep a year-group at school instead of letting much of it swell the unemployment figures; there was also some talk of attendant educational advantages in the proposal, but the whole prospect led to jealous rows between the churches and was dropped. Even Keir Hardie only urged feeding the unemployed rather than demanding that the Government create employment. The difficulty was that taxation increases on the better-off on a scale sufficient to fund employment projects for the large numbers of unemployed – such as road building, for example – as happened in Hitler's Germany with autobahns – was not a serious option in Britain at that time, for it would have had insufficient support among the better-off in the class-ridden society of the inter-war years. However, with the coalition government of 1931, three ministers – Thomas, Lansbury and Mosley – were charged with seeking some solution to high unemployment, but they diverged fundamentally in their favoured remedies – as did most of the economists they consulted – so that little could be agreed or done, despite unemployment in Britain peaking in April, 1930, to 1,650,000 out of a population of about 44 million. Unemployment figures continued high throughout the 1930s, only gradually being alleviated by slow economic recovery.

It might at first sight be thought a little surprising to find the better-off in society enthusiastic about a democratic system of government with a wide franchise, when the greater numbers of the less well-off would seem to constitute a potential threat to the advantaged position and privileges of the better-off. In the longer term it is probably accurate to believe that a democratic one-person, one-vote franchise may logically develop into some form of egalitarian socialism; but, in the shorter term, by providing the appearance of popular acceptance, democracy actually seems to safeguard the status quo and inhibit revolution, especially in Britain where the concerns of the better-off are ably supported by a privately-owned (and partly foreign-owned) press and media, which 'spins' its selection of news each day with what can sometimes seem like scant regard for impartiality. Many people rely on newspapers and the media generally to help in the formation of their opinions on day-to-day events. So, inevitably, headlines, and what is written below them, have a persuasive effect especially when a consistent line is taken, and competent journalist employed to deride (for instance) all supposedly leftwing views. There was a time when newspapers were believed to aim for an Olympian detachment in reporting current affairs; nowadays, most reveal a preference on most issues and argue them forcefully and persuasively. It is rare for them to present a debatable matter with prejudice undetectable – even on seemingly non-political concerns such as fox hunting. It is almost as if they feel they have to tell their readers what opinions to hold. In Russia, there was no democracy in 1917, let alone a semblance of a free press to help protect the country from violent revolution; but, paradoxically in Germany, it was a democratic election in 1933 which brought Hitler to power, now explained as a miscalculation of the German better-off, who imagined that they could control him. But that is only part of the story, for it was mainly the failure of the previous German administration to provide work for six million unemployed which gave Hitler the opportunity to gain this power, and very popular with the people of Germany – judged by the street cheers – did he become in tackling the problem.

In Britain it was one of the achievements of successive governments eventually to reduce unemployment figures to acceptable proportions by the end of the 20th century, some administrations motivated by conviction, others also perhaps by respect for the ballot box. Newspapers rarely trumpet such good news, for they are in business to improve circulation to make money, and they believe, probably correctly, that the public, on balance, prefers to read criticism and scandal rather than good news and praise – it is more exciting. So, as unemployment figures lessen, press coverage of it reduced, the issue having become more one of relief than despair – and therefore less newsworthy. But the changeover of British industry to high-technical work and away from heavy, labour-intensive production such as shipbuilding – which at present is more economically suited to lower-wage countries – could possibly lead to a future increase in unemployment in Britain, unless the education system can encourage more students to study scientific and technical subjects in the hope of producing mindsets more suited to employment in expanding high-tech. industries. It sometimes seems to require firm, dictatorial government – such as Augustus Smith wielded in Scilly between 1834 and 1972 – to advance the general prosperity of a region, even if it seems at the time to a minority, who are obliged to change their life and residence completely, a horrible action. Augustus Smith was probably influenced by Samuel Smiles and others who advocated *Self-Help*, and his changes can be justified by the result that they brought great and lasting benefit to the entire community in Scilly.

APPENDIX 8

PREFACE TO BIBLIOGRAPHY
Five books of the eighteenth and nineteenth centuries are of importance to anyone interested in studying the Isles of Scilly. These are:
(1) Heath, Robert. *A Natural and Historical Account of the Islands of Scilly* (1750)
(2) Borlase, William. *Observations on the Ancient and Present State of the Islands of Scilly* (1756)
(3) Troutbeck, John. A *Survey of the Ancient and Present State of the Scilly Islands* (1794)
(4) Woodley, George. *A View of the Present State of the Scilly Islands* (1822)
(5) North, I.W. *A Week in the Isles of Scilly* (1850, 1st edition; revised edition by L.H. Courtney in 1867)

Heath published his *Natural and Historical Account of the Isles of Scilly* in 1750 (the full title contains 142 words) from notes he had compiled while doing duty as an officer of the garrison on St Mary's. Dr Borlase, the antiquarian, wrote his '*Observations ...*' in 1756, a book which has been described as 'a useful work but one containing a great deal of speculation'. William Borlase was born at Pendeen in 1695 and died at Ludgvan in 1772, where he was rector.

Nearly forty years after Borlase's book, the Reverend Troutbeck, Chaplain of the Isles of Scilly from 1780 to 1796, published his *A Survey of the Ancient and Present State of the Scilly Islands*. He does not mention Heath's book but seems to have read it closely, and he writes of eighteenth century records, the originals of which no longer exist. Jessie Mothersole in her book, in a chapter dealing with smuggling entitled 'Former Industries', says that smuggling had been a very popular employment in Scilly and that even the clergy engaged in it. She instances a report – we know not on what foundation – that the Rev John Troutbeck had to leave the islands 'from fear of the consequences of having taken part in it'. Troutbeck had been educated at Queen's College, Oxford, and was Chaplain in

St Mary's till 1796.

In 1822 George Woodley of the SPCK (and minister on St Martin's and St Agnes), wrote his guidebook to Scilly entitled *A View of the Present State of the Scilly Islands* in which he criticised earlier works, especially Troutbeck's and Heath's, saying of the latter: 'In a word Heath's account may be read once for curiosity but will never be referred to with pleasure.'

In 1850 another clergyman, the Rev I.W. North, published his *A Week in the Isles of Scilly*, seeming to cram into seven days more than the average visitor nowadays manages in a month.

Of the large number of general books written about Scilly in the first half of the 20th century, two are worth picking out as perhaps the best:
(1) Mothersole, Jessie. *Isles of Scilly* (1910)
(2) Grigson, Geoffrey. *The Scilly Isles* (1948)

[Of recent works the most challenging and respected is *Exploration of a Drowned Landscape* by Charles Thomas, dealing with the early history of Scilly.]

Of magazines relating to Scilly the three most important are:
(1) *The Scillonian* (now biannual since 1975, formerly four times a year) published since 1925.
(2) *Scilly Up To Date*, about nine issues published each year since 1985 by A.H. Read & Son, the Island Printers.
(3) *The Tresco Times*, informative, readable and free.

The following bibliography may be described as extensive to about 1990; after that many books have been published about the Scillies, but it has been assumed that the reader who is interested in the bibliography will most appreciate a list of the older books, some out of print and possibly unfamiliar, rather than modern ones which can be perused and purchased in local bookshops. Cornwall public libraries have a copy of most of the better-known modern works, and there is also a magnificent private library at Penzance, known as the Morrab Library, which is wonderfully stocked. However, it is the public library which is in Morrab Road; the private library occupies an imposing house in sub-tropical Morrab Gardens.

BIBLIOGRAPHY until 1990

Date	Title	Author
c1222	*Heimskringla* (translated by Morris and Magnússon, 1891-95, in Saga Library – for Olaf Tryggvessön's connection with Scilly)	Snorri Sturluson
1478-1480	*Itineraries* (English translation 1969)	William of Worcester
1534-1543	*Itinerary in England and Wales* (published 1710, republished 1907 and 1964)	John Leland
1602	*The Survey of Cornwall* (reprinted 1811)	Richard Carew
1642	'A Petition from the Island of Scilly' in *A Natural and Historical Account of the Islands of Scilly* (published 1750, reprinted 1967)	Thomas Banks
1646	*A relation of the Surrender*	John Haslock
1651	*A True Account of the late Reducement of the Isles of Scilly*	Jos. Lereck
c1651	*Memorials*	Whitlock
1669	*Travels of Cosmo the Third, Grand Duke of Tuscany, through England during the reign of Charles the Second* (English translation published 1821)	Lorenzo Magalotti
1676	*Memoirs of Lady Fanshawe* (published 1829)	Lady Fanshawe
c1695	'Some Memorialls toward a Natural History of the Sylly Islands' in *The Scillonian*, No. 159	Anon
1702	*South Devon with a Description of the Scilly Islands*	C.S. Ward
1710	*Itinerary in England and Wales* (republished 1907 and 1964)	John Leland
1750	*A Natural and Historical Account of the Islands of Scilly* (republished 1967)	Robert Heath
1754	'An Account of the Great Alterations which the Islands of Sylley have undergone since the Time of the Antients' in *Philosophical Transactions of the Royal Society*, No. 48	Dr William Borlase
1754	*Antiquities, Historical and Monumental, of the County of Cornwall* (first edition) ... repub. 1973	Dr William Borlase
1756	*Observations on the Ancient and Present State of the Islands of Scilly* (republished 1966)	Dr William Borlase
1756	Review of Dr William Borlase's book in *Literary Magazine*	Dr Samuel Johnson
1769	*Description of England and Wales* Vol. 2. (Published by Newberry and Carnan)	
1785	*Voyages aux Montagnes d'Écosse et aux Isles Hebrides, de Scilly, d'Anglesey Etc.* Vol. 1	M. Guillaume Borlase
1792	*A Geographical Description of the Scilly Isles* (republished in 1976 and 1977 in *Cornish Studies*, Nos. 4 and 5)	Graeme Spence
1794	*A Survey of the Ancient and Present State of the Scilly Islands*	Rev John Troutbeck
1800	*An Account of All the Scilly Islands* (republished 1976 and 1977 in *Cornish Studies*, Nos. 4 and 5)	Henry Spry
1804	*The History of Cornwall* (supplement by Whitaker)	Rev R. Polwhele
1810	*The Report of the Surveyor-General of the Duchy of Cornwall ... concerning the Formation of a Safe and Capacious Roadstead within the Islands of Scilly*	Benjamin Tucker
1810	*The Climate of the Isles of Scilly*	T.T. Macklin
1811	*Observations on the Tin Trade of the Ancients in Cornwall*	Sir Christopher Hawkins

1811	*The Survey of Cornwall* (reprint of 1602)	Richard Carew
1814	*Magna Britannia*, Vol. 3.	Lyson
1816	*A History of Cornwall*	Fortescue Hitchens and Samuel Drew
1816	*A Guide to the Mount's Bay and the Land's End*, first edition. (Third edition 1828)	A Physician (John A. Paris)
1817	*Historical Survey of the County of Cornwall*, Vol. 3	C.S. Gilbert
1818	*A Report Detailing the Extreme Miseries of the Off-islands of Scilly*	Rev. George C. Smith
1821	*Travels of Cosmo the Third, Grand Duke of Tuscany, through England during the reign of Charles the Second (1669)* (English translation of publication of 1669)	Lorenzo Magalotti
1822	*A View of the Present State of the Scilly Islands*	Rev. George Woodley
1824	*Excursions in the County of Cornwall*	F.W.L. Stockdale
1828	*The Scilly Islands and the Famine*	Rev. George C. Smith
1829	*Memoirs of Lady Fanshawe* (1676) republished	Lady Fanshawe
1831	'List of rare plants found in the Neighbourhood of Penzance' in *Loudon's Magazine of Natural History*, No. 4	E. Brewer
1834	*The Cornish Tourist*	Anon
c1840	*Sketches in Scilly*	Lady Sophie Tower
1841	*Narrative of the Loss of the Steamer 'Thames' on the Rocks of Scilly*	Rev. George Woodley
1845	*A Guide to Penzance and its Neighbourhood including the Islands of Scilly*	J.S. Courtney
1848	*Thirteen Years' Stewardship of the Islands of Scilly*	Augustus Smith
1850	'At the Scilly Isles' (*Argosy* Vols. 17 and 18)	C.W. Wood
1850	*A Week in the Isles of Scilly* (first edition. Revised by L.H. Courtney in 1867)	Rev. I.W. North
1850	*On the Geology of the Islands of Scilly*	Joseph Carne
1851	*A Handbook for Travellers in Devon and Cornwall*, first edition. (Tenth edition 1882)	Thomas C. Paris
1852	*Scilly and its Legends*	Rev. H.J. Whitfeld
1853	'Wild Flowers and Ferns of the Isles of Scilly observed in June and July' in *Transactions of the Natural History and Antiquaries Society, Penzance*, No. 2.	L. and M. Millett
1855	*Tourist Guide to Devonshire & Cornwall including the Scilly Isles*, first edition. (26th edition, altered title, 1931). Published by A. and C. Black	
1855	*A Londoner's Walk to the Land's End and a Tour of the Scilly Islands*	Walter White
1858	*Sea-side Studies at Ilfracombe, Tenby, the Scilly Isles, and Jersey*, first edition. (Second edition 1860)	George H. Lewis
1859	'On the Geology of the Scilly Islands' in *The Geologist* (Vol. 2)	Rev. Francis F. Statham
1859	*Scilly Inseln und Jersey: Naturstudien am Seesstrande. Küstenbilder*	G.H. Lewes
1860	*The Beautiful Islets of Britaine*	Walter Cooper Dendy
1861	*Rambles in Western Cornwall*	J.C. Halliwell
1861	*Excursions in the County of Cornwall, etc.*	J.C. Halliwell
1861	*Lyoness (revisited)*	Tonkin and Row
1861	*Rambles beyond railways*	G. Smith
1862	*Catalogue of Plants – Scilly Isles – June 1862*	F. Townsend

212

1862-3	'Barrow at Samson, Scilly' in *Journal of the Royal Institution of Cornwall*, No. 45	A. Smith
1863	'Narration of the Discovery and Opening of a Kist-Vaen on the Island of Samson, at Scilly, 3rd September 1862' in *46th Annual Report of the Royal Institution of Cornwall*	Augustus Smith
1863	*The Cassiterides: An Inquiry into the Commercial Operations of the Phoenicians in Western Europe, with particular reference to the British tin trade.* (This book challenges two earlier works: *History of maritime and Inland Discovery* by Cooley, and *Historical Sketch of the Astronomy of the Ancients* by Sir C. G. Lewis, both of which seem to have argued that the Phoenicians never traded with Cornwall, let alone with Scilly).	George Smith
1864	'Contributions to a Flora of the Scilly Isles' in *Journal of Botany*	F. Townsend
1865	*Yachting Round the West of England*	Rev. A.G. L'Estrange
1865	*Cornwall and its Coasts*	Alphonse Esquiros
1866	'Sir Cloudesley Shovel' in *48th Annual Report of the Royal Institution of Cornwall*	T.Q. Couch
1867	*A Week in the Isles of Scilly*, first edition. (Fifth edition, altered title, 1897)	L.H. Courtney
1868	*Vast Sinkings of Lands*	R.A. Peacock
1868	*Sevenstones Lightship*	Augustus Smith
1869	*Ornithology of Cornwall and Scilly*	E.H. Rodd
1869	*Down Channel*	R.T. McMullen
1869	*Sailing Directions for Approaching the Islands of Scilly*	Capt. William Rowett
1870	'The Agriculture of the Scilly Isles' in *Journal of the Royal Agricultural Society of England*	Lawrence Scott and Harry Rivington
1870	'Additions to the Flora of the Scilly Islands' in *Journal of Botany*, No. 8.	M.A. Lawson
c1870	*Excursions through Cornwall*	J. Kinson
1871	*Notes on the New Merchant Shipping Code* – Pilotage	Augustus Smith
1872	'The Crown of Scilly' and 'List of some of the plants growing all the year round in the ground of the late Mr. Augustus Smith, at Tresco, in the Scilly Islands' in *Gardeners' Chronicle* for 1872	Anon
c1872	'Meteorology of West Cornwall and Scilly 1871' in *39th Annual Report of the Royal Cornwall Polytechnic Society*	W.P. Dymond
1873	*The Orkneyinga Saga*	Joseph Anderson
1873	*Traditions and Hearthside Stories of West Cornwall*, second series	William Bottrell
1873	*New Guide to Penzance, St Michael's Mount, Land's End, Logan Rock, Lizard, St Just, St Ives, etc.*, first edition (Second edition, altered title, 1875)	J.H.H. (John H. Hancock)
1873	*Scilly and its Emperor*	'S.F.T.' (Lady Sofia Tower)
1873	*Observations on the Current to the West of Scilly*	J. Rennell
1875	*Guide to the Scilly Islands*	J.C. and R.W. Tonkin
c1875	*Island Scenery*	J. Knapp
1876	'A Botanical Trip to the Scilly Isles' in *Hardwicke's Science Gossip*, No. 162	W. Curnow
1876	*The Cornwall Calendar and Register*, first issue	Percy & Co.

213

1877	'On the uses of the landed gentry' in *Short Stories on Great Subjects*	J.A. Froude
1877	'Notes on the Scilly Isles together with some Cornish Antiquities' in *Journal of the British Archaeological Association*, No. 33	S.M. Mayhew
1878	'The Scilly Isles as a Health Resort' in *British Medical Journal*	Barham
1878	*Tourist's Guide to Cornwall and the Scilly Isles*, first edition. (Seventh edition 1895)	Walter H. Tregellas
1880	*The Birds of Cornwall and the Scilly Islands*	E.H. Rodd
c1880	'Meteorology of West Cornwall and Scilly 1870 to 1879 and Observation on Sea Temperatures' in *47th Annual Report of the Royal Cornwall Polytechnic Society*	W.L. Fox
1881	'Tresco Abbey' in *Gardeners' Chronicle*, No. 84	J.G. Mitchinson
1882	*Guide to the Isles of Scilly*, first edition. (Third edition 1893)	J.C. and R.W. Tonkin
1883	*The Shipwreck of Sir Cloudesley Shovel*	J.H. Cooke
1883	*Sixty-eight Years' Experience on the Scilly Islands*	Robert Maybee
1884	'The Gardens at Tresco Abbey' in *The Garden*, No. 26	C.A.M. Carmichael
1884	'The Legend of the Lionesse' in *The Western Antiquary*, No. 4.	Robert Hunt
1884	'Ten Days in Scilly' in *Science Gossip*, Vol. 20	B.P.
1886	'Tresco' in *Gardeners' Chronicle*, No. 26	
1887	*Tourists' Companion*	E.W. Crofts
1888	'The Scillonians' in *Gentleman's Magazine*	Frank Banfield
1889	*Cornwall as a Winter Resort*, first edition (Third edition 1986). Published by W. Brendon & Son	
1890	'The Flora of the Scilly Isles' in *Transactions of Penzance Natural History and Antiquaries Society*, No. 3	Rev. H. Boyden
1890	*The Industries of Scilly with Special Reference to Narcissus Growing*	James G. Owen
1890	*Cornish Feasts and Folklore*	M.A. Courtney
1890	'Market-gardening in the Scilly Islands' in *Journal of the Royal Agricultural Society of England*, No. 1.	E. Brewer
1890	'The Progress of the Narcissus Culture in the Isles of Scilly' in *Journal of the Royal Horticultural Society*, No. 12	T.A. Dorrien Smith
1891	'Plants growing in Tresco Abbey Gardens' in *Transactions of Penzance Natural History and Antiquities Society*, No. 3	A. Henwood Teague
1891	*The Winter Resorts of Cornwall*. Published by E.L. Longley	
1892	*Sailing Tours Part 2. The Nore to Tresco, Isles of Scilly*, first edition. (Second edition, 1899)	Frank Cowper
1893	*The Age of the Saints: a Monograph of Early Christianity in Cornwall*	W. Copeland Borlase
1893	'Additional Records for the Scilly Isles' in *Journal of Botany*, No. 34	A. Somerville
1893	'A Summer Holiday in Cornwall and the Scilly Isles' in *Proceedings of the Holmes Natural History Society*	
1894	*Dragonet on Our Islands*	George R. Sims
1894	*The Lepidoptera of Cornwall and the Islands of Scilly*	W.E. Baily
1894	*A Summer in the Scilly Islands*	J.W. White

1894	*Ancient and Holy Wells of Cornwall*	M. and L. Quiller Couch
1894	Articles on Scilly by Rev. E.H.C. Stephenson in *The Evangelist Monthly*	Rev. Alfred Whymper (editor)
1895	*The Climate of the Isles of Scilly*	T. Thornton Macklin
1895	'Ten Days in Lilyland' in *Gardeners' Chronicle*, No. 17	H.T.W.
1896	'The Flower Trade at Scilly' in *The Times*, 29 May	Anon
1896	*Evenings with Grandmama: recollections of the Scilly Islands*	Rebecca Forfar
1896	*The Story of Atlantis*	A.P. Sinnett
1897	The Scilly Isles (Newnes Guide)	
1897	*Fair Lyonesse. A Guide to the Isles of Scilly*	James G. Owen
1897	*Lyonesse. The Homeland Handbooks*, first edition. (Seventh edition, altered title, c1913)	John C. Tonkin and B. Prescott Row
1898	Article in *Journal of the Royal Agricultural Society.*	
1898	'An August Visit to Tresco Abbey Gardens' in *The Garden* No. 54	S.W. Fitzherbert
1899	*A Book of Cornwall*, first edition. (Third edition 1912)	Rev. S. Baring-Gould
c1900	*The Wolf Rock Lighthouse*	J.N. Douglas
1900	*Life of Sir James Nicholas Douglass*	Thomas Williams
1902	'Early March in Tresco Abbey Gardens' in *The Garden*, No. 61	S.W. Fitzherbert
1902	*South Devon with a Description of the Scilly Islands* (Thorough Guide Series)	C.S. Ward
1904	*A Pictorial and Descriptive Guide to Penzance, St. Ives, Land's End and the Scilly Islands* (sixth edition)	Ward, Lock & Co.
1904	*The Cornish Riviera.* Published by the Great Western Railway	
1906	*Cornish Notes and Queries*	Peter Penn (editor)
1906	'The Birds of Scilly' in *The Zoologist*, July, August and September	James Clark and Francis R. Rodd
1906	*Isles of Ictis*	Emm. Green
1906	*History and Geography of Cornwall*	Thurstan C. Peter
1906	*Victoria County History of Cornwall*	William Page (editor)
1906	*The Geology of the Isles of Scilly*	George Barrow
1907	*Scilly and the Scillonians*	J.G. Uren
1907	*Leland's Itinerary in England and Wales.* (Re-issue 1964)	Lucy Toulmin Smith (editor)
1908	*The King's General of the West: Life of Sir Richard Grenville, Bart., 1600-1659*	Roger Granville
1909	*Flora of Cornwall*	F. Hamilton Davey
1909	1909 'Notes on the Flora of the Scilly Isles' in *Transactions of the Botanical Society of Edinburgh*, No. 24	W.W. Smith
1909	*Cassiterides and Ictis – Where are they?*	Thurstan C. Peter
1909	*The Romance of Smuggling*	Rev. Athol Forbes
1909	'Additional Notes on the Fauna of the Scilly Islands' in *Journal of the Royal institution of Cornwall*, Vol. 17, Part 3	Rupert Valentin
1909	*Cornish Characters and Strange Events*	Rev. S. Baring-Gould
1909	*Flora of Cornwall ... including the Isles of Scilly*	F. Hamilton Davey
1910	*The Cornish Coast (South) and the Isles of Scilly*	Charles G. Harper

1910	*The Isles of Scilly*, first edition. (Third edition 1919)	Jessie Mothersole
1912	*England's Riviera*	J. Harris Stone
1913	'Government of Isles of Scilly' in *Journal of the Royal Institution of Cornwall*, Vol. 19. Part 2, No. 60	Anon
1913	'The Culture of early flowers in Cornwall and the Scilly Islands' in *Kew Bulletin*	W. Dallimore
1914	'Plants of Scilly' in *Journal of Botany*, No.52	J.W. White
1919	*Black's Guide to Cornwall* (22nd edition)	A.R. Hope Moncrieff (editor)
1920	'Tresco Abbey Gardens, Scilly Isles' in *Kew Bulletin*	A.W. Hill
1921	'Plants of the Scilly Isles' in *The Naturalist*	W.B. Haley
1922	'A supplement to F. Hamilton Davey's *Flora of Cornwall* (1909), *Journal of the Royal Institute of Cornwall*, Vol. 21	Edgar Thurston and Chambré C. Vigurs
1923	*Life of William Douglass*	Thomas Williams
1924	'The Isles of Scilly' in *Regional Architecture of the West of England*	A.E. Richardson and G. Lovett Gill
1924	*Some Notes on Wild Nature in Scillonia*	C.J. King
1924	*The Cornish Tourist or Excursions through Cornwall*	Anon
1925	*The Godolphins*	Brigadier F.C. Marsh
1925	*The Isles of Scilly: The Visitors Companion in Sunny Lyonesse*, first edition. (Fourth edition c1937)	Alexander G. Gibson and Herbert J. Gibson
1925	'The Lepidoptera of the Scilly Isles' in *Entomologist*, No, 58	K.G. Blair
1925	*The Scillonian*, No. 1 (Magazine published quarterly until No. 200, Winter 1974-75, and then bi-annually)	
1926	'Flower growing for market in the Isles of Scilly since the Great War' in *Journal of the Royal Horticultural Society*, No. 51	A.A. Dorrien Smith
1927	'The Cassiterides, and the Ancient Trade in Tin' in *Journal of the Royal Institution of Cornwall*, Vol.22 Part 2	T.A. Rickard
1928	'The Granites of the Scilly Isles and their relation to the Dartmoor Granites' in *Quarterly Journal of the Geological Society of London*, No. 84	C.W. Osman
c1928	*A Holiday in the Scilly Isles*	Alexander G. Gibson and Herbert J. Gibson
1929	'Scilly under the Godolphins' in *Old Cornwall*, No. 9.	J.E. Hooper
1929	'The Spiders of the Scilly Islands' in *Proceedings of the Zoological Society of London*	W.S. Bristowe
1930	'The British and Irish Maniola jurtina L. (L.E.P.)' in *Entomologist*, No. 63	P.P. Graves
1931	'Blake's Reduction of the Scilly Isles in 1651' in *The Mariner's Mirror*, Vol. 17, No. 3	Rev. J.R. Powell
1931	'The Beetles of the Scilly Isles' in *Proceedings of the Zoological Society of London*	K.G. Blair
1931	*Cornwall Bird Watching & Preservation Society, First annual report covering Cornwall and Isles of Scilly*	
1931	'The Depopulation of Samson' in *The Scillonian*, No. 28	E.N.V. Moyle
1931	*B.C.B. Magazine*	E.A. Fenn (editor)

c1931	*King's Popular Guide. A Concise Guide to the Scilly Isles*, first edition. (Second edition c1932)	C.J. King
1932	'Cornwall and Scilly' in *The County Archaeologies*	H. O'Neill Hencken
1932	*The Archaeology of Cornwall and Scilly*	H. O'Neill Hencken
1932	*Cornish Seafarers*	A.K. Hamilton Jenkin
1933	'Where our Flowers come from' in *The Scillonian*, No. 7	Alex Gray
1933	'Travels of St. Samson of Dol' in *Aberystwyth Studies*	E.G. Bowen
1933	*Cornwall in the Great Civil War and Interrenum 1642-1660*, first edition. (Second edition 1963)	Mary Coate
1933	*St Michael's Mount*	Rev. T. Taylor
1934	*Isles of the Island*	S.P.B. Mais
1934	'The Early Days of the Scillonian Flower Industry' in *Royal Horticultural Society Daffodil Year-book*	Gordon W. Gibson
1935	*St Samson in Cornwall*	G.E. Doble
1935	*The West Country*	R.A.J. Walling
1935	'Further Notes on the Spiders of the Scilly Islands' in *Proceedings of the Zoological Society of London*	W.B. Bristowe
1935	'Tresco Abbey' in *Gardeners' Chronicle*, No. 98	E. Brown
1935	*British Regional Geology, South-West England*, first edition. (Fourth edition by E.A. Edmonds, M.C. McKeown and M. Williams 1975)	H. Dewey
1936	*Beast Book for the Pocket*	Edmund Sanders
1936	*Edward the Eighth – Our King*	A.V. Groom
1936	*The Isles of Scilly Standard Guidebook*, first few editions.	E.L. Bowley Later editions R.L. Bowley
1937	'The Call of the Sea' in *Strand Magazine* (August)	F.J. Mortimer
1937-1938	'The Building of Star Castle' in *Old Cornwall*, Vol. 3, Nos. 2 and 3	J.E. Hooper
1938	*St Mawes*	G.E. Doble
1938	'The Garden Isles of Scilly' in *The National Geographic Magazine*, Vol. 74, No. 6	W. Robert Moore
1939	*Sailing on the South Coast*, first edition. (Fourth edition, altered title, by K. Adlard Coles 1968)	
1939	*The Island News*, first issue 10 June. Weekly newspaper published by The Island Duplicating Office	
1940	'Notes on the Flora of the Isles of Scilly' in *The Journal of Botany*, Vol.78, No. 931	T.E. Edward Lousley
1941	'Isles of Scilly' in *The Land of Britain* (Report of Land Utilisation Survey of Britain)	B.S. Robertson
1941	*Tudor Cornwall*	A.L. Rowse
1941	'The Dual Nature of the Megalithic Colonisation of Prehistoric Europe' in *Proceedings of the Prehistoric Society*	G.E. Daniel
1944	'Isles of Scilly' in *Transactions of the Plymouth Institution* Vol. 18	R. Hansford Worth
1945	*Cornwall and its People*	A.K. Hamilton Jenkin
1945	'Note on Pirates Beheaded on Tresco', in *Devon & Cornwall Notes & Queries*, No.22	H.P.R. Finberg
1945	*Butterflies*	E.R. Ford
1945	*The Fortunate Islands*, first edition. (Ninth edition 2004)	Editions 1-4 E.L. Bowley, Editions 5-9 R.L. Bowley

1945	St. Martin's, St. Helen's and Teän, first edition. (Second edition 1948)	Rev. H.A. Lewis
1946	'A Survey of the Status of Birds breeding in Cornwall and Scilly since 1906' in British Birds, Vol. 39, No. 1	Lt.-Col. B.H. Ryves and Miss H.M. Quick
1946	Islands round Britain	R.M. Lockley
1946	'Ancient Causeway from St Mary's to Tresco' in The Scillonian, No. 20	G.F. Leechman
1946	The Coastline of England and Wales	J.A. Steers
1947	British Lighthouses	J.P. Bowen
1947	'Tresco under Three Reigns' in Journal of the Royal Horticultural Society, No. 72	Right Rev. J.W. Hunkin
1947	Footpath Guides, No.4: The Isles of Scilly	E.A. Belcher
1948	'The Isles of Scilly' in Countrygoer (Summer No.)	Geoffrey Grigson
1948	The Scilly Isles, first edition. (Second edition 1977)	Geoffrey Grigson
1949	Ancient Monuments of the Isles of Scilly	B.H. St. J. O'Neil
1949	The West in English History	A.L. Rowse
1949	'A Roman-British Hut in Scilly' in The Scillonian, No. 24	B.H. St. J. O'Neil
1949	'Excavation of a Bronze Age House in Scilly' in The Scillonian, No. 24	B.H. St. J. O'Neil
1950	The Prehistoric Chamber Tombs of England and Wales	Glyn E. Daniel
1950	Shipwrecks on the Isles of Scilly	Charlotte Dorrien Smith
1950	'Notes on the flora of the Scilly Isles and the Lizard Head' in Watsonia, No. 1	J.E. Raven
1951	The Buildings of England: Cornwall	N. Pevsner
1951	The Birds of Scilly as Recorded at Tresco Abbey	Anon
1952	The Islands of England	J.H. Ingram
c1952	Guide to Tresco Abbey Garden, first edition. (Second edition by T.M. Dorrien Smith c1956)	A.A. Dorrien Smith
1953	The Scilly Isles	C. Vyvyan
1953	'Acanthus mollis L. in St. Agnes, Isles of Scilly' in Watsonia, No. 2	B.W. Ribbons
1954	'The Excavation of a Cist-grave Cemetery and Associated Structures near Hugh Town, St. Mary's, Isles of Scilly, 1949-50' in Archaeological Journal, No. 111	Paul Ashbee
1954	'Isles of Scilly' in Britain Today, No. 216	Cécile Wilkinson
1955	'An Old Map of Scilly' (1550-94) in The Scillonian, No. 122	Kenneth Sisam
1955	Memoirs of a Birdman	Ludwig Koch
1955	Spring Blooms in the Scillies' in The Field, No. 205	C. Wilkinson
1956	'The Names of Samson and St Helen's' in The Scillonian, No. 126	Kenneth Sisam
1956	Isles of Flowers, first edition. (Second edition 1963)	Ernest Kay
1956	'A Little-Known Isle of Scilly (White Island, St Martin's) in Country Life, No. 119	G. Grigson
1956	Hobnails and Sea-boots	Wendy Aldridge
1957	St Agnes Bird Observatory Report (First annual report. Discontinued after 1963-1964 report)	J.L.F. Parslow (editor)
1957	'Farming the Fortunate Isles' in Geography, Vol. 42, Part 2, No. 196	A. Downes
1957	'The Wreck of Sir Cloudesley Shovell' in The Mariner's Mirror, Vol. 43. No. 4	J.W. Damer Powell

1957-58	'Geological Association Excursion' to the Scilly Isles in *Circular*, No. 597	A.J. Dollar
1958	*Isles of Scilly Visitor's Handbook*	Maxwell Fraser
1958	'Idrisi on Lyonesse' in *Journal of Celtic Studies*, No. 11	H.W. Bailey and Alan S.C. Ross
1958	'Some Preliminary Observations on the Lepidoptera of the Isles of Scilly' in *Entomologist's Gazette*, Vol. 9, No. 3	Austin Richardson and Robin M. Mere
1958	*Scilly Isles Survey*	The British Travel and Holidays Association
1958	*The Lost Land* (underwater exploration in the Isles of Scilly)	John Dunbar
1959 and 1960	'Wrecks of the Isles of Scilly' in *The Mariner's Mirror*, Vols. 45, No. 4 and 46, No. 2	Juliet du Boulay
1960	*Castles and Cannon*	B.H. St. J. O'Neil
1960	*St Mary's, Isles of Scilly Year Book*. Annual publication published by the Church Publishers.	
1960	'Salakee Down Chambered Cairn, St Mary's Scilly', in *Excavations on Defence Sites, 1939: Mainly Neolithic-Bronze Age*	W.F. Grimes
1960	'English Excursions' in *Country Life*	G. Grigson
1960	'A Sub-tropical Garden in Britain (Tresco)' in *Gardener's Chronicle*, No. 148	M. Savonius
1960	'Deer on the Isles of Scilly' in *127th Annual Report, Royal Cornwall Polytechnic Society*	F.A. Turk
1960	*The Isles of Scilly*	G. Forrester Matthews
1960	'The Last Voyage of Sir Clowdisley Shovel' in *Journal of the Institute of Navigation*, Vol. 13	W.C. May
1961	'The Palaeopathology of Early British Man' in *Journal of Royal Anthropological Institute*, No. 91	D. Brothwell
1961	'Some Naval Problems of Scilly in Napoleonic Times' in *The Mariner's Mirror*, Vol. 47	M. Mortimer
1961	'The Seven Stones Light Vessel, 1840-43' in *Devon and Cornwall Notes and Queries*	C.E. Welch
1962	*Atlas of British Flora*	F.H. Perring and S.M. Walters
1962	*Tresco, Isles of Scilly, Official Guide*	Ann Faber
1962	'Sea-boots Among the Daffodils' in *The Geographical Magazine* Vol. 35, No. 1	William Sansom
1963	*Map Collectors' Circle, No. 3: The Isles of Scilly*	Margaret Palmer
1963	*Scilly and the Scillonians: A Pictorial History*	F.E. Gibson
1963	'Eupithecia phoeniceata in Britain' in *The Entomologist's Record*, Vol. 75	Austin Richardson
1963	'Further Observations on the Lepidoptera of the Isles of Scilly' in *The Entomologist's Record*, Vol. 75	Austin Richardson
1963	*Cornwall and the Isles of Scilly*. Published by Shell Mex and BP. Ltd.	
1964	*An introduction to the Geology of Cornwall*	R.M. Barton
1964	*Birds of the Scilly Isles*	Hilda M. Quick
1964	*The Itinerary of John Leland in or about the years 1535-1543*, Vol. 1	Lucy Toulmin Smith (editor)
1964	'Excavation of a Celtic Hermitage on St Helen's, Isles of Scilly, 1956-58' in *Archaeological Journal*, No. 121	Helen O'Neil

1964	'Postal Affairs of the Isles of Scilly' in *Stamp Collecting* (24 July)	P.J. Elkins
1964	'Tresco Abbey Gardens' in *North Wales Gardener*, No. 9	J.D.H. Smith
1965	*The Grip of the Islands*	Mary Gillett
1965	'Early Daffodils in the Isles of Scilly' in *The Daffodil and Tulip Year Book for 1965*	Rodney W. Ward
1965	*Ancient Europe*	Stuart Piggott
1965	*The Bells of the Isles of Scilly*	Frederick Sharpe
1965	*Le Problème des Cassitérides et les sources de l'étain occidental dupuis les temps protohistoriques jusqu'au début de notre ère*	Jacques Ramin
1965	*A Landscape Charter for the Isles of Scilly*	G.A. Jellicoe
1965	*Wreck and Rescue Round the Cornish Coast*, Vol. 2	Cyril Noall and Grahame Farr
1966	*Airway to the Isles*	Philip Cleife
1966	*Antique Maps of Cornwall and the Isles of Scilly*	R.C.E. Quixley
1966	'Die Scilly Inseln' in *Erdkunde*, Vol. 20	Eva Leuze
1966	'The Lichen Flora of Bryher, Isles of Scilly, and its Geographical Components' in *Lichenologist*, Vol. 3.	D.S. Ranwell
1967	'Excavations on Nor'nour in the Isles of Scilly, 1962-6' in *Archaeological Journal*, No. 124	D. Dudley
1967	The 'Torrey Canyon' (Government White Paper Cmnd.3246). Published by HMSO	
1967	*Portrait of the Isles of Scilly* (First edition)	Clive Mumford
1967	*The Torrey Canyon. Report of the Committee of Scientists on the Scientific and Technological Aspects of the Torrey Canyon Disaster.* Published by HMSO for Cabinet Office	
1967	*The Wreck of the Torrey Canyon*	Crispin Gill, Frank Booker and Tony Soper
1967	'England's Scillies, the Flowering Isles' in *National Geographic*, Vol. 132, No. 1	Alan Villiers
1967	'George Eliot in the Scillies' in *The Cornish Review*, No. 5	Rosalind Wade
1967	*Tresco Abbey Gardens*	Laura Maconochie
1967	*Report on Isles of Scilly Steamship Co. Ltd. and Related Matters*	Peat, Marwick, Mitchell & Co.
1967	'The Pleistocene Deposits of the Isles of Scilly' in *The Quarterly Journal of the Geological Society of London*, Vol. 123, No. 489	G.F. Mitchell and A.R. Orme
1967	Report on the Animal Remains from Nor-Nour' in *Journal of the Royal Institution of Cornwall*, No. 5 new series	F.A. Turk
1967	'Flora of the Scillies' in *Gardeners' Chronicle*, No. 161	M.B. Gerrans
c1967	*Excavation of HMS Association*	Bob Rogers
c1967	*Shipwrecks Around the Isles of Scilly*, first edition. (Second edition 1971)	Frank Gibson
1968	'Scilly and the Royal Air Force' in *Western Morning News* (25 October)	Leslie Hunt
1968	*The Legendary History of Olaf Tryggvason*	Gwyn Jones
1968	'Notes on Flint Industries on Samson, Bryher and Tresco' in *The Scillonian*, No. 175 and 176	H. Minett-Smith

1968	'Grass-marked Pottery in Cornwall' in *Studies in Ancient Europe*	
		Charles Thomas
1968	*Critical Supplement to the Altas of British Flora*	F.H. Perring
1968	*Cornish Lights and Shipwrecks*	Cyril Noall
1968	*A Sea Miscellany of Cornwall and the Isles of Scilly*	Richard Gillis
1968	'Spirobis Species (Polychaeta: Serpulidae) from the Isles of Scilly' in *Journal of Marine Biology Association*, UK. No. 48	
		Tegwyn Harris
1968	'List of Marine Algae from the Isles of Scilly' in *British Phycological Bulletin*, No. 3	
		G. Russell
1968	*Some Lovely Islands* (chapter on St Agnes and the Gugh), first edition. (Second edition 1982)	
		Leslie Thomas
1968	*Wild Flowers in Cornwall and the Isles of Scilly*	Jean A. Paton
1969	*Cornwall Bird-Watching and Preservation Society Scilly Islands Report*. (First annual report covering Isles of Scilly only. In 1976 the title was changed to *Isles of Scilly Bird Report*)	
1969	'The Pilot Gigs of Cornwall and the Isles of Scilly' in *The Mariners' Mirror*, Vol. 55, No. 2	
		R.H.C. Gillis
1969	*The Impact of Tourism on the Ecology and Amenity of the Isles of Scilly*	
		University College of London
1969	*William of Worcester; Itineraries, edited from the unique MS. CCC Cambr. 210.*	
		John Harvey (editor)
1969	*Augustus Smith of Scilly*	Elisabeth Inglis-Jones
1969	*Island Treasure*	Roland Morris
1969	'The Marine Flora and Fauna of the Isles of Scilly' in *Journal of Natural History*	
		L.A. Harvey
1969	'A Bryophyte Flora of Cornwall' in *Transactions of the British Bryological Society* Vol. 5, Part 4	
		Jean A. Paton
1970	*Scilly 1801-1821 ... Through War and Peace*	Michael Tangye
1970	'The Impact of Recreation on the Ecology and Amenity of the Semi-natural Areas: Methods of Investigation Used in the Isles of Scilly' in *Biological Journal of the Linnean Society*, Vol.2, No.4	
		F.B. Goldsmith, R.J.C. Munton and A. Warren
1970	'Shipwreck in the Isles of Scilly, 1433' in *Oakum*	P.A. Kennedy (editor)
1970	'King Charles's Castle, Tresco, Scilly' in *Post-medieval Archaeology*, Vol. 4	
		J.J. Miles and A.D. Saunders
1970	*The Isles of Scilly* (visitors' handbook)	F.E. Gibson
1970	'Mammalian and Avian Remains from Possible Bronze Age Deposits on Nornour, Isles of Scilly' in *Journal of Zoology*, No. 162	
		J.C. Pernatta and P.T. Handford
1970	*The Standard Guidebook to the Isle of Tresco*	R.L. Bowley
c1970	*Valhalla – The Tresco Ships' Figurehead Collection* Published by National Maritime Museum	
1971	*Council of the Isles of Scilly, Report on the Water Resources of St Mary's*	
		Binnie & Partners
1971	*The Isles of Scilly: an Economic Survey and Report*	South West Economic Planning Council
1971	*A Report on the Naval Air Command Sub Aqua Club Expedition to the Isles of Scilly*	
		R.H. Graham and F. Shaw
1971	*The Blizzard of '91*	Clive Carter

1971	*Seashore Life in Cornwall and the Isles of Scilly*	Stella M. Turk
1971	*Cornish Shipwrecks Volume 3: The Isles of Scilly*	Richard Larn
1971	'Environment on Record' (Geogram survey of Tresco) in *The Geographical Magazine*, Vol. 44, No. 2	Max Nicholson
1971	*The Flora of the Isles of Scilly*	J.E. Lousley
1971	*Shipwrecks on the Isles of Scilly* (reprint of 1967 edition with amendments)	F.E. Gibson
1971	'Unusual Polychaeta from the Isles of Scilly' in *Journal of Natural History*, No. 5	Tegwyn Harris
1972	'The Marine flora and fauna of the Isles of Scilly: Polychaeta' in *Journal of Natural History*, No. 6	Tegwyn Harris
1972	*Pieces of Land*	Kevin Crossley-Holland
1972	*The Wreck Detectives*	Kendal McDonald
1972	*Island Camera*	John Arlott, Rex Cowan and Frank Gibson
1972	*The Hamilton Collection*	Ann Birchall
1972	*Instructions to Recorders*. Published by Biological Records Centre	John Heath and Diana Scott
c1972	*Nature Trails and Wildlife Conservation in the Isles of Scilly*, first edition. (Second edition c1973)	P.Z. Mackenzie
1972-73	'Gilstone Legends' in *London Diver* Nov-Dec. 1972 and Jan-Feb. 1973	John Pickwell
1973	'Rosevean: Ulysses' Silent Ship' in *The Dublin Magazine*, Vol. 10, No. 2	John Ryan
1973	'Culture and Change in the Isles of Scilly' in *The Explanation of Culture Change*	Paul Ashbee
1973	*Endowed Charities for the Relief of Need in Cornwall and the Isles of Scilly*. Published by the Cornwall County Council and the Council of Social Service for Cornwall	
1973	'Improbable Legends Surrounding the Ship wreck of Sir Clowdisley Shovell' in *The Mariners' Mirror*, Vol. 59, No. 2	J.G. Pickwell
1974	*Shipwreck*	John Fowles
1974	'Wrecks Round the Scillies' in *Buried and Sunken Treasure*	Richard Larn
1974	*Victorian and Edwardian Cornwall*	John Betjeman and A.L. Rowse
1974	*Ancient Scilly*	Paul Ashbee
1974	*Scillonian Quiz Book*	R.L. Bowley
1974	*Visitor's Guide to Archaeology in Scilly*	Luke Over
c1974	*A Historical Sketch Book of the Isles of Scilly Lifeboats*	The Isles of Scilly Ladies' Lifeboat Guild
1975	'Scilly – Britain's Smiling Islands' in *Reader's Digest*, Vol. 106, No. 636	John Ennis
1975	'The Distribution of Bumblebees in Cornwall and the Isles of Scilly' in *Cornish Studies*, No. 3	W.E. Almond
1975	*Lighthouses of England and Wales*	Derrick Jackson
1975	'The Dutch East Indiaman *Hollandia* wrecked on the Isles of Scilly in 1743' in *The International Journal of Nautical Archaeology and Underwater Exploration*, Vol. 4, No. 2	Rex and Zélide Cowan, and Peter Marsden

1975	*Gigs and Cutters of the Isles of Scilly*	A.J. Jenkins
1975	*The Isles of Scilly*	Crispin Gill
1975	*South West Water Authority. The Isles of Scilly. Report on Supplies on St Mary's*	J.K.D.
c1975	*Valhalla Maritime Museum Tresco*	Anon
c1975	*Rod Fishing in the Isles of Scilly*	John Bourdeaux
1976	*Lugworm Island Hopping*	Ken Duxbury
1976	*South West Water Authority. The Isles of Scilly. Report on Groundwater Resources on St Mary's*	D. Battersby
1976	*A Check-list of the Birds of Cornwall and the Isles of Scilly*	R.D. Penhallurick
1976 and 1977	'A Buried Soil at Innisidgen, St Mary's, Isles of Scilly' in *Cornish Studies*, Nos. 4 and 5	G.W. Dimbleby
1977	'The Names of the Eastern Isles' in *The Scillonian*, No. 205	Charles Thomas
1977	*The Cassiterides: My Lovely Islands*	Lis Hargreaves
c1977	*Wild Flowers of Scilly* No. 1 Coastal Habitats No. 2 Marshes, Stonewalls, Hedgerows and Windbreaks No. 3 Bulb Fields and Waste Places	David Hunt
c1977	*Tresco: A Pictorial Guide to the Island*	Robert and Emma Dorrien Smith
1978	*A Preliminary Handlist of the Guide Books to the Isles of Scilly (from 1816)*	Charles Thomas
1978	*Butterflies of Scilly*	M.H. Bletcher
1978	*Castaway & Wrecked*	Rex Cowan
1978	*A Guide to Bird-watching in the Isles of Scilly*	David Hunt
1978	*Islands*	John Fowles and Fay Godwin
1978	*The Birds of Cornwall and the Isles of Scilly*	R.D. Penhallurick
1978	*The Orkneyinga Saga: The History of the Earls of Orkney*	Hermann Pálsson and Paul Edwards
1978	'John Lethbridge, Diver' in *History Today*, Vol. 28	Zélide Cowan
1978	'The Old Church on Tresco' in *The Scillonian*, No. 207	Michael Tangye
1978	'Types and distributions of pre-Norman fields in Cornwall and Scilly' in *Early Land Allotment in the British Isles* (British Archaeological Report 48)	Charles Thomas
1978	'Island Holidays' in *Countrygoer* (summer)	Geoffrey Grigson
c1978	*Scilly Divers*	'Norm' (J.N. Gooding)
c1978	*Treasure Trove Islands*	Roland Morris
c1978	*Sea Angling in the Isles of Scilly*	Graeme Pullen
1979	*Cornwall and Scilly Peculiar*	David Mudd
1979	*HMS Colossus*	Roland Morris
1979	'Scilly: A Mecca for Birdwatchers' in *Country Life*, Vol. 165, No. 4266	D.I.M. Wallace
1979	*Sir Richard Grenville of the Civil War*	Amos C. Miller
1979	*Three Early Accounts of Scilly (1707, 1792, 1800)*	Charles Thomas (editor)
1979	'By Air to Lyonesse' in *Air Pictorial*, Vol.41, No. 11	M.J. Ingham
1979	*Gold and Silver Treasure* (Auction catalogue of artefacts from *Association, Hollandia*, etc.)	W.H. Lane & Son
1979	'A Glossary of Spoken English in the Isles of Scilly' in *The Journal of the Royal Institution of Cornwall*, Vol. 8, Part 2	Charles Thomas

1979	'An Archaic Place-name Element from the Isles of Scilly' in *The Bulletin of the Board of Celtic Studies*, No. 28	Charles Thomas
c1979	*Guide to the Natural History of Scilly. Nature Trails and their Habitat*	Anon
c1979	*The Savage Sea*. (Shipwreck photographs)	Frank Gibson
1980	'King Arthur's "Lyonesse"?' in *Popular Archaeology*, Vol. 1, No. 11	David Chance
1980	*My Scillonian Home*	Frank Gibson
1980	*Prijs der Zee*. (Hollandia, etc.) Published by Ryksmuseum, Amsterdam	
1980	*Isles of Scilly Survey*	Vivien Russell
1980	'But is "Lyonnesse" a Scilly Story at all' in *Popular Archaeology*. Vol. 1, No. 11	Peter Fowler
1980	*South England Pilot Volume V. The Scilly Isles*, first edition. (Second edition, altered title 1983)	Robin Brandon
1980	*Sunken Treasure*	Mark Williams
1980	*Scillonian Gigs of Today*	G.G. Tucker
1980	*The Observer, Island Britain* (Magazine supplement weeks 6-24 August)	Patrick Heron
c1980	*Tresco Abbey Garden*	P. Clough
1981	'Vegetation History of the Isles of Scilly' in *Environmental Aspects of Coasts and Islands* (BAR International Series 94)	G.W. Dimbleby, J.R.A. Greig and R.G. Scaife
1981	'George Bonsor: An Archaeological Pioneer from Spain on Scilly' in *Cornish Studies*, No. 8	Paul Ashbee
1981	'The Lord of Goonhilly' in *National Trust Studies 1981*	Charles Thomas
1981	*Sea and Shore Birds of the Isles of Scilly*	David Hunt
1981	*The Country Life Book of Britain's Offshore Islands*	
1981	*Tresco: Paradise Island*	Frank Gibson
1981	*Draft Structure Plan*	Council of the Isles of Scilly

1981	*Isles of Scilly Structure Plan*
	    Explanatory Memorandum.
	    Consultant Version (February 1981)
	    Explanatory Memorandum (August 1981)
	    Report of Survey (August 1981)
	    Proposed 1st Alteration (November 1981)	

c1981	*Old Scillonian Recipes*. (From notes made by Mary Ellen Jenkins in 1904)	
c1981	*H.M.S. Association: Sank 1707*. A Diver's Report	Mac Mace
1982	'Finds from the Hollandia' in *The International Journal of Nautical Archaeology*, Vol. 11. No. 4	Rex Cowan and S.B. Engelsman
1982	*The Scillonian and His Boat*	Alf Jenkins
1982	*The Nature of Cornwall*	Rennie Bere
1982	*Solar Energy & Dowsing in the Isles of Scilly*	A.P. Tabraham
1982	*Another Taste of Tresco* (Recipes)	Michael Shea
c1982	*The Birdwatchers. With Tall Tales of Scilly*	'Norm' (J. N. Gooding)
c1982	*A Yachtsman's Guide to Scilly*	'Norm' (J. N. Gooding)
1983	*A Bibliography of the Entomology of the Smaller British Offshore Islands*	Kenneth Smith and Vera Smith
1983	*A visitor's Guide to Cornwall and the Isles of Scilly*	Rita Tregellas Pope

224

1983	*Cost of Living Report: Town Comparisons – St. Mary's*	Reward Regional Surveys Ltd.
1983	*Isles of Scilly Project. Summary of Topic Papers*	Graham Moss Associates
c1983	*Shipwrecks around the Isles of Scilly*	Frank Gibson
1984	*The Wildlife of the Royal Estates*	Robin Page
1984	*Star Castle and its Garrison*	Francis and Pam Adams
1984	*The Isles of Scilly Comprehensive Land Use and Community Project*	Graham Moss Associates
1984	*A Photographic Year in the Isles of Scilly*	Frank Gibson
1984	'Excavations at Bar Point, St Mary's, Isles of Scilly 1979-80' in *Cornish Studies*, No. 11	John G. Evans
1984	'The Excavation of a Cottage on Samson, Isles of Scilly, 1977' in *Cornish Studies*, No. 11	Howard Mason
1984	*Little Arthur Farm Trail*	R. Morton
1984	'The numbers of landbird species on the Isles of Scilly' in *Biological Journal of the Linnean Society*	Timothy M. Reed
1984	'The Parliamentary Survey of the Duchy of Cornwall; part 2 (Isles of Scilly to West Antony, & Manors in Devon)' in *Devon & Cornwall Record Society* volume 27	J.G. Norman Pounds (editor)
1984	'A history of Flandrian vegetation in the Isles of Scilly: palynological investigations of Higher Moors and Lower Moors peat mires, St Mary's' in *Cornish Studies*, No. 11	
1984	'A study of vertebrate remains from May's Hill, St Martin's' in *Cornish Studies*, No. 11	F.A. Turk
1984	'The Short-lived Settlement on Samson, Isles of Scilly' in *Vernacular Architecture*, Vol. 15	Harry Gordon Slade
c1984	*Wild Flowers of Scilly*	David Hunt
1984 and 1985	'The Sub-fossil Flora of Cornwall and the Isles of Scilly' in *Cornish Biological Records*, Nos. 7 and 8	C.N. French
1985	*British Birds from Nature. The Tresco Collection*	Frances Mary Isabella Smith
1985	*Scilly Up To Date* (first issue May 1985)	A.H. Read & Son (publisher)
1985	*Tresco, England's Island of Flowers*	Ronald King
1985	*Isles of Scilly Archaeological Plan* (commissioned by English Heritage)	Jeanette Ratcliffe
1985	*A Check-list of the Birds of the Isles of Scilly*	S.J.M. Gantlett
1985	'Dog-welks: An Introduction to the Biology of Nucella lapillus (L)' in *Field Studies*, No. 6	J.H. Crothers
1985	'Two different patterns and shell-shape variation in the dog-welk Nucella lapillus' in *Biological Journal of the Linnean Society*	
1985	'Scale Insects (Homoptera: Coccoidea) of Tresco, Isles of Scilly' in *Entomologist's Gazette*, Vol. 36	D.J. Williams
1985	*Confessions of a Scilly Birdman*	David Hunt
1985	*Sir Clowdisley Shovell's Disaster in the Isles of Scilly –1707*. Historic Maritime Series No. 1.	Richard Larn and Peter McBride
1985	*Exploration of a Drowned Landscape*	Charles Thomas
1985	*A History of British Helicopters and its Predecessors*	

	since 1947	P. Lo Bao
1985	*The Isles of Scilly Eye Witness 1958-1984*	Frank Gibson
c1985	*Scilly – Isles of Flowers*	Frank Gibson
1986	*Gig Racing in the Isles of Scilly*	Frank Gibson
1986	*The Isles of Scilly Field Guide* by Quatenary Research Association	J.D. Scourse (editor)
1986	*Tin in Antiquity*	R.D. Penhallurick
1986	*Death on the Isles of Scilly*	John Purchas
1987	*To The Sunset Bound* (Civil air services)	M.J. Ingham
1987	*The Duchy of Cornwall*	Crispin Gill (editor)
1987	*Structural Controls on Tor Location, St Mary's, Isles of Scilly* by Department of Geography, University of Aberdeen	Peter G. Knight
1987	*Some Aspects of Contemporary Geochemistry and Sedimentology in the Isles of Scilly*	Ian Foster
1987	'Scilly Isles – Rocks & Wrecks' in *World Magazine* (June)	Rob Stratton
1987	'Museums' (Valhalla figureheads) in *World Magazine* (June)	Louise Roddon
1987	*The Story of the Isles of Scilly Lifeboats*	Jeff Morris
1987	So near and yet so far' in *Flight International*, 3 October	Harry Hopkins
1987	'Scilly Isles. The first 50 years of air services' in *Aviation News*, 16-19 November	M.J. Ingham
1988	*Isles of Scilly Golf Club. Official Handbook*	
1988	'A Celebration of Fifty Years of Air Services' in *Air-Britain Digest*, Vol. 40, No. 1	Peter Hughes
1988	*Views and Likenesses. Photographers & their Work in Cornwall and Scilly 1839-1870*	Charles Thomas
1988	*The Duchy Review* (First issue, published annually) Published by the Duchy of Cornwall	
1988	*Exploring Underwater. The Isles of Scilly*	Mark Groves
1989	*Atlantic Helicopter*	M.J. Ingham
1989	*Isles of Scilly Structure Plan. Proposed 1st Alteration*	
1989	*War Over the West*	Eddie Walford
1989	*The Chemistry of Shallow Lakes: A Comparative Study of Five Coastal Lagoons in the Isles of Scilly*	T.C. Jardine
1989	*Environmental change in south west England. A comparative study of sediments of five shallow lakes on the Isles of Scilly*	Karen M. Bardell
1989	*Water Resource Management on the Isles of Scilly*	Richard Wainwright
1989	'The Names of the Batteries on the Garrison' in *From Cornwall to Caithness – Some Aspects of British Field Archaeology.* (BAR British Series 209)	Charles Thomas
1989	*Islands Apart*	John Hunt
1990	*The Isles of Scilly Standard Guidebook* (48th edition)	R.L. Bowley
1990	*Visitor's Companion to the Isles of Scilly* (new edition)	F. Gibson
1990	*Scillonian War Diary 1914-1918* (three volumes)	compiled by John P. Osborne
1990	*Scillonian War Diary 1939-1945* (two volumes)	compiled by John P. Osborne
1990	*The Fortunate Islands* (eighth edition, revised)	R.L. Bowley
1990	*A Precious Heritage* – published by Isles of Scilly Environmental Trust	

Illustrated Catalogues of Shipwreck Artefacts for Auction

1969	14 July. *Association*	Sotheby & Co
1970	28 January. *Association*	—
1972	18 April. *Hollandia*	—
1973	21 September. *Hollandia*	W.H. Lane & Son
1974	24 September. *Association*	—
1975	26 September. *Association, Duoro, Hollandia, Thomas W. Lawson, Princesse Maria,* and *Schiller*	—
1979	30 November. *Association, Eagle, Hollandia,* and *Juno*	—
1983	1 June. *Association,* and *Hollandia*	—

Antiquaries Journal

1921	Roman altar	
1933	Megalithic monuments	H. O'Neill Hencken
1934	A cist; Iron Age finds on Teän	C.F. Tebbutt
1941	Celtic monastery on St Helen's; Cliff Castles	C.A.R. Radford
1949	Cist at St Martin's	H.A. Lewis
1952	Excavation of Knackyboy Cairn;	B.H. St. J. O'Neil
	Beads from Knackyboy Cairn	J.F.S. Stone
1953	Enamelled Penannular Brooch	B.H. St. J. O'Neil
1954	A triangular cist	B.H. St. J. O'Neil
1955	Excavation of homestead at Halangy Down, 1950	
		Paul Ashbee

Antiquity

1927	Lyonesse	O.G.S. Crawford
1928	Stone Cists	O.G.S. Crawford
1941	Grooved stone cists	S. Piggott
1979	Early walls	Peter J. Fowler and Charles Thomas

Cornish Archaeology

1962	Harry's Walls – new interpretation	A.D. Saunders
1963	Chambered tombs	Paul Ashbee
1965	Isles of Scilly Museum Association;	M. Mackenzie
	Excavations at Halangy Down	Paul Ashbee
1966	Excavations at Halangy Down 1965 and 1966	Paul Ashbee
1967	Thumbnail scrapers;	P.Z. Mackenzie
	Recent Discoveries	Mary Mackenzie
1968	Excavations at Halangy Down 1967 and 1968;	Paul Ashbee
	Prehistoric and historic mammals – Teän and St Agnes	F.A. Turk
1970	Excavations at Halangy Down 1969 and 1970;	Paul Ashbee
	Excavations at Nornour 1969 and 1970, interim report	S.A. Butcher
1971	Prehistoric and historic mammals – Nornour; Samson;	F.A. Turk
		D.S. Neal
	Flint arrowhead from Bryher	P.Z. Mackenzie
1972	Prehistoric habitation sites;	Alec Gray
	Unusual worked flint	P.Z. Mackenzie
1975	Recent fieldwork;	Charles Thomas

1976	Coarse storage vessel from Pendrathen;	John R. Samuels
1978	Smuggler's cache on Tresco	Michael Tangye
	Bant's Carn restored and reconsidered	Paul Ashbee
	Excavations at Nornour, 1969 to 1973, pre-Roman settlement;	Sarnia A. Butcher
	Borlase 'Stone Altar' on Tresco;	Norman Quinnell
	16th century outwork to King Charles' Castle;	Norman Quinnell
	Excavations at Bar Point	Paul Ashbee
1979	Porthcressa cist-graves postscript	Paul Ashbee
1980	Bar Point excavations;	J.G. Evans
1981	Prehistoric vessel from Tresco	John Samuels
1982	New view of Scillonian entrance-graves;	Paul Ashbee
	Roman altar;	Paul Ashbee
	Possible medieval cross base	Michael Tangye
1983	Hallangy Porth excavations 1975 and 1976, final report;	Paul Ashbee
	Little Bay, St Martin's, settlement excavations ;	David S. Neal
	Iron Age spiral bronze ring;	Paul Ashbee
	Possible font fragment	Michael Tangye
1986	Ancient Scilly; retrospect, aspect and prospect	Paul Ashbee

Proceedings of the West Cornwall Field Club

1952-1953	Two stone cists	Paul Ashbee
1953-1954	Fieldwork, 1950)	Paul Ashbee
1954-1955	Urn from Par Beach;	Paul Ashbee
	Flint Industries	Paul Ashbee
1956-1957	Megalithic Tombs on Teän	Charles Thomas
1960-1961	Cist-graves in Poynter's Garden	D. Dudley

Isles of Scilly Museum Publications

No. 1	*Fish around the Isles of Scilly*
No. 2	*Birds in the Isles of Scilly*
No. 3	*Shipwrecks around the Isles of Scilly*
No. 4	*Flowering Plants and Ferns in the Isles of Scilly*
No. 5	*The Pilot Gigs of Cornwall and the Isles of Scilly*
No. 6	*The Shipwreck of Sir Cloudesley Shovell*
No. 7	*Nornour*
No. 8	*Scarcer Maps and Books of Scilly*
No. 9	*Robert Maybee, The Scillonian Poet*
No. 10	*A Short Guide to the Isles of Scilly Museum*
No. 11	*A Short Guide to the Geology of the Isles of Scilly*
No. 12	*The Buildings of Scilly*
No. 13	*Lepidoptera of the Isles of Scilly*
No. 14	*The Kelp Industry in Scilly*
No. 15	*Isles of Scilly Survey*

FICTION

	Cornubia	G. Woodley
c1876	*The Watchers on the Longships*	F.J. Cobb
1890	*Armorel of Lyonesse*	Sir Walter Besant
1895	*Wrecked off Scilly*	M. Onley
1896	*A Man of Moods*	H.D. Lowry
1899	*The Watchers* (reprinted 1960)	A.E.W. Mason
1899	*Miranda of the Balcony*	A.E.W. Mason

1904	*The Marvellous History of King Arthur in Avalon, and the Lifting of Lyonnesse*	Geoffrey Junior
c1905	*The Pillar of Light*	Louis Tracy
1906	*Bazin's Gold*	E. Cornish
1907	*Major Vigoureux*	'Q' (Sir Arthur Quiller-Couch)
	Tom Tiddler's Ground	'Q' (Sir Arthur Quiller-Couch)
1913	*Maze of Scilly – Sea Tales of Scilly (1707-1822)*	E.J. Tiddy
1926	*The Dominant Law*	D. Lewis
	Fairy Gold	Sir Compton Mackenzie
	Lost Land of King Arthur	J.C. Waters
	Marazan (2nd edit. 1964)	Nevil Shute
1939	*The Flowery Isles; or The Lost Land of Lyonesse*	Mary Rhys
	Dangerous Waters	J. Cox
1954	*The Riddle of Samson* (second edition 1957)	A. Garve
	Wrack	Maurice Drake
	Enter the Saint (The Death Penalty)	L. Charteris
	Black Gull	D. Lamport
1956	*Cat in Gloves*	Denis Delaney (Peter Green)
1957	*Seven Red Roses*	Leila Mackinlay
1958	*Daffodil Island* (second edition 1960)	Judith M. Berrisford
1965	*The Eastern Beacon*	Mary Ray
1968	*Death in the Scillies*	H.C. Davis
1969	*The Mermaid's Daughter*	Joyce Gard
1971	*The Strangers*	Ann Schlee
1975	*The Scillies Trip*	John Banfield
1977	*The Happy Year*	Margery Hicks
1983	*The Proprietor*	Ann Schlee
1984	*Hell Bay*	Sam Llewellyn
1985	*Sweet Ellen*	Sarah Francis
	Pegleg	Sam Llewellyn
	Why the Whales Came	Michael Morpurgo
1989	*Full Circle*	Martina West
1990	*The Silver Lady*	Martina West
	The Island Beyond Beyond	Martina West

POETRY

1866	*Roathmere and other Poems*	Sarah Elizabeth Tonkin
	The Ballad of the Royal Anne	Crosbie Garstin
1891	*Songs of the West*	Rev. S. Baring-Gould and H. Fleetwood Sheppard
1925	*Lyonesse*	B.M. Warrand
1946	*The Isles of Scilly and Other Poems*	Geoffrey Grigson
1949	*Here comes she home*	Geoffrey Fyson
1970	*Mary Wilson: Selected Poems*	Mary Wilson
1979	*Mary Wilson: New Poems*	Mary Wilson
1979	*To Scilly*	Alec Gray
1980	*A Journey to Scilly*	Mary Wilson
1985	*Seating on the Pebbly Beach*	D.A. Leonard
1987	*Touching a Man*	D.A. Leonard
1989	*Karlo Dog (an Airedale)*	D.A. Leonard

Many excellent books on the Scillies have been published since 1990. Here is a small selection:

The Cita	Richard Larn
St Martin's Ancient Port	Glynis Cooper
Scilly's Wildlife Heritage	Adrian Spalding
Shipwreck around the Isles	F.E. Gibson
Isles of Scilly Photographic Memories	Zelide Cowan (Francis Firth)
The Last Piece of England	Richard Barber
Star Castle and its Garrison (new edition)	Adams
The Victorian Titanic	Keith Austin
Steamers and Ferries of Cornwall and the Isles of Scilly	Alan Kittridge
Sir Cloudesley Shovell	Simon Harris
Islands	John Fowles and Fay Godwin
Tresco Abbey Garden	Mike Nelhams
South-West Granite	Peter Stanier
Castaway and Wrecked	Rex Cowan
Admiral Shovell's Treasure	Peter McBride and Richard Larn
Dive the Isles of Scilly and North Cornwall	Richard Larn and David McBride
All in a Lifetime	Matt Lethbridge
Granite Land	Jenny Leather
The Illustrated Encyclopaedia of Arthurian Legend	Ronan Coghlan
Lost Patrols: Submarine Wrecks of the English Channel	Innes McCartney
Scilly at War	R.L. Bowley
The Isles of Scilly Standard Guidebook, 55th edition 2004/5	R.L. Bowley

INDEX